Janner's
Product Liability

GREVILLE JANNER

Janner's
Product Liability

Cartoons by Tobi

BUSINESS BOOKS
COMMUNICA - EUROPA

First published 1979

ISBN 0 220 67008 0

Printed in Great Britain by T. J. Press (Padstow) Ltd.,
for the publishers, Business Books Ltd.,
24 Highbury Crescent, London, N5.

For
SONYA AND SHIMON PERES
with fond admiration

OTHER BOOKS BY THE SAME AUTHOR INCLUDE:

Janner's Compendium of Employment Law

The Employer's Guide to the Law on Health and Safety at Work

The Employer's and Personnel Manager's Handbook of Draft Letters of Employment Law

The Employer's Guide to the Law on Employment Protection and Sex and Race Discrimination

The Director's Lawyer and Company Secretary's Legal Guide

The Director's and Company Secretary's Handbook of Draft Legal Letters

The Director's and Company Secretary's Handbook of Draft Contract Letters

The Business and Professional Man's Lawyer

The Businessman's Guide to Letter-writing and to the Law on Letters

The Businessman's Guide to Speech-making and to the Laws and Conduct of Meetings

The Businessman's Guide to Travel and to Profits Abroad

The Caterer's Lawyer and Restaurateur's and Hotelier's Legal Guide

The Manufacturer's Lawyer and Factory Manager's Legal Guide

The Motorist's Lawyer

Coping with Crime

The Employer's Lawyer

Motorists — Know Your Law

Farming and the Law

Your Offices and the Law

Your Property and the Law and Investor's Legal Guide

The Personnel Manager's Lawyer

The Businessman's Legal Lexicon

Contents

x   *Product Liability*

Introduction

UK manufacturers, distributors and even retailers are rightly anxious at the advance of 'product liability'. But while recognising the profound impact which new law may have on their business profits, few have either understood or (still less) guarded against these changes. This book is designed as the businessman's practical and readable guide to this crucial area of law.

In Britain, the liability of manufacturers, distributors and retailers for the goods they supply depends upon fault. This applies in the rules on contract, tort (civil wrongs — in particular: negligence) and crime. Except for one comparatively minor corner of the law (the 'strict liability' of employers to employees who suffer death or injury through defects in equipment they supply) 'no fault' means no liability.

Soon, though, we are likely to have 'no fault liability' or 'strict liability' in many legal spheres, as recommended by the Law Commission, the Scottish Law Commission, the Royal Commission on Civil Liability and Compensation for Personal Injuries (the Pearson Committee) and (above all) by the EEC Draft Directive on Liability for Defective Products.

To win damages for breach of contract, the plaintiff must show that he suffered damage as a result of a breach by the defendant of a binding term in a legally enforceable contract. No breach, no damages.

To win a negligence action, the plaintiff must prove that

the defendant owed him a duty to take care; breach of
that duty; and damage flowing from the breach. No failure
to exercise proper care . . . no negligent act or omission . . .
no liability.

Section 6 of *The Health and Safety at Work etc. Act,
1974,* provides (in broad terms) that designers, manufacturers, importers and suppliers of equipment and of other
'articles' and of substances for use at work must take such
steps as are 'reasonably practicable' to ensure that they are
safe. Those who do what is 'reasonably practicable' commit
no offence, even if a product is both defective and
dangerously so.

In civil law, employers must take reasonable care not to
submit employees to unnecessary risk and they must comply with their statutory duties. The mere fact that an employee is injured at work will give him no right to damages.
Exception (as we have seen): under *The Employers' Liability
(Defective Equipment) Act, 1969.* And, of course, an
injured employee's right to Industrial Injuries Benefit does
not depend upon proof of negligence or breach of statutory
duty on anyone's part.

You are injured in a road accident and claim damages
from another road user? Then you will have to prove positively that the defendant was at fault. The burden of proof
rests on you.

Proposals for legislation include recommendations for
'strict liability' on manufacturers, designers, exporters,
suppliers and distributors of products . . . on employers, for
the results of industrial accidents . . . and of a right for
injured road users to claim damages, without having to prove
that someone else was to blame. Different commissions or
reports make differing recommendations. But it is inevitable
that change is on the way. Strict liability in one form or
another will soon be upon the world of industry and commerce. Hence this book.

Here, then, are the legal rules, presented in as clear and
lively a form as possible. While it is hoped that some lawyers
may be pleased to revisit previous stamping grounds where
future business is about to run rampant — and even to have
the frontiers of that expanding territory pushed forward — this
is essentially a book for those in industry and commerce who

have to cope with the emanations of Parliament and of the courts.

In the same way, you will find summaries of the recommendations of the various commissions and of the EEC Directive. Their essentials are reproduced in appendices.

In addition, every businessman needs to know how far the law will still allow him to reduce or to remove his normal responsibilities through the insertion of exclusion clauses in his contracts. The new rules are set out in *The Supply of Goods (Implied Terms) Act, 1973,* and *The Unfair Contract Terms Act, 1977* — both of which are explained and also included (in full) as appendices.

Finally, a book of this complexion must include at least some reference to insurance. After all, one of the great problems in the United States as well as other countries where strict liability has already arrived is the pure misery of obtaining insurance — at bearable cost or at all. And British concerns dealing with those countries are today faced with potential litigation which means insurance costs at a level which is driving some of them out of the market.

As manufacturers, designers and others who 'put goods into circulation' become increasingly vulnerable from the law, so they must seek an increasing shield from the insurer. Insurance law itself is exceedingly complicated and this book is no place for a full analysis. But I have included some of the basic legal rules on insurance and (much more important) two most valuable chapters on product liability insurance practice, written by Oliver Prior, Executive Director of Bland Payne — my warmest thanks to him.

To those who have given me such prodigious help in the production of this work, my warmest thanks. I am especially grateful to: His Honour Judge Brian Clapham; to my assistants Kathy McLeod and William Sandover; to my wife; and to my son, Daniel.

The Temple   Greville Janner, QC, MP
London EC4
January 1979

"THEY'RE VERY CONSIDERATE HERE — LAST TIME I GOT
FOOD POISONING THEY SENT ME A 'GET WELL' CARD
ON THEIR STANDARD WRITTEN TERMS . . . !"

Part One

CIVIL LAWS — THE LAWS ON 'TORT' AND 'DELICT'

Chapter 1

Introduction

The civil law gives rights to individuals, firms, companies and
other citizens — individually or in some group or corporate
capacity — to claim legal remedies against each other. To succeed in an action in 'tort' (or, to use the Scots expression, in
'delict'), the plaintiff must satisfy a court 'on the balance of
probabilities', on three separate matters.

First: the defendant must 'owe a duty of care' to the
plaintiff. There must be some relationship which gives rise to
a duty upon the defendant to take care to avoid acts or
omissions which cause damage to the plantiff. The extent of
this 'duty of care' has grown to cover most people who are
(*a*) affected by the wrongful act or omission and (*b*) are not
'too remote'.

Second: the defendant must have behaved in some way that
is inconsistent with his duty. The plaintiff must prove 'negligence' (or some lack of due care).

Finally: it is not enough that the defendant acted in breach
of his duty of care. The plaintiff must prove that as a result
he suffered injury, loss or damage — once again, not too
'remote' from the initial wrongful act.

In the main, these are 'common law' rules. They have grown
up in the course of centuries through the binding effect of
court decisions. The basis of our legal system (as well as that
of the US and other 'common law countries') is that a higher
court is influenced by decisions of courts of equal standing and
bound to follow rules laid down in decisions of courts of
higher standing.

Of course, it is often possible to 'distinguish' one case from
another, that is, to make distinctions between decisions based
on the facts — in legal terms.

A judge may say: 'It was decided in the case of *X* v. *Y* that
such-and-such is the law. But that case was founded on facts

which are substantially different from those in the present case . . . .' Indeed, if a judge is sufficiently determined (as some, like the formidable Master of the Rolls, Lord Denning) he can generally find some ground for creating a distinction — even with a decision made by himself in another legal forum.

Most of our law of 'tort' has grown up through judges' decisions. These are contained in the Law Reports and much of the law in this book has been combed out of cases. To avoid interfering with the readibility of the text, but so as to provide lawyers and others who wish to examine the cases in more detail, I have collated references to the Law Reports in Appendix 2.

So case piles up on case, decision upon decision, Law Report on Law Report. The reprints of the most important ancient decisions chosen by *The All England Law Reports* (1558 to 1935) take 37 volumes. The up-to-date *All England Law Reports* (from 1936 to 1978 inclusive) comprise 124 volumes. As a wise teacher used to say: 'No lawyer can hope to know all his law — only where to find it. And he must also know his judges . . . and how to handle them, individually and collectively. . . .'

Even with statutes such as *The Employers' Liability (Defective Equipment) Act, 1969, The Occupier's Liability Act, 1957*, and *The Animals Act, 1971*, the vast bulk of our law on the tort of negligence comes from cases. The judges seek out a duty of care; breach of the duty; damages. Duty of care and damage is not enough — the second essential — breach of duty or 'fault' must be proved. Strict liability (or 'no fault' liability) for products is likely to emerge from statute.

Parliament rules supreme. It may overrule any court decision. Unlike the principle enshrined in the United States Constitution, to ensure a 'balance of power' between executive and judiciary, even the learned law lords (the House of Lords sitting in its judicial capacity) cannot declare an Act of Parliament to be 'unconstitutional' and therefore void.

The courts can only interpret the wishes of Parliament, not override them. They may regret the effect of Parliament's wording and even point the way to change, but they cannot effect that change. Alone among our courts, the House of Lords may overrule or override its own decisions, in the light of the advance (or retreat) of thought. It cannot deflect the moving finger of parliamentary legislation.

So profound alteration in our law on product liability will probably come mainly from Parliament and soon.* It is likely before long to place 'strict liability' on many of those who should be legally 'caring': manufacturers certainly; intermediate parties — distributors, erectors, installers, plus those who service or maintain plant or equipment, probably; even the retailer or other ultimate seller, potentially; with importers and others also at risk.

When (and if) this occurs, new liabilities will be created. However: the older ones will remain. The basic law is likely to be founded upon the existing rules, which will be extended. Meanwhile, sufficient unto the day be the insurance thereof, provided that those who are likely to be involved are prepared.

The following chapters describe and define the 'duty of care' which rests upon us all in most industrial or commercial circumstances. This duty overlaps in many cases with the (separate) duty created by the law of contract — a duty which is initially the result of legally binding agreement between parties, but one with which Parliament has recently interfered by placing limits on the contracting parties' rights to limit or exclude the rights of others. Part 2 of this book covers contractual liability and Part 3 the law on exclusions. Employers owe duties to take care for their employees, through the (special) contracts between them and those who work for them — contracts which result from individual or collective bargains or both. Both the common law and statutory rules are covered in Part 3, with special reference to harm caused to employees through defective products.

Finally, every community establishes minimum standards of behaviour, required by that society at the particular time. The laws of criminal responsibility have already been stretched towards products – primarily through Section 6 of *The Health and Safety at Work Act, 1974*. Once again, through a combination of judge-made and statute law, standards have evolved. These are built into Part 4 of the book.

*Professor Anthony Jolowicz — an eminent expert in this field — recently stated that, in his view, strict liability is already being imposed in the UK through court decisions. Its arrival in the USA, France and the Federal Republic of Germany has largely been by that route.

Chapter 2

The ultimate consumer and the snail in the bottle

The manufacturer owes duties defined by the individual contract and by contract law towards those with whom he has a contractual relationship. But thanks to the decision of the House of Lords in the remarkable case of the dead, black snail, he must also take due care to protect 'the ultimate consumer' of those products. That 'consumer' is his 'neighbour'; and even though he is a total stranger, he may sue the manufacturer for damages. True, he must prove fault (or 'negligence'). But one day soon, even that ultimate liability to the eventual sufferer may be 'strict'.

Miss Donoghue was a shop assistant who was taken out by her friend for refreshment at a local cafe. The proprietor duly opened a bottle of ginger beer, ordered for her by her friend, and poured some of it into a glass. The bottle was opaque and the contents were invisible. Miss Donoghue drank.

The hospitable friend then poured the remainder of the beverage into the tumbler. And out swam the limp and slimy remains of the most famous snail in legal history. Not surprisingly, Miss Donoghue not only suffered gastric illness but also 'severe shock'.

Miss Donoghue could scarcely have sued the lady friend, who had bought the defective drink for her. If you serve up poison to a friend, the fact that she does not pay for it will not free you from potential liability. But clearly, Miss Donoghue's friend was not at fault.

Or Miss Donoghue might have sued the cafe, with whom the friend had a contract in which there was an implied term that the food would be palatable and would poison neither her nor her friends. But the proprietor was not to blame. Nor did the sufferer have any contract with him.

Next up the line came the distributor. He was liable to Miss Donoghue neither in contract nor in tort. So she took a huge plunge backwards and sued the manufacturer, Mr Stephenson.

Sadly, Mr Stephenson himself died before the case was heard, no doubt himself suffering from deferred shock.
But the case reached the House of Lords, where a majority led by Lord Atkin held that the plaintiff was entitled to succeed on the basis of a duty of care owed in the 'tort' or civil wrong of negligence. This duty exists independently of contract. Lord Atkin said: 'The rule that you are to love your neighbour becomes, in law: You must not injure your neighbour; and the lawyers' question: 'Who is my neighbour?' receives a restricted reply. You must take reasonable care to avoid acts or omissions which you can reasonably foresee would be likely to injure your neighbour.'

So entirely independently of any contractual duty, you must avoid taking action which you 'can reasonably foresee' would be likely to injure 'your neighbour'.

Who is your 'neighbour', in law?

Lord Atkin: 'The answer seems to be persons who are so closely and directly affected by my act that I ought reasonably to have them in contemplation as being so affected when I am directing my mind to the acts or omissions which are called in question.'

As another judge once put it: 'One man may owe a duty to another, even though there is no contract between them. If one man is near to another, or is near the property of another, a duty lies upon him not to do that which may cause a personal injury to that other, or may injure his property.'

This rule includes cases of the supply of goods 'to be used immediately by a particular person or persons, or one of a class of persons, where it would be obvious to the person supplying, if he thought that the goods would in all probability be used at once by such persons before a reasonable opportunity for discovering any defect which might exist — and where the thing supplied would be of such a nature that a neglect of ordinary care or skill as to its condition or manner of supplying it would probably cause danger to the person or property of the person for whose use it was supplied, and who was about to use it.'

Before Donoghue's case, the duty seems to have been confined to goods 'used immediately' and 'at once, before a reasonable opportunity of inspection'. Now, 'reasonable foreseeability' was stretched much wider.

Lord Atkin, again: 'A manufacturer puts up an article of food in a container which he knows will be opened by the actual consumer. There can be no inspection by any purchaser and no reasonable preliminary inspection by the consumer. Negligently, in the course of preparation, he allows the contents to be mixed with poison . . . .' If the rules of law did not permit the sufferer to obtain damages from the manufacturer, then its principles would be 'remote from the ordinary needs of civilised society'. 'Where there is so obviously a social wrong', the remedy must be available.

By Scots and English law alike, 'the manufacturer of products which he sells in such a form as to show that he intends them to reach the ultimate consumer in the form in which they left him, with no reasonable possibility of intermediate examination,* and with the knowledge that the absence of reasonable care in the preparation or putting up of the products might result in injury to the consumer's life or property, owes a duty to the consumer to take that reasonable care.'

The doctrine of the 'ultimate consumer' then spread out across the field of law.

A Dr Grant contracted dermititis after wearing underwear manufactured by Australian Knitting Mills Limited. The garments contained 'an excess of bisulphate soda'. The determined efforts of the defendant's lawyers to make a distinction between internal consumption and external wear were dismissed by the court. The doctor was the 'ultimate consumer' of the garments.

A solicitor's managing clerk, named Haseldine, went to visit a client who lived on the fifth floor of a block of flats. A porter showed him to the lift. When it reached the second floor, it stopped, reversed direction, and sped downwards, stopping with a violent jerk at the bottom, in the basement. Mr Haseldine suffered severe spinal injury.

The lift had been in use for some 35 years and a firm of engineers (A & P Steven Limited) were under contract to maintain it. Mr Haseldine sued the owners of the building and the engineers.

The Court of Appeal held that the owners were not to

* See also Chapter 5 on intermediate examination.

blame as they had employed competent contractors and had reasonably acted on their advice. But the lift had been left in a dangerous condition through the negligence of the engineers; there was no reasonable opportunity for intermediate examination; so the engineers were liable to the visitor, who (in effect) was the 'ultimate consumer' of the engineers' services.

So the *Donoghue* v. *Stephenson* principle extended from the manufacturer of the goods to the supplier of services. Engineers, consultants, erectors, installers, repairers, maintenance men — all owe a duty to take care not merely for the safety of those with whom they contract, but also with anyone whom they ought reasonably to contemplate would be affected by their negligent act or omission.

In the case of *Green* v. *Fibreglass Limited,* the court again emphasised that the obligation of the repairer or engineer in this sort of case 'has nothing to do with the law of contract'. It depends upon negligence — which is quite separate.

Vacwell Engineering Company Limited manufactured equipment designed to produce transistor devices. A Mr Neale was in charge of their applied physics department and worked side by side with a Russian, one Strouzhinski, in Vacwell's laboratory. While washing the labels off samples in two adjacent sinks, prior to using them in the manufacturing apparatus, there was a sudden white flash; Mr Strouzhinski was killed; Mr Neale was injured; and Vacwell's premises were seriously damaged. Vacwell sued BDH, the suppliers of the chemicals, alleging that they were delivered without any adequate warning notice of the industrial hazard which might arise in their use.

There was no suggestion of any absolute duty on BDH to give warning of industrial hazards of dangerous chemicals 'whether they could have discovered them by the exercise of reasonable care or not'. But (said Mr Justice Rees), they did owe a duty 'to take reasonable care to ascertain major industrial hazards of chemicals marketed by them and to give warnings of such hazards to their customers'.

If that duty had been complied with, the explosion hazard 'would have come to light and a suitable warning would have been given'. This would have prevented Vacwell dealing with the ampoules as they did. The damage was foreseeable; there was no fault on Vacwell's part; the manufacturers were liable.

The same reasoning was applied by a court in *Boots* v. *Devilez*, a case brought against the manufacturers of corn solvent (and explained in detail in Chapter 4). The plaintiff was using the substance while dressed in his birthday suit. His hands were wet. The bottle slipped. The solvent allegedly spilled over his private parts — which duly dissolved.

'There had never been such an accident in the past', said the manufacturers. 'How lucky', replied the court.

'The user ought to have realised that corn solvent would dissolve other, more valued parts of the body than corns', they argued. 'Not so', said the court. 'That which will dissolve one substance will not necessarily dissolve another.' They owed a duty of care to the ultimate consumer. They should have labelled the product, 'Danger!'.

There, the health hazard was all too obvious. In the sad case of *Wright* v. *Dunlop Rubber Company Limited,* the court applied the same rules to carcinogenic substances. If, for instance, employers operate a system under which employees are allowed to put oily rags into their pockets and the oil eventually causes cancer of the scrotum, the employers will be liable because they have been negligent.

So 'ultimate consumers' include not only private but also business buyers; not only employers but also employees — all those whom you should expect to suffer as a result of your negligent act or omission, if you apply your mind to the problem.

Chapter 3

Negligence and individual liability

If you are negligent at work, could you be forced to pay damages to anyone who suffers as a result? If, for instance, you drive negligently and as a result your company's insurers have to pay damages, could they force you personally to indemnify them because you were at fault? Or could negligence in your design department impose liability on the individual designer, if it could be shown that his fault caused damage to someone else?

In the case of *Lister* v. *Romford Ice and Cold Storage Company Limited,* the House of Lords held that an employer was not bound to take out a policy which would cover the personal liability of a servant who was negligent in the course of his employment and that no term was implied into a contract of employment that an employee is entitled to be indemnified by his employers against claims or proceedings 'or acts done in the course of his employment'.

Happily, by a majority of two to one, the Court of Appeal came to a different conclusion in the later case of *Morris* v. *Ford Motor Company Limited.* Lord Denning and Lord Justice James held, in effect, that employees are indeed entitled to be indemnified against civil claims arising out of negligence committed during the course of their employment.

Lord Denning said that it would not be 'just and equitable' that employers should lend their name to their insurers to sue their own servant for damages, so as to make him personally liable. 'Their insurance company has received premiums and should bear the loss. It should not seek to make the individual employee personally liable.

'Everyone knows that risks such as these are covered by insurance. So they should be, when a man is doing his employer's work, with his employer's plant and equipment and happens to make a mistake.

'To make the servant personally liable would not only lead to a strike. It would be positively unjust. *Lister* v. *Romford Ice and Cold Storage Limited* was an unfortunate decision. Its ill-effects have been avoided only by an agreement between insurers not to enforce it. . . .

'I would apply this simple principle: Where the risk of a servant's negligence is covered by insurance, his employers should not seek to make that servant liable for it. At any rate, the court should not compel him to allow his name to be used to do it.'

Lord Justice James agreed. To allow insurers to claim an indemnity against the employee 'would be unacceptable and unrealistic . . . in an industrial setting'.

So even where insurers decide not to abide by a 'gentleman's agreement', the courts will enforce 'realism and justice' upon them — at least in an 'industrial setting'.

Naturally, the negligent employee will have to account to

his own employer and if his negligence was sufficiently serious or persistent, he may be dismissed 'fairly'. Again, no insurer and no employer can protect the individual against his personal liability in criminal law — whether under the Health and Safety at Work Act, the Road Traffic Act or any other. But at least he now knows that his master is 'vicariously liable' in civil law, even though he bears his own burden of blame under the laws of crime.

Chapter 4

The danger of warnings

Very sensibly but not at all helpfully, *The Occupiers' Liability Act, 1957,* says that a warning 'may or may not' be enough to enable the occupier to comply with his 'common duty' of care. The danger of warnings for those who give them? That they may believe that a warning is of itself enough. It may be — or it may not be. All depends on the nature and extent of the warning, and of the hazard, and the likelihood that the person who sees or hears it will take sufficient heed.

As with premises, so with products. Warnings should certainly be given, but whether or not they will free the giver from liability will depend on all the circumstances of the particular case.

The sad saga of Mr Devilez, who spilled Boots' corn solvent onto his John Thomas, shows the courts do lay store on warning. Neither the fact that no one appears to have suffered the same fate previously nor Boots' plea that 'surely you don't have to tell someone to be careful not to pour corn solvent over his private parts', availed the unfortunate defendants. A stern warning should have been placed on the bottle, such as (presumably): 'Handle with care . . . Keep away from all personal projections . . .'

If you know or ought to know of the danger then you should take reasonable care to ensure that others are warned. Manufacturers owe a duty to distributors; distributors to retailers; retailers to customers; and, doing the legal leap-frog, manufacturers to 'ultimate consumers'.

Messrs Barnes delivered a container of nitric acid to carriers, Messrs Russell. They gave no warning of the dangers of the contents, although they knew or ought to have known of the dangers. The container exploded and one of the carrier's employees (Mr Farrant) was injured. Messrs Barnes were held liable for the dangerous product. They should have given due warning.

The Army & Navy Co-operative Store sold a tin of chlorinated lime to Mrs Clarke, as a disinfectant powder. They knew of accidents caused by the substance so they should have realised that the tin might cause danger. When Mrs Clarke was injured by the substance, she won damages because she was given no warning.

Messrs Jeffery manufactured a cleaning fluid which they modestly dubbed 'the pluperfect liquid'. Unfortunately when it came into contact with cast iron, it emitted fumes of highly inflammable nitrogen.

Anglo-Celtic Shipping Company Limited employed Messrs Elliott to repair one of their ships and instructed them to use the 'pluperfect' wonder liquid to clean a condenser. The workman came towards the condenser carrying a naked flame. Anglo-Celtic sued both Elliotts and Jefferys for dam — ages arising out of the resultant explosion.

Neither the plaintiffs nor Elliotts knew of the special danger from the pluperfect liquid. The manufacturers either knew or ought to have known. The article was dangerous in itself and the instructions failed to give any adequate warning to the users. So they were liable to compensate the sufferers.

Some dangerous substances are dealt with by statute or statutory instruments. Readers concerned with the manufacture of pharmaceuticals, medicines, foods or drugs will know of the various Acts, Rules and Regulations. These cover not only labelling and warning, but in some cases also packaging. Recent regulations on child-resistant containers, for instance, were something of a triumph for back-bench campaigning in which some of us took special pride.

Section 6 of the Health and Safety at Work Act (see Part 4) places a further criminal responsibility on manufacturers to give adequate information to enable their products to be properly used. Manufacturers of a substance containing a small quantity of cadmium marketed it in sticks,

bundled together with a warning around the outside. A
chandler separated a bundle and sold the sticks separately. A
plumber used one of them as a brazing alloy, inhaled cadmium fumes, and died.

The company's insurers duly paid up. The company was
grateful that the Health and Safety at Work Act was not then
in force.

Harrods Limited defended an action brought by a Mrs
Fisher. They supplied a fluid for cleaning jewellery in a
plastic bottle with a plastic bung and screw top. The fluid
contained components which could damage eyesight.

Mrs Fisher squeezed the bottle; the bung burst out; and
fluid shot into and damaged her eye. The court held that
Harrods should have warned that the fluid must be kept away
from eyes.

The more obvious the danger, the less the need to warn.
Conversely, the less obvious the danger, the more obvious the
need to warn against it.

Too many people are poisoned by household bleaches.
Adults read warnings; children are poisoned.

Some kitchen cleansing substances are not only marketed
in tubs like those used for margarine but actually look like
that delectable substance. Both may be on the same shelf in
the same kitchen at the same time. Common-sense requires
the cleanser to be marked with a warning.

However, no one need tell the housewife that a carving
knife cuts fingers, nor an industrial user that the blade of a
saw may remove a finger. Latent, not patent, dangers require
maximum warning.

In the old case of *British Chartered Company of South
Africa* v. *Lennon Limited,* Lennon dispatched cattle dip
marked with labels intended for smaller tins. The British
Chartered Company used the substance in accordance with
the incorrect instructions. They had realised there was something wrong with the quantities marked but presumed that
the substance and not the label had been altered. The court
held the manufacturers negligent and liable.

Mrs Watson was injured by a dye applied to her hair by
Buckley Osborne Garratt & Company Limited. Preliminary
'patch testing' would have revealed the plaintiff's sensitivity
but the defendants had advertised that no testing was needed.

So they and not the hairdressers were negligent and liable to compensate the customer.

➜ Rapidol Limited supplied hairdressers with a dye of their own manufacture. The bottles and accompanying brochures warned that the dye might be dangerous to certain skins and that patch tests were necessary.

A hairdresser named Ashford thought that she knew better. Ignoring the warning, she applied the dye to Mrs Holmes hair, without testing. Result: dermatitis. Mrs Holmes sued both the hairdresser and the manufacturer.

The Court of Appeal held that the warning given by the manufacturers was sufficient to alert a hairdresser to the potential dangers of the substance; that more could not be expected of the manufacturers; and that it would be 'unreasonable and impossible' to expect them to give a warning in such form that 'it must come to the knowledge of the particular customer who was going to be treated'. The hairdresser was in breach of contract with her customer and was also liable in negligence. The manufacturer discharged his duty to 'the ultimate consumer' by giving the warning to the hairdresser.

* * *

➜ In broad terms, where common-sense requires warnings, so does the law. If in doubt, warn, and ensure that the warning is itself correct and adequate, within the bounds of reasonable practicability.

Chapter 5

Intermediate examination

So the liability in the 'tort' of 'negligence' rests on the supplier of the product, where there is no reasonable prospect of 'intermediate examination'. But when can blame be laid against the distributor, the wholesaler, the retailer or anyone else who physically comes into possession of the property before it reaches 'the ultimate consumer'? When is 'intermediate examination' reasonably practicable?

Suppose that you are a supplier of components. If you mass-produce the goods, you will probably recognise that a percentage (however small) will be defective. If one of these is incorporated into the eventual product, that product will itself be defective — possibly, dangerously so. How far, then, can you expect your customer (or, perhaps, what we might call 'the ultimate manufacturer') himself to test the items?

If you yourself are to inspect each tiny item, your quality control department will multiply and so will the (probably originally modest) cost of the individual product. Therefore you rely on the customer.

In criminal law, if your customer gives you a *written* undertaking that he will carry out all necessary research and testing, you are in the clear. Otherwise, you may have to rely on his good sense or his industrial knowledge or commercial intelligence.

In the law on the sale of goods, Section 14 of the Sale of Goods Act (Appendix 3) specifically excludes liability for goods which are not fit for the purpose supplied, where the buyer did not rely on the seller's skill or judgment. Whether or not he did so is a question of fact. And so is the likelihood or feasibility or reality of 'intermediate examination'.

The manufacturer or other supplier who wishes his customer to examine goods should say so. Include a term, if you wish, in your own written, standard terms. A judge may (under *The Supply of Goods (Implied Terms) Act, 1973,* — see Chapter 23) hold that this clause is 'unfair' or 'unreasonable' and therefore void, but he may not. Your customer may not even challenge the exclusion, probably because he does not know his law or because he sees the exclusion as reasonable and fair in the circumstances. Alternatively — and better still — why not draw your customer's attention to the need for intermediate testing or examination by him? Do so orally by all means. But if you wish to prove your case, then take the trouble to write.

These rules are important, of course, even today when 'fault' must be proved by the plaintiff. They will become more vital in future, when the law will impose liability without fault — and when fault will therefore become relevant when enabling the parties sued to impose or to apportion blame as between their erring or innocent selves.

Now let us look at some of the decided cases on 'intermediate examination'.

In *Griffiths* v. *Arch Engineering Company (Newport) Limited*, the plaintiff was injured by a portable pneumatic grinding machine hired by sub-contractors from a plant-hire company. He was given permission by the sub-contractors to use the machine; the grinding wheel shattered because the speed of the machine was too fast for the diameter of the wheel; and the question was — should the sub-contractors or the plant-hire company or both be held liable?

The plant-hire people maintained that 'intermediate examination' should have been carried out by the sub-contractors. However, the judge emphasised that 'the mere existence of a reasonable opportunity for intermediate examination will not exonerate a manufacturer or hirer out of a chattel'. The proper question is: 'Whether he should reasonably have expected that the person to whom he has passed the article would use the opportunity for inspection in such a way as to give him an indication of the risk and the means of warning any subsequent user of the article.'

The possibility or probability of intermediate examination 'is merely one facet of the wider principle . . . Was there a reasonably foreseeable risk that the plaintiff who was in fact injured would sustain such injury if no precautions were taken to guard against the risk? There is a lot to be said for the view . . . that the customer would rely on his supplier and assume that what his supplier handed out to him was sound and in proper order — particularly if he was paying for it.'

So the possibility of intermediate examination is not enough to free the supplier from liability. Was it reasonably to be expected that the intermediate party would inspect?

In *Clay* v. *A.J. Crump & Sons Limited*, builders employed demolition contractors to demolish an old building and building contractors to erect a new one on the same site. They employed an architect to prepare plans and supervise. A wall collapsed and injured Mr Clay, a labourer employed by the building contractors. He sued the architect, the demolition contractors and the building contractors. The trial judge held that all three were partially liable and this view was upheld by the Court of Appeal.

The architect had argued that the building contractors

should have examined the wall. But the court held that the architect knew or ought to have known that the building contractor's examination would be likely to be cursory, in reliance on his having left the site safe; that he had failed to take steps to satisfy himself that the wall was safe to be left, although he had had the opportunity of doing so; and that the fact that the building contractors had the last opportunity to examine the wall did not, in the circumstances, break the chain of causation. The architect's negligence was one of the causes of the plaintiff's injuries. Blame was shared and so, therefore, were the damages.

This decision was followed in the case of *Driver* v. *William Willett (Contractors) Limited.* Here, a firm of consulting safety and inspecting engineers had agreed to advise the employers on safety requirements in compliance with the relevant regulations. They had not advised the employers to discontinue the unsafe use of a hoist. They were 60 per cent responsible for the accident, even though the employers themselves were negligent and could have avoided the accident, had they followed the rules.

Even a local authority building inspector may be responsible on the same basis. In *Dutton* v. *Bognor Regis Urban District Council,* the Court of Appeal held that the inspector owed a duty of care to the purchaser of the house. His failure to make a proper inspection before he gave his approval imposed liability on his employers, even though the building contractors had been negligent.

These rules are, of course, of great importance to all consultants and others who are not necessarily as expert as their title suggests. They are bound to carry out their jobs in a proper and workmanlike manner and to use that degree of skill reasonably to be expected of a person of their standing, experience and repute. If they fail so to do and as a result someone is hurt, they cannot avoid responsibility merely because of the possibility of intermediate examination. The 'chain of causation' may have begun with their faulty advice. Alternatively, they may have had the opportunity to break the chain and to avoid the accident, by the giving of the correct advice or information. Either way, they may be liable in law.

Again, whether the courts are dealing with a defective

product, in the sense of something manufactured, or a dangerous structure, the rules are essentially the same. If, but only
if, there was not only a probability of intermediate examination and this examination could, should and would have
rectified the defect, will someone higher up the chain be
likely to throw off the entire responsibility onto those lower
down it.

Of course, if the intermediate examiner discovered the defect and failed to do anything about it, the situation would
be very different – as was illustrated in the case of *Taylor* v.
Rover Company Limited & Others. Mr Taylor was injured
when a splinter of steel flew from the top of a chisel which
he was hammering. He lost his eye. The hardness in the chisel
was caused by negligence in the original heat treatment. However, the employers kept the chisel in circulation after they
had discovered the defect. There was actual knowledge of
the defect. 'This was a dangerous chisel . . . it ought to have
been taken out of circulation . . . It was the keeping of the
chisel in circulation with the knowledge that it was dangerous that caused the accident.'

So if intermediate examination of the defective product
does take place and reveals that defect, then the manufacturer may avoid liability even though he was originally at
fault. The chain of causation was broken and the link between him and the sufferer has been cut. The sole, effective
cause of the damage was the supervening intervention.

Chapter 6

Liability of the volunteer

Even the businessman performs kindnesses. He may give
presents – presumably, in the hope of oiling the wheels of
commerce. Provided that he does not act dishonestly or
secretly, so as to be in breach of the Prevention of Corruption Acts, the law will not be concerned with his motives.
Exception: where the gift goes to employees of public
authorities – local or national, government or nationalised

industries. In such cases, corruption is presumed against both parties and it is up to the accused to prove his innocence.

Again, businessmen give references, both trade and personal. The recipient in all probability is a total stranger. True, they themselves may rely upon the courtesies of the business world. Finally, advice and information are often exchanged by those who design, manufacture, distribute or sell industrial products.

So to what extent are you free from liability if you give information or advice which turns out to be wrong? Does the law protect the volunteer? The answer first appeared in the case of *Hedley Byrne & Company Limited* v. *Heller & Partners Limited.*

Hedley Byrne were thinking of extending £17,000 credit to a company called Easipower Limited. In response to an enquiry they made to Heller & Partners, they received a reference: 'Respectably constituted company, considered good for its ordinary business engagements'. A figure of £100,000 per annum was 'larger than we are accustomed to see' − but it appeared to Hedley Byrne that they should have no problems over £17,000, which they duly invested.

Shortly afterwards, Easipower went into liquidation. Hedley Byrne sued and the trial judge said: 'I have no hesitation in holding that Mr Heller was guilty of negligence in giving such a reference without making plain − as he did not − that it was intended to be a very guarded reference . . . Properly understood, according to its ordinary and natural meaning, the reference was not justified by facts known to Mr Heller.'

The case eventually reached the House of Lords, on three points. First, Heller's protested that they had not been negligent. Second, they maintained that there was in any event no legally enforceable duty on their part to take care. They were, after all, only volunteers, supplying a free service for which (they said) they should not be held liable in law. And third, they relied upon their disclaimer. As usual with banks and others, the reference was given 'without legal responsibility'.

The Law Lords unanimously held that even a volunteer must normally take proper care in circumstances such as these. The supplier of the reference knows that its recipient intends to rely upon it and he 'owes a duty of care' to that recipient, even though he is merely performing a kindness.

Lord Morris: 'If, in a sphere in which a person is so placed that others could reasonably rely on his judgment or his skill or his ability to make careful enquiry, a person takes it on himself to give information or advice to, or allows his information or advice to be passed on to, another person who — as he knows or should know — will place reliance upon it, then a duty of care will arise.'

In normal circumstances, a volunteer may only be under a duty to give honest advice. But, as one businessman to another, the duty now goes further. And breach of that duty will give rise to an action for damages for negligence, if the recipient of the free advice suffers loss.

Fortunately for the bankers, though, the judges decided that the disclaimer was effective. You could not reasonably say that a giver of advice 'without responsibility' should have legal responsibility heaped upon him. There was a clear notice, excluding the normal rights. Therefore the question as to whether or not the merchant bankers had in fact been negligent did not arise. They won their case.

So the moral for any giver of advice or information, paid or unpaid (but especially for the gratuitous provider of the milk of commercial kindness) is: disclaim, loud and clear. By all means give advice, information or references, directly or through your staff, but always add a disclaimer. The words 'without responsibility' or 'without legal responsibility' are the right ones — not 'without prejudice', 'ex gratia' or (still less) 'E & OE'. Any or all of these might suffice, but when we know from the House of Lords that 'without legal responsibility' provides full cover, why take chances?

This is a rule, of course, which you should not only follow for yourself but one about which you should instruct all your staff. Anyone who gives references, or any other sort of advice or information, should disclaim. 'Failure to include a disclaimer in references or advice will be regarded as a serious disciplinary offence.'

There is a possibility that these rules will be affected by the new, anti-exclusion clause legislation. The Unfair Contract Terms Act provides that where a business contract or notice contains an exclusion clause on someone's own, standard written terms, it will only be upheld if it 'satisfies the test of reasonableness'. If disclaimers in references were ever held to be 'unfair' or 'unreasonable', who then would give references, free, and out of the kindness of their commercial hearts?

So as it is likely that the rules in *Hedley Byrne* v. *Heller* will remain effective, consider how they have been affected by two, important later cases.

In *Mutual Life and Citizen's Assurance Company Limited and Another* v. *Evatt,* Mr Evatt claimed damages against Mutual Life for negligent advice given to him gratuitously. He was a policy holder in Mutual Life; he had asked for advice concerning the safety of investments in another company which, together with Mutual Life, was a subsidiary of a third; and — without any disclaimer — Mutual Life had told him that the company in question was 'financially stable and that it would be safe to invest in it'. Mutual Life knew that Mr Evatt would rely on the advice given and therefore (he maintained) when he suffered financial loss through relying on that advice, he was entitled to damages as the advice was given negligently.

The House of Lords held that, even if Mr Evatt were able to establish all the facts alleged and to prove negligence, that 'would establish no more than that the company could have provided him with reliable advice if it had chosen to make the enquiries requisite to provide the material necessary to form a reliable judgment . . .'. He did not aver that Mutual Life to his knowledge 'carried on the business of giving advice on investments or in some other way let it be known to him that they claimed to possess the necessary skill and competence to do so and were prepared to exercise the necessary diligence to give reliable advice to him on the subject matter of the enquiry.' So the law did not impose a duty of care on Mutual Life in those circumstances.

The Mutual Life case narrowed the effect of *Hedley Byrne* v. *Heller*. By a majority of three to two, the House of Lords held that 'in the absence of contract, the maker of a statement of fact or the giver of an opinion owed to a person whom he could reasonably foresee would rely on it in a matter affecting his economic interest a duty to be honest in making the statement'. But there was no 'duty of care' unless the relationship between the adviser and the advised was 'a fiduciary one or possessed some other characteristic which would give rise to such a duty'. Unless there was a relationship of the utmost good faith, a contractual relationship, or at least the relationship of business adviser, then there is apparently no duty of care.

Finally, remember the words of Lord Denning: 'If a man, who has or who professes to have special knowledge or skill, makes a representation by virtue thereof to another, be it advice, information or opinion — with the intention of inducing them to enter into a contract with him, he is under a duty to use reasonable care to see that the representation is correct, and that the advice, information or opinion is reliable. If he negligently gives unsound advice or misleading information or expresses an erroneous opinion, and thereby induces the other side into a contract with him, he is liable in damages.'

More of this (in Part 2). Please take care when you confer on another your 'advice, information or opinion' however gratuitously. The milk of human kindness may prove an extremely expensive legal substance.

Chapter 7

'Interference with goods'

The Torts (Interference with Goods) Act, 1977, came fully into operation from 1 June 1978. It changes a mass of legal rules and procedures which operate when one person fails to take proper care of the goods of another. It repeals *The Disposal of Uncollected Goods Act, 1952*, and substitutes new, simplified procedures which apply when you get lumbered with other people's property which they fail or refuse to collect or pay for. Here is a breakdown of the main features of this statute.

*   *   *

If you receive another person's property into your possession, he is the 'bailor' (who has 'bailed' his goods to you) and you are the 'bailee'. If (as is likely) the 'bailment' occurs as a result of a contract, then your rights and duties and those of the bailor will depend (as always) upon the terms of your agreement.

All too often, the parties to a contract fail to spell out all the terms. For instance, what is to happen if the goods are lost, damaged or destroyed while in your care? In the absence of some special arrangement to the contrary, the bailor must (in broad terms) take as much care of other people's goods as if they were his own. He will not be automatically liable to pay compensation merely because they go astray while in his hands. He 'owes a duty of care' to the bailor; and damages will be payable if he is in breach of that duty.

Equally, in contracts where the bailee is to expend time or materials on the bailor's property, he (the bailee) will have a 'lien' on the goods – the right to keep them until they have been paid for. Similar rights are enjoyed by a warehouseman.

In the past, all these rights could (in the main) be excluded by agreement. Today, *The Unfair Contracts Terms Act, 1977* applies to all contracts for the provision of services – including those of a bailee. Where the deal is set out in the bailee's own written, standard terms, most exclusion clauses will only be valid if they are reasonable. In any event, any clause which seeks to restrict or exclude liability for causing death or personal injury is itself a dead letter.

If a bailee wrongfully detains goods belonging to the bailor, the bailor used to sue for 'detinue' – for the return of goods detained and for damages for their wrongful detention. The Torts (Interference with Goods) Act abolishes 'detinue'.Today, if (for instance) you wrongfully refuse to return your customer's article, then he would bring proceedings for 'wrongful interference' with goods – for 'converting them' to your use. If the plaintiff gets damages equal to the full value of the goods, then his right to them will be extinguished. Conversely, if you put up the defence that you 'acted in the mistaken but honest belief that you had a good title' to the property, then even if you are wrong, an allowance will be made as against any damages payable for the value of any improvement which you may have made to the goods, (e.g. by repairing them).

Now suppose that several prople claim ownership of an article and you are happy to give it up only to the true owner. The Act provides a procedure to be followed. You should put the case into the hands of your lawyer, to get on with following the rules.

The most important part of the Act is undoubtedly Section 12, which deals with uncollected goods, in three circumstances:

1 Where you retain them in your possession when your customer is in breach of his obligation to take delivery of the goods or to give directions for their delivery; or

2 Where you could impose such an obligation by giving notice to your customer, but you cannot trace him or communicate with him; or

3 Where you can 'reasonably expect to be relieved of any duty to safeguard the goods on giving notice to the bailor', but (once again) cannot track him down.

In the above cases, you may 'impose an obligation on your customer to take delivery of the goods or to give directions for their delivery'.

The procedures are laid down in the first Schedule to the Act and they start by your giving a notice to your customer, in writing, and either by delivering it or leaving it at his address or by post (recorded delivery, please). The notice will specify your name and address; give details of goods concerned and say that they are ready for delivery; and specify how much you expect to be paid for the goods before you hand them over.

If you have taken in an article for 'repair or other treatment', there will normally be an express or implied term that it will be handed over when the job has been done. In that case, you may give notice at any time after completion of the work. And a similar rule applies if you have taken in the article 'for valuation or appraisal, or for storage or warehousing'.

Next, you should give a similar notice of your intention to sell the goods. The period between the giving of the notice and the date specified when you intend to sell it must be 'such as will afford the bailor a reasonable opportunity of taking delivery of the goods'. If the bailor has to pay money to the bailee and if that amount became due before the notice was given, the period should be not less than three months − otherwise, 'reasonableness' will (as always) depend upon all the circumstances of the case.

If you do sell having given your notices − or if you cannot track down the bailor, so as to warn him − then, provided you are 'reasonably satisfied that the bailor owns the goods', you will be entitled as against him to sell. If you do so, you will not free yourself from the owner's rights − if he turns up, he can demand the value of the goods (less the cost of putting them right or storing them). But the bailor will have no legal claim against you − other than for the balance of proceeds of sale, after deduction of your account for repair, storage and/or the cost of sale.

Alternatively, if you wish to be even safer in your approach, you may apply to the court for authority to sell. And anyway, while the rules are new, it is as well to get your solicitor to check out their operation in practice and to help you where necessary.

Finally, remember that these rules apply only in England and Wales. The Disposal of Uncollected Goods Act was repealed for Scotland, and now there are new rules on bailment in Scotland which differ from those in England and Wales. If you dislike the way that Parliament has laid down the rules for you, then − in this area at least − you could normally change them by agreement. So make your own contracts and expect to be bound by them.

Chapter 8

Passing off and trade marks

The name of a well known product is likely to be the seller's greatest asset. He may have spent a fortune on building up the goodwill which attaches to that name. If he has been able to register it, then he has the sole right to use it and will be able to take proceedings for infringement of his trade mark. But even if he has not registered the name, he may still take steps to prevent other people's goods from being 'passed off' as his. It is a civil offence (as opposed to a criminal one) to 'pass off' goods as being those of someone else.

In one famous case, the manufacturers of Babycham champagne perry discovered that when customers went into a certain public house and asked for 'Babycham', champagne perry of a different brand was being poured into their glasses. So the manufacturers of the other drink were cashing in on the popularity of the Babycham label. Babycham brought a 'passing off' action and obtained an injunction — an order restraining the publican from passing off champagne perry not manufactured by them as being Babycham.

So if a customer comes into a shop and asks for 'Brand W wool', it will not do to wrap up 'Brand V wool', leaving the customer to believe that he is getting the brand she asked for. If someone demands an 'A Line Corset', she must not be sold a 'Z line', in such a way that she may be deceived.

This is not to say, of course, that a seller must give the customer that which he asks for. There is nothing whatsoever to prevent a retailer, for instance, when asked for 'Brand W' wool from saying: 'We don't stock Brand W, I'm afraid. But I have some Brand V, and I think that you'll find it just as good. It's also rather less expensive . . . .' Alternatively, when asked for 'A line' corsets, their manufacturers have no valid complaint if the shopkeeper, honestly expressing his bona fide belief, tells the customer, 'We think that A line are unshapely. Would you like to try the latest Z line?'

The essence of 'passing off', then, lies in the probability that members of the public will be deceived. If a manufacturer can show that people have actually been deceived, then he will probably win his case. But he is not bound to show actual deception. It is enough if he shows the likelihood that deception will arise.

Take the famous case of *Daks* v. *Kidax*. The manufacturers of the world-famous Daks slacks tried to prevent the use of the name Kidax, on the ground that members of the public would be likely to believe that these were kiddies' Daks. But they lost their case. They could prove no actual deception and as Kidax had been on the market for a long time, the court was unwilling to accept that deception was likely in the future.

Of course, deception may arise not only from the name but also from the make-up or presentation of the product. Suppose, for instance, that 'D line' corsets had become famous for the D-shaped box in which they were sold. Another manufacturer produces a product with an entirely different name, but markets it in the same shaped box. There may be just as active 'passing off' here as if the name had been identical. Once the particular box had become associated in the minds of the public at large with a particular company's goods, that company acquires a right to the sole use of that make-up for the class of goods in question, just as successfully as if the design had been registered.

'But suppose that we manufacture, say, woollen garments and either the name or the make-up happens to be similar to that of one already on the market — but we don't know of this. We have no intention of deceiving anyone. Could the other manufacturers do anything about it?'

Certainly. To succeed in a 'passing off' action, the plaintiffs do not have to show any actual intention to deceive anyone.

'So it's really up to us to make sure that we don't come too near to anyone else's name or to the way in which they market their products?'

Correct.

'What can an aggrieved manufacturer do about it?'

He can apply to the court for an injunction, restraining the competing manufacturer from putting out goods in the deceptive way or under the deceptive style in question. If the goods are already in the factories, he can seek an injunction, to prevent their sale in the way complained of. He may also recover damages, if he can show that as a result of the 'passing off', his trade was adversely affected.

Naturally, if the plaintiffs succeed in this sort of action, the defendants may suffer heavily. If you are at the wrong end of a 'passing off' action, you may lose all you have spent on wrapping, packing, naming the goods, printing or marketing them. If the design is deceptive, you may lose everything. If you are simply selling them, in so far as you have been actively doing the 'passing off', you may find that you have to pay the costs of a legal action and damages into the bargain. And while you may be entitled to an indemnity from your suppliers if they were responsible for the 'passing off', you may still yourself be held responsible in the first place.

So respect other people's goodwill.

Even if you give something away as part of a sales drive

this does not mean that you can pretend that it was the creation of someone else who did not create it. Merely because you do not charge for an object does not mean that you can pass that object off as your own, if it was someone else's — and that other person had not given his permission. And if you sell premium goods, because the people who buy from you are going to give away the goods, rather than sell them, you are no more entitled to use other people's names on those goods than you would be if you were selling them directly to the public or if your customer was going to do so. All this was made abundantly clear in the High Court case of *Societé Anonyme Unic* v. *Lindeau Products Limited.*

Towards the end of 1961, Lindeau Products sold over a million pens to Lever Brothers, to be given away with packets of Omo. It was the defendants' business to sell promotion ideas 'to leading companies', and it was their suggestion that this give-away should be attached to the purchase of this famous detergent. After all, a gift will add brightness and lightness to the lives of the giver and the receiver — provided that the receiver buys more of the goods with which the gift is handed out.

Anyway, all would have been well were it not for the fact that the pens each had the word 'Everglide', written in very small letters around the button at the top of the pen'.

Unfortunately for Lindeau Products, 'Everglide' was a registered trade mark. It had been registered 'in respect of pens and parts of pens' by Societé Anonyme Unic, of Rue Juliette Dodu, Paris. As soon as they discovered what had happened, they sued for an injunction and for damages. After all, anyone who goes to the trouble of registering a trade mark and succeeds in his application is entitled to protect the goodwill which lies in that trade mark. Anyone who infringes that goodwill by using the trade mark without permission is liable to be dragged into court and to be restrained by an order of that court from continuing his wrongful behaviour in the future — and damages will be assessed to compensate the proprietors of the mark.

When the case came to court, Lindeau Products argued that when pens were bought by Lever Brothers, the purchasers were 'completely unaware of the existence of the mark on the pens'. The pens were then 'distributed as gifts without re-

ference to any brand'. The defendants were therefore, it was
said, entitled to raise a defence under Section 5 of *The Trade
Marks Act, 1938.*

Consider, first, Section 4. This says that, in general, 'the
registration . . . of a person . . . as proprietor of a trade mark
. . . in respect of any goods shall, if valid, give or be deemed
to have given to that person the exclusive right to the use of
the trade mark in relation to those goods. Without prejudice
to the generality of the foregoing words, that right shall be
deemed to be infringed by any person who, not being the
proprietor of the trade mark or a registered user thereof
using by way of a permitted use, uses a mark identical with it
or so nearly resembling it as to be likely to deceive or cause
confusion, in the course of trade, in relation to any goods in
respect of which it is registered, and in such a manner as to
render the use of the mark likely to be taken either

a   as being used as a trade mark; or
b   in a case in which the trade mark is used upon the goods
     or in physical relation thereto or in an advertising circu-
     lar or other advertisement to the public, as importing a
     reference to some person having the right either as
     proprietor or as registered user to use the trade mark or
     to goods with which such person as aforesaid is con-
     nected in the course of trade.'

This Section is drafted as widely as possible to protect the
registered owner of a trade mark. Compare the incomplete
protection given by the Act to a person whose trade mark is
not registered. As Section 2 puts it: 'No person shall be
entitled to institute any proceedings to prevent, or to recover
damages for, the infringement of an unregistered trade mark,
but nothing . . . shall be deemed to affect any rights of action
against any person for passing off goods as the goods of
another person or the remedies in respect thereof.'

Reverting to a trade mark infringement, one of the defences
is provided by Section 5. This says: 'In any action for infringement of the right to the use of a trade mark given by
registration . . . no injunction or other relief shall be granted
to the plaintiff if the defendant establishes to the satisfaction
of the court that the use of which the plaintiff complains is
not likely to deceive or cause confusion or to be taken as
indicating a connection in the course of trade between the

goods and some person having the right either as proprietor or as registered user to use the trade mark.'

It was upon this exception that Lindeau Products relied. 'There was no deception, confusion, or suggestion of a connection in the course of trade', said Counsel for the defendants. After all, how could there be? The buyers (Lever Brothers) did not know of the mark and the goods were sold 'without reference to the brand'.

During the course of the evidence, witnesses were asked whether they could read the word written around the button at the top of the pen. Some managed to read it with the naked eye, but others needed a magnifying glass. The Judge, Mr Justice Ungoed-Thomas, was satisfied that 'the word had been used on the pens as a trade mark', but he questioned whether the sale of the pens to the distributors of the detergent or the distribution of the pens to the public constituted an infringement of the mark.

Eventually the Judge decided against the defendants. 'It seems a matter of inevitable inference', he said, 'that among the persons who bought the packets of detergents there would have been some conversant with trade marks used on ball-points, who would have recognised the mark and assumed the pens to have been connected with the plaintiffs. The plaintiffs will be granted an injunction to restrain further infringement of their mark, and an inquiry as to damages.'

Now, this was no joke for the defendants. The damages might well be heavy. The court costs would not be light. And the injunction might leave them with literally thousands of ball-points on their hands—the fact that these were not to be sold but merely to be given away would make them no less of a waste. What may be 'free' to the lucky members of the public to whom they are given, is far from free to the buyers of the premium product.

The moral, then? Be careful of the names which you apply to products, even those you give away. If you are infringing someone's trade mark, you will be in trouble.

Nor is that the end of the matter as we have already seen. Passing-off actions can be as effective as actions for infringements of trade marks.

You will note that while you must take care not to deceive the people to whom you sell goods, you also have a responsibility which goes a stage further. You must not let those to whom you sell goods deliberately or unconsciously deceive those members of the public to whom they pass those goods on. You must not 'put into their hands that which may become an instrument of deception towards others'. That was, in effect, what Lindeau Products did when they handed over to Lever Products the pens with the 'Everglide' registration mark. Lever Brothers were not deceived. The brand name was no part of their bargain. But when they gave away the goods to the public, members of the public might well have been deceived into thinking that those pens were the product of the plaintiff's work. The fact that the pens were given away rather than items to be sold, was completely irrelevant.

How you 'put into the hands of the public' the goods concerned is irrelevant. If those goods become 'instruments of deception' you are in trouble. In these days when so much advertising is lavished and so little expense is spared in the building up of a trade name, its infringement seldom goes unnoticed. If the mark has been registered as a trade mark, then an action may lie for infringement of that mark. But even if it has not been registered, to be at the wrong end of a passing-off action brings joy to no one.

"CAN I MAKE YOU AN OFFER, 'SUBJECT TO HUSBAND'?"

Part Two
CONTRACTS

Chapter 9

Introduction

A contract is a legally binding agreement made between two
or more parties. Liability of the parties under that contract
normally depends upon the terms of the agreement. These
may be either express or implied.

An express term is one which has been explicitly agreed
. . . the price, the quantity, the nature or quality of the goods,
plus the delivery date and the like. Additional terms are implied, sometimes as a result of court decisions, sometimes
thanks to *The Sale of Goods Act, 1893.*

The first place to look to discover whether or not one contracting party can hold the other liable under the agreement
is at the agreement itself — which may be oral, in writing or
partly oral and partly written. There is no legal requirement
that a contract involving a product must be written to be
binding. Only in rare cases will the law not enforce a deal
because of the absence of writing. The main terms of a contract for the transfer of an interest in land, or of guarantee, or
of hire purchase, or of insurance, must be in written form. In
most other cases, an oral deal is as binding as a written one.

In practice, the trouble with an oral contract, of course,
arises when the parties disagree on its terms. Can they prove
an express agreement? What implications should be drawn
from the words used — and what were they?

So wise contractors either initially put or later confirm the
important terms, in written form. Where liability depends
upon contract, look for writing; and then see whether there
are further terms to be implied.

Normally, only those who are party (or 'privy') to a contract can acquire rights under it. With the exception of
collateral warranties (representations made usually by manufacturers but sometimes by dealers, to induce customers to
enter into contracts with others — details in Chapter 14)
where there is no 'privity of contract', there can be no good
contractual claim.

As we have seen (in Part 1), a duty may be owed to total strangers under the rules on negligence. But liability for a product is generally owed in contract only to other parties to the deal.

So in this Part, we examine contractual liability for products; the nature of 'privity of contract', and exceptions to it; and we look especially at implied terms concerning the quality and fitness of products (generally made under *The Sale of Goods Act, 1893*) and at the limits placed on the power of contracting parties to reduce or exclude contractual liability through contractual terms, notices or disclaimers. *The Supply of Goods (Implied Terms) Act, 1973* and *The Unfair Contract Terms Act, 1977*, have brought about massive changes in this field.

So also has the famous Romalpa decision. This established that the seller of goods may not only retain their ownership until he has paid for them but even trace the proceeds of sale of those goods, when they pass into the hands of third parties. We look at the Romalpa rules generally, but with specific reference to defective products.

Remember, though, that a claim arising in a contract due to a defect in a product depends upon proof of an express or implied term; of breach of that term; and of damage flowing from the breach. Once again, no default under the contract means no right to damages. In contract law, the only strict liability arises from the agreement of the parties. A manufacturer may become his customer's insurer. But until the law changes (as it probably will) in this area too, no fault means no liability in law.

* * *

Before you can understand how contractual protection may be removed, you must know the basic essentials of a valid, binding contract. Where those essentials are present, the contract is binding. Subject to restrictions on exclusions, all parties to the agreement are bound by it. Conversely, if any essential of the contract is missing, either party may refuse to proceed. Exclusion clauses are irrelevant because the agreement as a whole is totally ineffective.

Suppose, then, that you are a supplier of products. You recognise that the risks involved in the sale are greater than its potential profits? You are worried at the rights which the buyer will have, if the product is defective? Before you worry about the effectiveness of the exemption clauses, you should look and see whether the contract as a whole is viable. If you understand the rules which now follow, the chances are very good that you can emerge unscathed from the entire, ill-conceived operation.

Or are you a purchaser who has acquired a good deal? Maybe there are no exclusion clauses or you are satisfied that they are unreasonable and would not be enforceable, thanks to the new statutes? You wish to know whether you can force the unwilling supplier to honour his obligations? Once again, consider whether your contract contains all the essential terms. The absence of even one will destroy the entire deal.

Chapter 10

Offers, acceptances, counter-offers and 'invitations to treat'

The first stage in making a binding contract is the 'offer'. 'I offer to produce these goods for you. . . .' 'I offer to buy these products from you. . . .' 'We will distribute these items on your behalf. . . .'

If you advertise goods in a catalogue or exhibit them in a trade fair or in a shop window, you are not making an 'offer' but only inviting others to offer to purchase from you. You are issuing a so-called 'invitation to treat'. Therefore, when your customer says: 'I'll take those goods . . . I'll buy that machinery . . . I accept your offer . . .', he is in law himself *making* the offer.

At this stage, you may reject that offer or accept it on different terms. That is why no one in *civil* law is forced to sell goods at the price marked, to any particular customer or at all. Provided that he does not discriminate against customers on grounds of sex or race, he may contract or not, as he sees fit.

In *criminal* law, the rules are different. *The Trade Descriptions Act, 1968,* makes it an offence to advertise or to offer goods for sale at a price lower than that at which you are in fact prepared to supply them. Most wrongful acts (including, frequently, the marketing of a dangerous or defective product) produce both potential civil and criminal consequences (see Chapter 29 — with special reference to manufacturers' liability under Section 6 of the Health and Safety at Work Act). In this instance, though, the supplier is generally civilly in the clear but criminally at risk.

To be capable of acceptance, an offer must also be *unconditional*. 'I can supply you these goods at your price, if I can get the board to agree . . .', is not an 'offer' which the customer can accept. 'I offer you this job subject to references . . .', or 'We will gladly supply this product, if we can obtain the necessary materials . . .', are both statements of intent, but not acceptable offers.

Note, though, the vital distinction between a 'conditional offer' and an 'offer subject to conditions'. 'We offer to supply these goods subject to our usual terms of trading, printed on the back hereof . . .' is a firm, acceptable and 'unconditional' offer to supply the goods on the terms stated. Every offer is made 'on conditions'. But no acceptable offer is 'conditional'.

Similar rules apply to 'acceptances'. Particularly, to be effective, an acceptance must be both 'unconditional' and the other party's terms must be accepted.

If you write: 'We thank you for your order which we accept, subject to . . .', you are almost certainly giving a 'conditional acceptance', which has no legal effect whatsoever. You are not bound to satisfy the condition; meanwhile, the other contracting party may revoke his offer — for any reason or for none, but probably because he can do a better deal elsewhere.

More subtly, you are likely to send an 'acceptance' which is 'subject to our standard terms of trading'. If these differ substantially from the terms in the offer, you are not 'accepting' the offer made by the customer but (in law) making a 'counter-offer' — which he, in his turn, may accept or reject.

Suppose, for instance, that you are a supplier of products. Your customer's 'acceptance' includes a clause which im-

poses new responsibilities on you for research or testing or
which includes exclusion clauses which may have some legal
effect. Or suppose that you offer to supply goods on a certain date, specifying that 'while every effort will be made to
deliver on the stated date, no responsibility can be accepted
for delay, howsoever caused'. Your customer 'accepts' on
the basis that 'time of delivery shall be an essential term of
this contract'.

In all those cases, your customer is in reality saying: 'I do
not agree to purchase your products on your terms. I will
only do so on mine — which are different'. He is seeking to
substitute his terms for yours. He is offering to buy — not
accepting your offer.

Note that the names of the documents are irrelevant. You
may call your 'offer' an 'order', 'acknowledgement', 'quo-
tation', 'estimate' or any other name that suits your current
fancy or that of your lawyers. Equally, your customer may
put his terms into an 'acceptance', 'acknowledgement of
order', 'confirmation' or any other document. 'The law
looks at the reality and not at the form' — at the situation
created by the document, not at the name conferred upon
it.

So what happens in practice? The supplier makes his offer
— perhaps in a firm estimate, a quote or even in a letter. The
customer sends his 'counter-offer'. If the supplier spots the
differences and rejects them, he makes a 'counter-counter-
offer'. "We thank you for your 'acceptance' but we regret
that we cannot guarantee the delivery date as you ask . . . that
we are not prepared to undertake the additional research
and testing which would be required by your clause . . . that
we are not prepared to contract other than on the basis that
we retain title in the goods until payment is made." (See
Chapter 25 for the Romalpa rules).

At this stage, there is still no deal. Negotiations are proceeding — or, perhaps, have come to an abrupt end. There is
no contract, though. Either party may depart from the bargaining.

Now suppose that the supplier does not spot the differences
in the customer's terms and simply delivers the goods. By
delivering, he impliedly accepts the terms in the counter-
offer. So far as an exclusion clause is contained in that

counter-offer (for example) and is binding, the customer is in luck. Generally, he who contracts last contracts best — it is the last document in the chain that contains the 'agreed' terms. It is irrelevant that the agreement is implied rather than expressed.

Alternatively, maybe the supplier gets the last written word. Perhaps he puts in a counter-counter-offer and then delivers the goods, which the customer accepts. In that case, when the customer accepted the goods, he also accepted the suppliers' counter-counter-offer. The suppliers' terms prevail.

Chapter 11

Other essentials of a binding contract

If an unconditional offer has been unconditionally accepted, what other ingredients are essential for a binding contract?

First: some contracts must be either made in writing or evidenced by some note or memorandum in writing, if they are to be legally binding. In the past, writing was required for most contracts of any importance.

As discussed in the Introduction of this Part, the requirement for writing is almost solely limited to: contracts for the transfer of an interest in land; contracts of hire purchase, insurance or for the transfer of shares; and contracts of guarantee.

The expression: 'There was nothing in writing, so I hereby cancel' should be expunged from the business vocabulary. The absence of writing makes the terms of the deal harder to prove . . . and makes dispute and litigation much more likely in origin and unpredictable in outcome . . . but it does not normally affect the validity of the bargain. In cases for the supply, sale or distribution of products, writing is legally irrelevant.

Most deals may effectively be made by telephone. However, wise contractors confirm terms in writing, for the avoidance of dispute. Equally, if you receive someone else's purported confirmation of (perhaps) a telephone order or agreement to supply, check it with care. Failure to challenge an incorrect statement in a letter of confirmation is almost always fatal to denial of accuracy at a later stage.

Next, in England and Wales (but not in Scotland), a contract will not be binding unless there is some 'consideration'. Each party must give something in return for what he receives — if only one promise in return for another. 'In consideration of your agreeing to supply this product at that price, I undertake to pay that price. . . .'

In practice, 'consideration' generally becomes a live problem where you seek an option. 'Will you keep that offer open until tomorrow?' 'Can I have time to consult my board?' A simple agreement to give the option is not binding in law. 'Consideration' in such a case is normally called a deposit.

If you put down a deposit on goods and then decide not to proceed with the deal, the deposit is usually forfeited, although there is nothing to prevent you from coming to some other arrangement, like agreeing that the deposit money will be put on one side, as credit towards a future purchase. Conversely, if the deal goes off through the fault of the party who takes the deposit, it will be returnable.

Contracts on the sale of property are invariably paid 'subject to contract'. If no contract is made, the deposit is repayable. Equally, the party who takes the deposit on that basis is not bound to grant an option. It is merely 'an earnest of good faith' on the part of the proposed purchaser.

Suppose, then, that there is an unconditional offer, unconditionally accepted; that there is no need for writing and that the parties have exchanged promises so that there is 'consideration' for the deal. That leaves 'illegality' and 'capacity to contract'.

An illegal contract is void. (But see also page 77 for the case of *Shelley* v. *Paddock*.) Anyone who makes an agreement (for instance) to evade VAT or tax or customs duty is not bound by his wrongful act. Or suppose that you engage someone to work on a defence contract but you cannot get clearance for him. You may not be allowed to tell him why you are not prepared to honour your word, but the continuation of the contract of employment may be in grave peril.

Finally, parties must have 'contractual capacity'. A 'minor' — that is, someone under the age of 18 — cannot be held to a business contract, nor can he be forced to repay a loan. Only contracts for 'goods or services reasonably necessary for him at the time when he made the contract' will be binding. A business deal is never one for a 'necessary'. So do not give credit to youngsters or make advances on pay to young employees – unless you recognise that the law will not be able to help you, if they dishonour their obligations.

A company may make an effective contract within the limits laid down in the objects clause of its Memorandum of Association. Any contract which goes outside those powers is said to be *ultra vires*.

However, thanks to EEC legislation with which we have had to comply, even an *ultra vires* contract may now be enforced by the innocent, unwitting third party.

Equally, of course, a company may be bound by its deals in the same way as a private individual. As it is individuals who make contracts on behalf of companies – whether for the supply or purchase or distribution of products or for any other reason – we must now conclude this introduction to the law of contracts by considering some of the rules on agency. For instance, suppose that one of your staff enters into a contract to supply a product, and the liability under that contract is greater than you are willingly prepared to undertake. In what circumstances are you entitled to call off the deal on the basis that your employee or subordinate has no authority to make it?

Chapter 12

Agents — their liability and yours

Liability for your own mistakes and misdemeanours is bad enough. Liability for the misdeeds of others is worse.

Criminal responsibility (Chapter 29) rests on those individuals who have contravened the rules either personally or through their servants or agents. If you hand someone a gun to kill your enemy then your penalty, like your guilt, may exceed his. But if he takes his own unlawful initiative without your knowledge or consent and (at least under the Health and

Safety at Work Act) with no 'consent', 'connivance' or 'neglect' on your part, then he, not you, will be criminally responsible.

In civil law, though, you are 'vicariously liable' for the negligence of your employee; you take the benefit of all that he does correctly in the course of his work for you and you normally shoulder the burden of his misdeeds. If he is negligent in, say, the production of goods for you and on your behalf, then the 'ultimate consumer' who suffers will be entitled to look to you for his remedy. You may have a right to an indemnity from the actual 'tortfeasor', but if he is a 'man of straw', that remedy may not be worth having, so hopefully you are fully and properly insured.

To what extent can your servant or agent impose *contractual* obligations which other parties can enforce against you?

Naturally, you give certain power to those who operate for you or on your behalf. They have your 'actual' authority, normally within limits which you specify. You are bound by any deal made by your servant or agent within the limits of the authority you gave him.

What, though, if your agent exceeds your authority? Suppose, for instance, that he is offered a deal which he regards as both important and beneficial to his employers. Unfortunately, to tie up the arrangement he would have to go beyond the authority you gave him. If he is selling, perhaps the customer is offering a fraction less than he is authorised to accept; or if he is buying, the price may be a little more than he was told to pay.

Usually, your employee (or other agent) tries to contact you, his employer (or principal). To no avail. You are out, away, unavailable. So he is in a well known spot. If he exceeds his authority, he is likely to be in trouble. After all, what is the point of putting a limit on his powers and informing him of that limit if he is going to go beyond it on his own initiative? On the other hand, if he allows the deal to escape him, you may say, perhaps with total justification: 'Why didn't you use your initiative? What's the use of employing a person like you at your level, if you are not prepared to take a decision off your own bat?'

Precisely the same rules would apply to an agent who gave a warranty about a product which he is not authorised to give — or who recommends a product for an unsuitable purpose. If he is acting within the scope of his apparent or implied or ostensible authority, his employers will have to accept legal responsibility for the results of his incorrect statement.

In countries, companies and firms where an employee who makes a mistake is likely to suffer while one who does well rarely benefits, the employee will play safe and stick to his authority. Elsewhere, he is likely to shrug, to take the plunge and to hope for the commercial best.

If all goes well, the deal is approved — no problem. But if the contract goes sour for the employers or principals, they will not only protest to the employee, they will probably also contact the other party and say: 'We are very sorry, but Mr So-and-so had no authority to make the deal on our behalf'.

At this stage, the law will intervene on behalf of the innocent other party, deceived into entering the arrangement by his reasonable belief that your servant or agent was entitled to do the deal on your behalf. If you gave him your 'apparent' or 'ostensible' authority, the other party is entitled to rely upon it and to insist upon the carrying out of the contract in precisely the same way as if the individual concerned had your 'actual' authority.

You must take care, then, not to 'clothe' your servants or agents with authority which they do not possess. If you 'hold out' a servant or agent as entitled to make a contract on your behalf, then you are bound.

This concept is technically known as 'the doctrine of holding out' — which is not (as a solicitors' examination candidate recently suggested) a branch of the law on indecent exposure!

In each case, then, the law looks to see whether the employee or agent was 'held out' as having the authority which in actuality he did not possess. Would a person of his status or standing, with the credentials which you provided for him, reasonably be expected to be entitled to make the deal in question?

You might, of course, put the other party 'on notice' of the limits on the authority of the servant or agent. 'We enclose herewith details of the research and testing which we are willing and able to carry out, if required, on our products. No

employee is authorised by us to extend those limits without
my personal, written authority. . . .' Or: 'I am pleased to
introduce our Mr Black. He has authority to place orders on
our behalf up to a maximum of £. . .'

Alternatively, the other party may impliedly have notice
of limits on authority. You would hardly expect an office
boy to be able to place an order for intricate machinery, nor
the junior clerk for a major computer. But directors, company
secretaries, senior managers and other executives are likely to
have implied authority to take major decisions.

*   *   *

The above rules apply to situations where the relationship
of employee/employer or principal/agent provably exists.
With the former, there is seldom any real problem, at least in
the area of product liability. Difficulty is more likely to arise
when you deal with 'independent contractors' or 'self-
employed' agents.

If a manufacturer sells direct to his customer, then he
bears his own liability. If a retailer sells goods which he has
obtained from a distributor who got them from the producer,
each bears his own liability. But where you buy or sell through
an 'agent', is he really your 'agent' or is he acting as a
principal?

Section 6 of the Health and Safety at Work Act (Chapter
30) applies to 'importers'. If you import *directly* any articles
or substances designed or intended (respectively) for use at
work, then you are within the jurisdiction of our courts and
must bear the same responsibility as you would have done,
had you manufactured the products in the UK. If, on the
other hand, you import through an agent, the next question
must be: While he calls himself an 'agent', is he in fact the
principal? Is he doing the importing and then selling the goods
to you – in which case he bears the responsibility; or is he
acting for you and merely placing the order on your behalf,
leaving you with any legal liability?

The same questions arise if you sell through an 'agent'. Is
he buying the goods from you then selling them on as
'principal' – even if he says that he has the 'sole agency' for
a particular territory? Or is he really acting for you and on

your behalf, so that there is a direct contractual relationship between you and the customer whom he introduces to you?

Many commercial agencies are (legally, at least) nothing of the kind. Your agents may well have special privileges as a result of their contractual relationship with you, but they deal direct with their customers — even though they stand to gain if you do well and to lose if you fail to honour your obligations.

*   *   *

If an employee's carelessness results in a product becoming defective, his employer will bear the legal responsibility. The employee's liability is far more theoretical than real.

The negligent employee, of course, is in breach of his contract with his employer. In appropriate cases, the employer may be entitled to dismiss him 'fairly'. An employee's 'conduct' is one admissible reason which *may* make a dismissal 'fair'.

However, the employer must also act 'reasonably' in treating the reason as sufficient to warrant depriving the employee of his livelihood. 'Reasonableness' depends upon all the circumstances of the particular case — not least, whether the employee was really told of his duties; whether he knew the likely results of his negligence; whether the employer operated a fair system for discipline and dismissals — including giving the employee the right to state his case and to appeal, where possible, to a higher level of authority.

So the employee will bear his personal responsibility towards his employer; and the employer will be liable in contract to those with whom he has 'privity of contract' — while in the tort of negligence, he (the employer) will bear a responsibility stretching outwards towards 'the ultimate consumer'.

Similarly, the agent has a contractual responsibility upwards towards his principal and downwards towards his customers. Subject to exclusion clauses (the law on which follows in Part 3) his duties depend upon those contracts. And as a principal, he bears the same responsibility as any other distributor or intermediary.

One final warning. The laws on agency are complex and an

agent may be entitled to benefit from a contract and, indeed, on occasion to obtain damages for breach of an agreement to which he was not a party. If you run into that sort of situation, you should take specific legal advice, based upon the particular facts of your case.

Chapter 13

Privity of contract

Only parties to contracts may take advantage of their terms. A 'third party' — that is, one who has no contractual arrangements with the others — may directly or indirectly benefit from the contract or lose if that contract is broken, but he cannot enforce it. One of the parties involved may take steps to protect his interest — but the third party is powerless. 'In the law of England, certain principles are fundamental. One is that only a person who is party to a contract can sue on it. . . .'

Messrs Dew entered into a contract with Dunlop to buy tyres and other goods from them at list prices, Dunlop having agreed to give them certain discounts. As part of the deal, Dews undertook not to sell to certain classes of customers at prices below the current list prices of the appellants. However, they were entitled to sell to a class of customer that included Selfridges at a discount substantially less than they were themselves to receive from Dunlop. In the case of any such sale, they undertook to obtain a written undertaking from the customer that he would observe those terms which they had themselves undertaken.

Selfridges agreed to buy Dunlop goods from Dew and gave the required undertaking not to cut prices. They broke that agreement and Dunlop sued.

So Dew bought from Dunlop and sold to Selfridges. There was no contractual relationship between Selfridges and Dunlop and therefore (said the House of Lords) they could not sue on the deal. Even though they had been wronged, they had no rights against Selfridges, who were strangers. They might possibly have sued their customers (Dew) for not enforcing the resale price maintenance arrangement. They could not leap over their customer and onto those who had no contractual relationship with them. There was no 'privity of contract' between Dunlop and Selfridges.

Now suppose that Dunlop had sold defective tyres to Dew who had sold them on to Selfridges. In the absence of some collateral warranty (perhaps contained in a 'guarantee' or 'warranty') from the manufacturer (details in next chapter, and in Part 3 on exclusion clauses) Selfridges would have had no contractual rights against Dunlop. The product was defective? Then their remedy in contract would lie against their supplier — Dew. If by some mischance Dew had gone out of business or into liquidation, Selfridges would have been left without remedy.

The same principle would have applied down the line — Selfridges' customer would sue them; they would bring Dew into the action as 'third party', and Dew in their turn could seek an indemnity from the manufacturer of the defective product as a fourth party.

If someone had suffered personal injury as a result of the defective tyre, that sufferer (as the 'ultimate consumer' of the product) could have jumped the queue and, like the lady who swallowed the soft drink polluted by the decomposing snail, he could have gone straight for the negligent manufacturer (see Chapter 2 and the case of *Donoghue* v. *Stephenson*).

So the principle in Dunlop's case goes far beyond the facts which, in any event, have been largely superseded by rules banning resale price maintenance. In the realm of liability for defective products, the principle of claims being restricted to those with whom the plaintiff has a contractual relationship remains supreme.

A curious variant on this theme appeared in the well known case of *Daniels & Daniels* v. *R. White & Sons Limited and Tarbard*. Mr Daniels was a street trader, dealing in second-hand clothing and furniture. He sued R. White & Sons, manufacturers and bottlers of (amongst other things) lemonade. Mr Daniel's wife joined him in the action, both alleging that the Whites had supplied 'a bottle of lemonade which in fact contained carbolic acid'. They included as a defendant a Mrs Tarbard, licensee of the Falcon Arms pub.

The plaintiffs alleged that Whites 'did not exercise reasonable care as manufacturers to prevent injury being done to
the consumers or purchasers of their wares'. Mr Daniels also
alleged that Mrs Tarbard was in breach of the warranty
implied (then as now) by the Sale of Goods Act, that the
lemonade would be 'reasonably fit for the purpose of
drinking, and that it contained no deleterious or noxious
matter and/or that it was of merchantable quality'.

'A perfectly sober gentleman', Mr Daniels not only drank
the polluted lemonade himself but gave some to his wife.
Both of them 'immediately realised that there was something
burning in the liquid . . . and at once thought that they had
been poisoned. . . .'

Whites were acquitted of any liability. Unlike the case of
Donoghue v. *Stephenson*, in which the manufacturer had
clearly failed to clean out the offending bottle, Whites (said
the judge) had taken 'reasonable care'. There was 'quite
adequate supervision' at the factory. The method of cleansing
the bottles was 'described as foolproof'. So the manufacturers
walked out of court, freed from blame and responsibility.

What, then, of the licensee who had retailed the defective
goods? There was a sale by description; a breach of the implied condition that the goods should be of merchantable
quality; therefore Mr Daniels — but not his wife — had a
good claim against Mrs Tarbard.

So Mrs Daniels lost her case. She had no contractual
relationship with the retailer nor (still less) with the manufacturer. So there was none of the 'no fault liability' which
the Sale of Goods Act in effect imposes on most sellers of
goods. Those who retail are bound (in general) to supply goods
which are 'of merchantable quality' and 'reasonably fit for
the purpose supplied'. The fact that they may have taken all
reasonable and proper care is irrelevant. They are in breach of
contract.

As Mrs Daniels had no contract with the licensee, she had
to show that her position was the same as that of the plaintiff in *Donoghue* v. *Stephenson*. She had to establish that
they owed a duty of care; that they were in breach of that
duty; and that damage flowed. *Donoghue* v. *Stephenson*
ensured no difficulty in proving a 'duty of care', as Miss
Donoghue was the 'ultimate consumer' of the liquid. She fell

ill and therefore suffered damage. But there was no negligence
. . . no breach of duty . . . no fault . . . and therefore no
liability in negligence.

When 'no fault liability' is introduced, people like Mrs
Daniel will succeed even without proof of negligence. Meanwhile, those who have a contractual relationship are generally
far better off when seeking damages than those who must
rely on the laws of negligence. Conversely, the absence of a
contractual relationship generally spells death to an action
for damages for breach of contract.

Chapter 14

Collateral warranties

The concept of 'privity of contract' means that only those
who are party (or 'privy') to a contract may obtain a legal
remedy against those who break it. Strangers may have rights
in tort, but only parties have rights in contract. There is,
though, one major exception – where the stranger can rely
on a so-called 'collateral warranty' – a promise given by
someone else who was not a party to the contract, in order
to induce the plaintiff to enter into an agreement.

The collateral warranty is generally a statement made by a
manufacturer or other person who stands to benefit by the
sale of a product to someone else, in order to induce that
other person to purchase. The manufacturer (or other bene-
ficiary) says (in effect): 'If you purchase my product, I will
give you the following warranties about the goods. . . .'

On page 224, we explain and analyse the nature of a
'warranty' (as opposed, for instance, to a 'condition').
Normally, either a warranty or a condition is a term of the
contract in question – a specific part of the contract itself. A
'collateral warranty', though, is one which does not form part
of the contract made between those who are 'privy' to the
agreement. It is only 'collateral' to it – but nevertheless one
which may be dragged into the centre of legal battle, as it
has been in the leading cases on the subject.

Motor dealers represented that a car was 'in perfect condition'. The purchaser paid a deposit to the dealer and then entered into a hire purchase agreement with a finance company. The contract for the purchase of the vehicle, then, was made between the buyer and the finance house. The dealer was a stranger to the transaction.

The buyer paid all instalments due, plus the usual option-to-purchase fee. The car became his.

Unfortunately, the car turned out to be in poor and unroadworthy condition and the buyer had to spend a large sum on repairs. He sued the dealers for damages for breach of warranty. They retorted that they were not parties to the bargain. The judge held that the dealers had 'given a warranty as to the condition of the car; that the plaintiff was induced by the warranty to enter into the hire purchase agreement; that the warranty was broken; and that the plaintiff suffered damage through the breach as he paid a larger sum under the hire purchase agreement for the car than it was worth and than he would have paid had the warranty not been given.'

The plaintiff was awarded damages — the difference between the value of the car at the date of the hire purchase agreement and the value it would have had if it had answered to the warranty. For the first time, a defendant had been made liable in an action founded in contract, even though he was not a party to that contract.

Under *The Consumer Credit Act, 1974,* both the finance company (which sells the car) and the dealer (who supplies it) are jointly liable to the consumer under the sale. Furthermore, any statements that the dealer makes in the course of negotiations are deemed to be made on behalf of the actual seller. The consumer has a remedy — and the dealer and the finance company can sort out between themselves who will bear the cost of the defect.

The decision in the car case was followed in a manufacturer's case, on typical lines. Paint manufacturers (Detel Products Limited) represented to the owners of the Shanklin Pier that their paint would be suitable for repainting the pier and 'would give a surface impervious to dampness, would prevent corrosion and the creeping of rust and would have a life of 7-10 years'. In reliance of this statement, the Pier authorities specified that their contractors should use Detel paint.

Unfortunately, the paint was not suitable for the protection of the pier and its life was 'of a very short duration'. Result: massive additional expense for the pier company and a claim for damages against Detel Products, who were not a party to the contract.

The court held that 'the consideration for the warranty in the usual case was the entering into of the main contract in relation to which the warranty was given. . . .' The warranty was collateral to the main contract. There was a separate arrangement between the manufacturers and the purchaser: 'Specify that our paint is to be used . . . ensure that the contractor purchases our product . . . and we will warrant that it will do the job required by you. . . .'

Shanklin Pier was entitled to rely on that collateral warranty. They won their case.

Next came *Yeoman Credit Limited* v. *Odgers & Others*, decided by the Court of Appeal. Briefly, a car dealer warranted that a vehicle was 'in perfect condition', as a result of which the purchaser entered into a contract with a finance company. The vehicle 'almost immediately proved unroadworthy because of persistent defects in the brakes', so the purchaser refused to pay instalments.

The Court of Appeal held that 'the hire purchase agreement was the purpose and the product of the warranty'. The damage suffered by the hirer was the 'loss directly and naturally resulting from the breach of warranty' and included 'the wasted instalments' and other amounts paid under the hire purchase agreement. The hirer was entitled to rely upon the collateral warranty given by the dealer, who was not a party to the contract with the finance house.

This decision was followed in the case of *Wells (Merston) Limited* v. *Buckland Sand and Silica Company Limited.* Buckland Sand warranted that their product conformed to a specified analysis and would be suitable for use in the growing of crysanthemums — the purpose for which (as Buckland well knew) Wells were buying the sand. The product did not conform to the warranty.

The judge held that there are 'two ingredients and two only . . . required in order to bring about a collateral contract containing a warranty: (a) The promise or assertion by A as to the nature, quality or quantity of the goods which B may reasonably regard as being made with the intention that it be relied upon and (*b*) acquisition by B of the goods in reliance on that promise or assertion'.

As Professor Bill Wedderburn (now Lord Wedderburn) had put it: 'The consideration given to the promise is no more than the act of entering into the main contract. Going ahead with that bargain is a sufficient price of the promise, without which it would not have gone ahead at all.'

It followed that those who had purchased the sand on the basis of the product maker's warranty were entitled to rely upon the promise or assertion given to them. The promise was broken; the assertion was incorrect; the manufacturers had to pay damages.

A similar conclusion was reached in an (earlier) case to which we have already referred in connection with the distributor's liability (Chapter 4). The claim was brought by a Mr Watson, who had his hair dyed by Mrs Buckley in her salon. He arranged to have it tinted 'to an auburn shade' and Mrs Buckley had recommended a new dye called 'Melereon'. She showed him the trade journal advertisement, which read: "Make your next hair dye order: 'Melereon' — the safe, harmless hair dye . . . no ifs or buts; it is a hair dye that will not harm the most sensitive skin; the hair dye which positively needs no preliminary tests."

Accepting the assurance that the new dye was safe and harmless, Mr Watson put his head into Mrs Buckley's hands — whence it emerged, itchy and ridden with dermatitis. Mrs Buckley had been in no way negligent and had applied the solution entirely in accordance with the maker's directions. Unfortunately, the dye contained a 4 per cent solution of acid, to be diluted to a 2 per cent solution before it was applied to the head. It was unsafe.

Following the principle in the famous snail case of *Donoghue* v. *Stephenson* (Chapter 2), Mr Watson could have sued the manufacturers. But (as, alas, is not unusual) their company dissolved even more effectively than their products. So he sued the hairdresser and the distributor.

The court held that the hairdresser had impliedly warranted that the solution was 'a merchantable hair dye' and she was therefore liable to him in damages for breach of contract. However, the distributors had been negligent and by their

advertisements had 'intentionally excluded interference with,
or examination of, the article by the consumer'. They had
therefore brought themselves into a direct relationship with
Mr Watson, to whom they were duly liable on their collateral
warranty.

Indeed, the judge went further. The product was itself a
dangerous one; 'an unusual standard of care was required';
and the distributors even on this ground 'owed a duty to take
care towards the plaintiffs'. As they were in breach of that
duty, they were liable to pay damages.

Finally: *Andrews* v. *Hopkinson*. The manager of a second-
hand car showroom described a saloon vehicle as: 'A good
little bus. I would stake my life on it'. He added: 'You will
have no trouble with it'. Mr Andrews paid his deposit and
entered into an agreement with a finance company.

About a week later, Mr Andrews was driving the car when
the steering mechanism failed and it collided with a lorry. He
was seriously injured. When the car was examined it was found
that a joint in the steering mechanism had failed. The car was
neither safe nor fit for use on the highway and the defect was
'long standing'. Although the fault was probably 'not dis-
coverable by an ordinary owner driver', it could easily have
been spotted 'by any competent mechanic'. Once again, the
hirer sued the dealer, rather than the finance company. This
time he claimed not merely the difference between the value
of the car as warranted and its value as delivered, but also
damages for his personal injury.

The court held that Mr Andrews' injuries were indeed 'a
direct and natural result of the breach of warranty' — so he
had a good claim against them in contract. In addition, he
was entitled to damages for the tort of negligence. The
dealers had failed to use 'reasonable diligence' either to
examine the car or to warn Mr Andrews that there was no
such examination.

So finally the two streams of the law — in contract and in
tort — flowed together, reaching the same legal outlet. The
dealers were strangers to the contract, but had formed a direct
relationship through their 'collateral warranty'. And as the
'ultimate consumer' of the dangerous product, the injured
Mr Andrews could leap over the contractual buyer and bring
a successful claim also under the law of negligence.

Chapter 15

Caveat emptor v. *caveat vendor*

Once upon a time, the buyer was expected to look after himself. *Caveat emptor* — let the buyer beware. Which was all very well when buyer and seller were engaged in comparatively simple transactions, normally on a more or less level basis. One farmer sells a cow; another buys it; the buyer must examine the beast and look for defects. One villager owns a horse which needs shoeing; the blacksmith does the job and his customer judges the result.

Unfortunately, these splendidly simple transactions — like methods and machines — grew more complex. By the end of the industrial revolution, most buyers had to rely on most sellers not to supply goods which were defective.

Finally, in 1893, Queen Victoria's Parliament recognised that buyers — private and business alike — required protection against their respective goods. Liability for products must (in contract at least) be placed on the seller.

There are two types of contractual term: 'express' and 'implied'. If the parties expressly come to an arrangement regarding quality or merchantability of goods, that (said Parliament) would remain a matter for them. However, in the absence of some agreement to the contrary, terms would now be implied into contracts, giving rights to buyers. Most important: terms would be implied that (generally) goods would be of 'merchantable quality' and 'reasonably suitable for the purpose supplied'.

The Sale of Goods Act, 1893 (as set out in full in its now amended form as Appendix 3 of this book) marked the mighty entry of interventionist, consumer legislation into the market place. But (in the main) its rules could still be excluded by mutual agreement. Manufacturers, distributors and retailers alike set about the excluding process, with brilliant results.

In each case, all that was required to exclude liability was an 'agreement to the contrary', negating the implied terms introduced by the 1893 Act. Naturally, no one produced a document called an 'agreement to the contrary' nor (still less) an 'exclusion of rights' clause. Instead, they conferred upon the unsuspecting buyer a so-called 'guarantee' — guaranteed

to provide rights considerably less extensive than those given
by Parliament under the Sale of Goods Act — or a 'warranty'
— which warranted unnecessary trouble.

Suppose, for instance, that you bought a defective vehicle.
Under the Sale of Goods Act, you were entitled to have it
put right at the seller's expense. Under the so-called 'warranty'
the manufacturer would (if he thought fit) replace parts which
(in his sole opinion) were defective in manufacture, but you
probably would have to pay for labour; for bringing the
vehicle to the works; and make no claim for any 'consequential loss, howsoever caused'. Instead of having rights which
could last six years (see page 228 on limitation of actions),
the guarantee usually lasted twelve months or a specified
number of miles, whichever passed first. Nor was there much
to choose between guarantees put out by the various vehicle
manufacturers. I was once commissioned to do a survey of
these documents for a well known Sunday national newspaper which advertised itself as *The Fearless Paper*. Having
collected and analysed all these horrific and disgraceful
documents, I produced and sent in a devastating breakdown.

The next day, the features editor telephoned. 'Sorry', he
said. 'It's a brilliant piece — but we can't use it.' 'Why not?'
'I am afraid that some of our most valued advertisers would
leave us. . . .' 'I thought that you were the fearless newspaper,
I said. 'So we are', he replied. 'But you need a newspaper to
be fearless in!'

So the entire weight of organised industry stood behind
these 'guarantees' and 'warranties', which were particularly
awful when supplied with electrical and other household
goods and appliances. 'If you ever banned these exclusion
clauses', argued their opponents, 'we would have to put our
prices up very considerably.'

They also added that the documents generally created a
new and otherwise non-existent relationship between the
customer and the producer. As we saw in Chapters 13 and 14,
contractual rights exist only where there is 'privity of contract'. But the manufacturers supplied 'collateral warranties'
which gave the buyers rights, however emasculated, against
the maker. If you bought from a dealer of substance, you
could look to him for your rights and remedies. You made
your deal with him and the Sale of Goods Act rights applied

as against him. But if he disappeared or went into liquidation, your rights against him would be worthless, so you would be grateful for even lesser remedies against the maker.

On balance, though, these 'guarantees' and 'warranties', with their massive exclusion clauses, provided industry and commerce with almost watertight protection. You manufactured, distributed or sold a defective product? Never mind. You might lose a customer for the future, but for the present your exclusion clause would protect you.

At last, in 1973, Parliament acted. It enacted the Supply of Goods (Implied Terms) Act. This statute applies, as its name indicates, to contracts for the supply of goods. It does not cover any provision of services. They were the subject of *The Unfair Contract Terms Act, 1977.* So now consider how these two crucial statutes have excluded the exclusions.

Part Three
EXCLUSIONS, EXEMPTIONS AND RETENTION OF TITLE

Chapter 16

Introduction

The simplest rules are those which brook no exceptions. If a defendant was convicted of murder, the judge was required to sentence him to death — leaving any prerogative mercy in the anxious hands of the sub-secretary. 'Any employee who smokes in a forbidden area *will* be dismissed.' As soon as you make an exception for a worker of unblemished record and long service, you open the door for a complaint from the next sacked miscreant that he is being 'victimised' — still: someone in authority may decide to give the wrongdoer another chance.

'Use may be made of these premises/goods at your entire risk' . . . 'No responsibility can be accepted for consequential loss or damage howsoever caused. . . .' Someone, of course, may make an *ex gratia* payment, to preserve goodwill and to avoid trouble — perhaps because he gets one of those useful letters from an MP: 'Knowing the high repute of your business, I thought that you would like to know, so that you could deal with the matter . . . I am being pressed to take other steps, but I hope that these will not be necessary. . . .'

As for manufacturers, distributors and other suppliers of goods, they have customarily and unsurprisingly attempted to keep their obligations to the minimum. Parliament created rights for the buyer? Then lawyers found ways to diminish, minimise or even to exclude or remove those rights altogether. That left the party who was morally guilty but legally blameless free to stretch points as he saw fit. 'The guarantee period has expired, but as a gesture of goodwill, we are prepared to. . . .'

As liability for defective products has grown, is growing and is almost certain to spread still further, the importance of exclusion or exemption notices, clauses or arrangements, grows proportionately. Unfortunately, for those who wish to rely on them, so has the determination of successive parliaments to exclude the exclusions. Hence *The Supply of Goods (Implied Terms) Act, 1973*, and *The Unfair Contract Terms Act, 1977*.

These two statutes are of paramount importance to the product manufacturer, distributor or retailer and to his legal adviser. In this Part, we dissect those statutes; put them into ordinary commercial and industrial context; and consider how they are (and in future how they are likely to) operate.

Thanks to detailed questioning and cross-questioning by delegates at a host of conferences and seminars at which I have explained these statutes, I recognise the practical worries which beset, confuse and aggravate both those concerned with products and their advisers. This Part deals specifically with those problems. There are, of course, a host of occasional and desperately intricate attendant problems which we must leave to the academics. Sufficient unto the once-in-a-legal-lifetime are the intricacies thereof.

For instance, for every occasion when you must consider that there has been a 'fundamental breach' of a contract or a 'breach of a fundamental term', there are likely to be hundreds when you will ask: "Is a court likely to regard this clause as 'reasonable' and hence enforceable?"

Here, then, is a breakdown of the law on exclusion clauses as they are likely to affect liability for defective products.

We have already considered the difference between liability in the tort of negligence and a liability in contract. The exemptions — like the substantive rules — also differ. But this time, logic and legislation both suggest that we should start with the basic rules of contract; then look at the power of the contracting parties to opt out; and then turn to the removal of non-contractual rights, knowingly or otherwise.

Chapter 17

Exemption clauses — your guide to the new rules

Before launching into an explanation of the effects of *The Supply of Goods (Implied Terms) Act, 1973* and *The Unfair Contract Terms Act, 1977,* (which I shall refer to hereafter as 'the 1973 Act' and 'the 1977 Act', respectively) here is a brief summary of the rules.

Negligence

Clauses which seek to reduce or remove liability for death or personal injury caused by negligence are void. Other 'anti-negligence' exemption clauses are generally valid if 'reasonable'.

Supply of goods

Exclusion clauses are void in contracts for the supply of goods to 'consumers' if they reduce or remove rights to non-defective goods, fit for the purpose supplied. A 'consumer' is a private customer. In non-consumer contracts (i.e. sales by a business seller to a business buyer) such exclusion clauses are valid — but a court has power to declare a particular clause void if it is 'unfair or unreasonable' in the circumstances.

Contracts for services

Other such exclusion clauses, and in particular those in contracts for the supply of services, must 'satisfy the test of reasonableness' to be valid *if*:
1   They are in 'consumer contracts'; or
2   They are in the contracting party's 'own standard, written terms'.

Reasonableness

'Reasonableness' depends upon all circumstances of the particular case — which include: the availability of the goods or services from some other source; the relative bargaining strength of the parties; and whether or not the other party knew of the existence of the clause and/or came to some special arrangement taking the exclusion into financial account.

Scotland

The above rules apply to the whole of the United Kingdom.

Exception: those rules relating to services (i.e. under the 1977 Act) apply in England, Wales and Northern Ireland whether the exclusion clause is contained in a contract or in a notice (contractual or non-contractual). In Scotland, they apply only where the clause is in a contract or in a *contractual* notice. In practice, the distinction will rarely have any practical effect.

Exceptions

Exceptions include insurance and international supply contracts.

Chapter 18

Exclusions in contracts for the sale of goods

The most important section in *The Sale of Goods Act, 1893*, (as amended by the new legislation) states that (in general) a buyer ('consumer' or business) is entitled to goods which are of 'merchantable quality' and 'reasonably suitable for the purpose supplied'.

The law provides three preliminary exceptions to the 'merchantability' rule.

1   The goods do not have to be perfect. They need only be 'reasonably saleable', i.e. the goods do not necessarily have to be without blemish.
2   Where the seller specifically draws a defect to the buyer's attention before the contract is made, then even if the defect in question renders the goods 'unmerchantable', the buyer has no lawful complaint.
3   If the buyer examines the goods before the contract is made, then, in so far as defects are 'patent' — such that the examination 'ought to reveal' — they need not be 'merchantable'.

Again, there are initial exceptions to the suitability rule:

1   Where the buyer neither 'expressly nor by implication'

makes known to the seller the purpose for which the goods are being bought, then he cannot be expected to know that purpose;

2   Where the circumstances show that the buyer does not rely 'or that it is unreasonable for him to rely' on the seller's skill or judgment, then it is up to him (the buyer) to be satisfied that the goods are 'reasonably fit' for the purpose for which they are purchased.

Now suppose that there is an ordinary contract for the supply of goods which contains, expressly or by implication, terms requiring that those goods should be neither defective nor unfit for the purpose supplied. Can the seller exclude liability by inserting the appropriate clause into the contract?

The 1973 Act makes a great divide between a 'consumer sale' — in which case the exclusion clause is void — and any other sale in which such a clause 'shall not be enforceable to the extent that it is shown that it would not be fair or reasonable to allow reliance on the term' (Section 55 of the 1893 Act as amended by Section 4 of the 1973 Act).

The 1973 Act defines 'consumer sale' as the sale of goods (other than the sale by auction or by competitive tender) by a seller in the course of business where the goods:

1   Are of a type ordinarily bought for private use or consumption; and

2   Are sold to a person who does not buy or hold himself out as buying in the course of a business.

Take cars. Ordinary saloon vehicles — as opposed to vans or lorries — are 'ordinarily bought for private use or consumption'. If you buy one for and on behalf of your business, then it is not a 'consumer sale', and an exclusion clause as to merchantability or fitness would be binding unless you can show to a court that it would not be 'fair or reasonable' in the circumstances of your case to allow the seller (or the manufacturer, as the case may be) to rely upon it.

If, on the other hand, you were buying the vehicle for your private use or that of your wife, you can accept any 'guarantee' or 'warranty' without worry. It will help you to establish a relationship with the manufacturer which might be useful if the dealer becomes either difficult or insolvent (see Chapter 14 as to collateral warranties). And exclusion clauses regarding quality or fitness are dead.

One day, a court may have to look into the hybrid case of the businessman who buys a saloon car ('of a type normally bought for private use'), but who intends to use it primarily for the purposes of his company, which will pay (perhaps) 90 per cent of the running and other costs. Is he buying the vehicle 'in the course of a business'? If it proves defective or dangerous, any clause which seeks to remove liability for death or personal injury due to negligence will be void (see Chapter 20). But a clause which attempts to exclude or reduce liability for property damage may still survive.

In most ordinary cases, though, the distinction between a 'consumer' and a 'non-consumer' is far more obvious. Are you buying the refrigerator or heater or other appliances for your home or for your office or works?

These rules have been in force since 1974. The lack of court decisions based upon them is not as curious as it appears.

Company 'A' sells a defective product to Company 'B' and then relies upon an exclusion clause. Company 'B' knows its basic law and says: "If you persist on relying on that clause, we will challenge you. The clause is clearly 'unfair' and 'unreasonable'." Company 'A' will retreat as fast as it decently can. After all, is such a clause – any such clause – likely to be both 'fair and reasonable'? If the effort to rely on the clause fails, will not other customers know of that failure? Reliance on the clause is unlikely to add lustre to the supplier's good name.

Alternatively, if the buyer does not know of his rights, he may allow the seller to get away with legal murder. There is nothing unlawful in including exclusion clauses, although many experts believe that there should be. If the buyer believes that the exemptions provided by the 1973 Act apply only to 'consumers' (one of the most common misconceptions), then more fool he.

Chapter 19

The Unfair Contract Terms Act, 1977 — and services

The limits on the power of exemption clauses attached to the sale or supply of goods are tightened still further by the 1977 Act. Sections 5-7 apply.

At first blush, Section 5 seems to carry the buyer's real protection very little further. But it extends (so far as may be necessary) the protection which already assists the consumer under the law of collateral warranties (see Chapter 14), by extending it to a claim for negligence.

The Section first applies to 'goods of a type ordinarily supplied for private use or consumption'. So it extends even to cases where goods 'ordinarily supplied' for consumer use are in the particular case bought for a business purpose.

'Where loss or damage *(a)* arises from the goods proving defective while in consumer use' and *(b)* results from the negligence of a person concerned in the manufacture or distribution of the goods, liability for the loss or damage cannot be excluded or restricted by reference to any contract term or notice contained in or operating by reference to a guarantee of the goods.'

Note that this Section does not apply to a guarantee given (for instance) by a retailer to his customer, nor when the goods are actually in business use; nor to business contracts. It does mean that, where the *Donoghue* v. *Stephenson* principle of liability to 'the ultimate consumer' in negligence applies (see Chapter 2), he need worry as little about exclusion clauses if he claims damages for negligence as he would if he claimed for breach of a collateral warranty.

Goods are regarded as 'in consumer use' when someone is using them or has them in his possession for use 'other than exclusively for the purpose of the business'. 'Exclusively' is the key word.

Anything in writing is a 'guarantee' if it 'contains some promise or assurance (however worded or presented) that defects will be made good by complete or partial replacement, or by repair, monetary compensation or otherwise.'

'This Section does not apply as between the parties to a contract under or in pursuance of which possession or ownership of the goods passes.' Retailers who wish to give special, additional rights to their customers may do so, exclusion clauses and all. But of course, they cannot exclude Sale of Goods Act rights but only add to them. The addition, though, may itself include exclusions.

Next: Section 6 — no more exclusions against 'title'. Section 12 of *The Sale of Goods Act, 1893*, implies an undertaking into contracts that the seller has a title to the goods that he is selling. You can theoretically only sell that which is yours; Section 12 (as amended by the 1973 Act) says that when you buy goods the seller impliedly warrants that he has a right to sell the goods. If he does not, because, for example, the goods might have been stolen, then he is liable to pay damages to the innocent purchaser. And Section 6 of the 1977 Act provides that 'liability for breach of the obligations arising from Section 12 of the Sale of Goods Act' — and from Section 8 of the 1973 Act, which makes corresponding provision 'in relation to hire purchase' — 'cannot be excluded or restricted by reference to any contract term'.

While the above rule applies to all contracts, Section 6(2) deals with consumer contracts only — arising from Sections 13, 14 and 15 of the 1893 Act, under which a seller gives an implied undertaking 'as to conformity of goods with description or sample, as to their quality or fitness for the particular purpose', or Sections 9, 10 or 11 of the 1973 Act, which makes corresponding provision in relation to hire purchase.

Once again (but, I repeat, in respect only to consumer contracts this time), these rights 'cannot be excluded or restricted by reference to any contract term'. However, you will not be surprised to find sub-section 3 providing that in *business* contracts (i.e. 'as against the person dealing otherwise than as consumer'), the above rights can be excluded or restricted by reference to a contract term — 'in so far as the term satisfies the requirement of reasonableness' (Chapter 23). And under Section 6, contracts of sale and of hire purchase are both covered.

See Appendices 3 and 4 for *The Sale of Goods Act, 1893,* and the 1973 Act, as amended.

Chapter 20

Negligence and exclusion clauses

The essence of 'strict' or 'no fault' liability is that it protects the sufferers irrespective of whether or not they can prove negligence on the part of the manufacturer, distributor or retailer. So to the extent that this concept becomes embedded in our law, the importance of excluding rights where negligence is proved will diminish.

Until the law is changed, proof of fault is required: negligence gives rights to total strangers (see, for example, Chapter 2 for the rules on the 'ultimate consumer'); and those who install, erect, maintain or repair products or who provide other services are particularly at risk.

So consider: how and to what extent can you reduce those risks by supplying your goods or services on the basis that you do not accept responsibility for harm caused through negligence?

* * *

Section 1 of the Unfair Contract Terms Act defines the word 'negligence' in three ways:

1   It means the 'breach of any obligation, arising from the express or implied terms of a *contract*, to take reasonable care or to exercise reasonable skill in the performance of the contract'.

Suppose that you contract to carry out research or testing on someone else's product. By law, you impliedly undertake to exercise reasonable care in doing the job. The common law will not permit you to say: 'There was nothing in the contract about taking care. . . .' So the same careless act or omission is likely to constitute *(a)* a breach of your contract and *(b)* negligence. In practice, the legal consequences may well be the same – although, as we keep seeing, the duties in negligence stretch much wider than those in contract.

2   The breach 'of any common law duty to take reasonable care or exercise reasonable skill (but not any stricter duty)'.

Irrespective of any contract, the law imposes duties – to avoid acts or omissions likely to cause harm to your 'neighbour' and to exercise such degree of skill and care as is appropriate, having regard to your status, training, qualifications and the like. You may even owe such a duty to a person for whom you are performing a totally gratuitous and kindly service, such as providing a reference (see Chapter 6).

This duty is mainly imposed by the common law arising through the decisions of courts. But it also appears in statutes such as *The Occupiers' Liability Act, 1957*, which imposed 'a common duty', owed by an occupier to all his lawful visitors. Nowadays, it is even owed to some who are technically 'trespassers', but to whom you owe a 'legal as well as a humanitarian' duty, because you know or ought to have known of their likely presence on your property.

3   The breach of the 'common duty of care' imposed by the Occupiers' Liability Act, then, is specifically referred to in the 1977 Act.

So 'negligence' may be a breach of a contractual or of a common law or of a statutory duty to avoid careless acts or omissions.

In the realm of product liability, 'negligence' may also be statutory or common law. Either way, it applies to 'business liability'. As with the Sale of Goods Act, the 1977 Act is not intended to prevent the exclusion of liability which might arise 'from things done or to be done by a person *not* in the course of a business (whether his own business or another's)', or from the occupation of premises '*not* used for business purposes of the occupier'.

Anyway, if there is a breach of duty, the rules apply whether that breach was 'intentional or inadvertent or whether liability for it arises directly or vicariously'. Whether the negligent act was committed by you personally or by your servant or agent . . . whether by employer or employee . . . the rules apply. Here they are:

Section 2: 'A person cannot by reference to any contract term or to a notice given to persons generally or to particular persons, exclude or restrict his liability for death or personal injury resulting from negligence.'

Where negligence causes 'death or personal injury', no exclusion is permitted. It matters not whether the exclusion clause is in a contract for the supply of goods; in a notice on a lorry or in a car park or given to a customer or to a stranger. If you are negligent (as defined) — personally or by the hand of some other person acting for you or on your behalf — the law will hold you liable.

So the Act makes a clear and radical distinction between 'liability for death or personal injury' and that causing 'other loss or damage'. 'In the case of other loss or damage, a person cannot so exclude or restrict his liability for negligence except in so far as the term or notice satisfies the requirement of reasonableness.'

An exclusion clause in a contract for the supply of goods to a consumer is void (see Chapter 23), and other specific rules apply to specified cases. But in the absence of such rules, a product manufacturer, distributor or retailer may still include a valid, binding clause in a contract or in a notice, excluding liability due to negligence which causes loss or damage *other than* personal injury or death — provided that the clause is 'reasonable'.

'Reasonableness' (as always) depends upon all the circumstances of the particular case, and because some of the circumstances are specifically defined both in the Supply of Goods (Implied Terms) Act and in the 1977 Act, they are the subject of Chapter 23.

Finally: 'Where a contract term or notice purports to exclude or restrict liability for negligence, a person's agreement to or awareness of it is not of itself to be taken as indicating his voluntary acceptance of any risk.'

Volenti non fit injuria proclaims the law. The essence of

this maxim is that a volunteer cannot complain of injuries which he voluntarily undertook. If you knowingly and willingly accept a risk, you cannot afterwards claim damages because that risk leads to precisely the sort of damage you accepted.

If you enter a boxing ring, you can scarcely complain if your nose is broken. Nor can you successfully sue the man who dislocates your shoulder in a rugby tackle. If you fall while ski-ing, you canot blame the proprietors of the ski slope, who failed to remove the rock from your path. And if you eat too much whipped cream and chocolate cake and suffer a stomach ache, you will have no claim against their manufacturers, processors or distributors — unless, of course, the food was poisoned,

Still, knowledge of a risk does not remove anyone's duty to guard against it. If you sell dangerous products, you must take all such steps as are reasonably practicable to protect those who may suffer through the danger, not only by keepin that danger to a minimum, but also by giving all due warnings

Neither danger money nor knowledge of the danger makes a person a 'volunteer'. He does not assume a risk because he knows of it. Nor (thanks to Section 2(3) of the 1977 Act) does agreement to or awareness of an exclusion clause (of itself) indicate acceptance of risk. There may be other indications of acceptance. But you cannot just say: 'Well, you knew of the clause . . . you accepted the danger, didn't you? So we are not liable in law. . . .'

To summarise, you are now responsible if your *negligence* or that of your servant or agent causes personal injury or death and you cannot remove that liability through any exclusion clause, whether in a contract or in a notice, whether addressed to an individual, a company, a firm or to the world at large. However, in the case of other loss or damage caused through negligence, you may exclude liability through a contractual clause or notice, provided that the exclusion satisfies 'the test of reasonableness'. The law allows you to include the exclusion, but sternly limits its effect.

Chapter 21

Exclusions from the exclusions of the exclusion

The Unfair Contract Terms Act, 1977, excludes or restricts
the effects of exclusion or exemption clauses. Schedule 1
excludes various contracts from the restrictions and exclusions on the restrictions and exclusions. A few of these affect
product liability.

The rules do not extend to 'any contract of insurance
(including a contract to pay an annuity on human life)'. So
your insurers are as entitled today as they ever were to limit
the rights you receive in return for the premium you pay.

Business people often ask: 'What are my rights against my
insurers?'. The reply is always and will remain: 'Look at your
policy . . . check on its terms . . . and especially, see the
exclusions'.

The Schedule also excludes 'any contract so far as it relates
to the creation or transfer of a right or interest in any patent,
trademark, copyright, registered design, commercial or technical information or other intellectual property, or relates to
the termination of any such right or interest'.

You cannot exclude criminal liability under Section 6 of
the Health and Safety at Work Act, in connection with the
unsafe design of a product. But a contract for the 'creation
or transfer' of rights in that design may contain effective
exclusion clauses, reasonable or otherwise.

Other exclusions from the coverage of the 1977 Act
include contracts: for the creation or transfer of an interest
in land: for the formation or dissolution of a company; for
marine towage or salvage; or for the carriage of goods by ship
or hovercraft.

Finally — and most important — Section 26: "The limits
imposed by this Act on the extent to which a person may
exclude or restrict liability by reference to a contract term do
not apply to liability arising under a 'contract for international
supply of goods'." This means a contract with the following
characteristics:

1   Either it is a contract for the sale of goods or it is one
     under or in pursuance of which the possession or owner-
     ship of goods passes; and
2   It is made by parties whose places of business (or, if
     they have none, whose habitual residences) are in the
     territories of different states (the Channel Islands and
     the Isle of Man being treated for this purpose as different
     states from the UK).

So if your place of business is in the UK and your supplier's
or customer's place of business is abroad, the exclusion rules
do not apply to your contracts. Their exclusion clauses and
yours will be effective or otherwise, irrespective of the 1973
or the 1977 Acts. (For the law on the enforcement of overseas or international contracts, see Part 5).

Chapter 22

General rules on exclusion

Here are answers to some of the most common questions
covering the general rules on exclusion clauses.

When is an exclusion clause part of a contract?
    Usually, when it is contained in a contractual document,
but it may also be in a notice. And on occasions, if the parties
know that a contract is on the basis of the exclusion concerned
it may be implied into the deal by the custom of the trade, or
by the course of dealing between the parties.
    To see whether a particular document is contractual, or
post-contractual and no part of the deal at all, see Chapter 10
where we look at essentials of a valid, binding contract). In
broad terms, the last document is generally the one containing
the binding term.

What is the effect of signing a document?
    Normally, it means that the person who applies his signature
cannot afterwards be heard to say that he did not know its
contents. Even if the document was obtained by fraud, it
would generally be binding unless it is of an entirely different

nature to that intended by the party concerned. In some cases, though, fraud has been held to render the entire contract void. *The Misrepresentation Act, 1967* (as amended by the new legislation) gives additional rights to a contracting party deceived by a false representation of facts (see Chapter 26).

Finally, consider the important case of *Shelley* v. *Paddock.* Miss Shelley bought a house in Spain from Mr & Mrs Paddock, who said that they were the agents for the owners of the property. Miss Shelley paid £80 deposit, and thereafter £12,000 as the balance of the purchase price, into the Paddocks' bank account in England. Unfortunately, the Paddocks had no right to sell the house. Miss Shelley sued for the return of her money.

Now, *The Exchange Control Act, 1947*, makes it a criminal offence to make a payment in the UK to or for the credit of a person resident outside 'the scheduled territories' (in broad terms: the sterling area) without obtaining Treasury consent. As no such consent had been obtained, the contract of sale was illegal and hence void.

Miss Shelley tried another route. She said: 'I have suffered damage due to the Paddocks' fraud'. She claimed damages not for breach of contract but in the tort (or civil wrong) of deceit or fraud. Instead of claiming the return of her money, she claimed damages, to compensate her for the loss of that same sum. And she won.

Are there any special rules for the interpretation of binding exclusion clauses?

Yes. The most important is what lawyers call the *contra preferentem* rule. If there is doubt as to the meaning of a clause of this sort, it will be interpreted against the person who seeks to rely upon it.

Also, an exclusion clause will be interpreted 'strictly'. A court will generally only enforce it if it is clear, precise and covers the situation in question. In other words, courts do not generally like these clauses, which take away people's rights. Therefore, if they can, they will interpret them out of existence.

Is an exclusion clause valid if it limits the amount of damages that can be recovered?

Yes. But a 'penalty clause' is void. Courts will enforce a term which requires a defaulting party to pay a sum which is 'a genuine pre-estimate of damage' — that is, a sum which represents what the parties really believed the breach would cost the innocent party. But where a clause is designed merely to encourage compliance by imposing a penalty on the contrac breaker, it is not enforceable.

Will an exclusion clause contained in a delivery note or in a receipt have any effect?

Normally, no. These are 'post-contractual documents'. They come after the contract is made and do not contain contractual terms. But they may be proof that the parties knowingly contracted on the basis set out in those documents.

We wish to enforce an exclusion clause. Will we have to prove its existence and its applicability?

Yes. The burden of proof normally rests on the person who seeks to rely on an exclusion clause. In addition, you may well have to prove that it 'satisfies the test of reasonableness' (see Chapter 23).

Can an oral promise overrule a printed exclusion clause?

Yes. Courts have held on several occasions that where an oral promise is 'repugnant' to the terms of a printed contract, the express, verbal promise can be relied upon. One problem with oral promises, of course, is that you have to prove their existence. But written exclusions are now subject to legislative restriction.

If a contract contains an exclusion clause, what is the effect of a misrepresentation made by the party relying on the clause?

If there is a misrepresentation, the exclusion clause is unlikely to be regarded as part of the contract between the parties. However firmly the courts normally lean against exclusion clauses, they do their utmost to help the innocent party where there has been a false factual statement.

Is it true that the courts will not enforce a bargain which is 'harsh and unconscionable'?

Be careful of this one. There have been a few cases where contracts have been set aside on this ground — but they are very few. There is a common, dangerous and totally incorrect belief that the Unfair Contract Terms Act enables people to avoid contracts which are 'unfair'. In general — subject to the 1893, 1973 and 1977 Acts and to the laws on fraud and misrepresentation — parties remain bound by their bargain. If *you* make a deal which *you* later regret, *you* cannot rely on the courts to get you off the legal hook.

Chapter 23

The test of 'reasonableness'

Life for the businessman and for the lawyer would be much easier if the law laid down precise, provable tests. Instead, it allows people to do that which is 'reasonable' or penalises them for being 'unreasonable'. For instance:

In general, a dismissal is 'unfair' if the employer has acted *'unreasonably'* in depriving the employee of his livelihood. But if he carried out a 'fair' (and hence *'reasonable'*) procedure; dismissed for one of the (very wide) *'reasons'*, now in *The Employment Protection (Consolidation) Act, 1978*; and acted *'reasonably'* in all the circumstances of the case, the dismissal will be 'fair.'

You may use *'reasonable* force' to eject a trespasser from your premises.

As an occupier of premises, you must take *'reasonable* care' for the safety of your lawful visitors. That is the 'common duty' imposed by *The Occupiers' Liability Act, 1957.*

Finally and above all, in a multiplicity of circumstances referred to in both *The Supply of Goods (Implied Terms) Act, 1973,* and *The Unfair Contract Terms Act, 1977,* exclusion or exemption clauses are only enforceable if they are *'reasonable'*.

* * *

In French, 'to be right' is *'avoir raison'* — literally: *'to have reason'*. The French make no distinction between that which is correct and that which is reasonable. In language, at least, 'reason' dictates 'right'.

Conversely, to be wrong is *'avoir tort'*. So a person commits a 'tort' where he does not have 'reason'. Lack of 'reason' or 'reasonableness' is the basis of 'civil wrong' or 'tort', in English law — which, thanks to William the Conqueror and other distinguished visitors to our islands, traces one of its sources to cross-Channel ideologies. Indeed, a trend which almost ceased hundreds of years ago has recommenced with Continental EEC Directives — including, of course, the one on product liability which (as we go to press) is still in draft.

So we accept the need for 'reasonableness'. But what does it mean?*

Where precision is possible, there are laws, regulations, specific rules, like those in the Factories Act, the Protection of Eyes Regulations, the Food and Drugs Act, the Building Regulations . . . But where precision is impossible . . . where the law must remain as flexible as the circumstances . . . the legislature falls back on the doctrine of 'reasonableness'.

The trouble here is that those who judge 'reason', and the 'reasonableness' which should flow from it, are almost as varied as the circumstances of the cases concerned.

In another sphere, every lawyer who deals with cases involving damages for personal injury knows that the amount of damages will depend not only upon the success of the case but also on the nature, temperament and generosity of the judge who hears it. Some are mean, others over-kind . . . some take particular illnesses especially seriously, while others play them down . . . .

The Court of Appeal will only interfere if awards of damages are (one way or the other) outside the limits laid down by precedent. It follows that when your case comes up for trial, you must hope for a judge whose view of 'reasonableness' (in your particular circumstances, of course) is similar to your own. And if you are trying to settle a case in advance, one of your problems (and certainly that of your lawyer) arises because you will not know until the morning of the trial which judge will decide your dispute.

Basically, 'reasonableness' is what you (or I) consider to be right. 'Unreasonableness' is the view of the other man.

*What is reasonably practicable under the Health and Safety at Work Act (Chapter 30) is a question of common sense and requires the making of a 'computation' — balancing the risk against the sacrifices involved in the measures necessary for averting it. (See *Edwards* v. *National Coal Board* in Index of Cases.)

In the days of the famous three-day working week, when the miners' dispute was the centre of business and political anxiety, there were two views of Edward Heath, Her Majesty's Prime Minister. Each was held by 'reasonable men'. On the one hand, Mr Heath was: 'Firm, dogged, resolute, stout-hearted and unwilling to give way to blackmail'. On the other, the same man in the same circumstances was: 'Stiff-necked, inflexible, rigid . . . with his mind closed to reason and common-sense.' You paid your political levy or contribution and you took your choice.

Not long ago, I received a letter: 'I read your rotten book', it said. 'I followed your awful advice. I am being prosecuted. I demand that you defend me. . . .'

It turned out that my unfortunate reader was a retailer who had read my advice: 'You may use reasonable force to evict a trespasser from your premises'. When an unwanted customer refused to leave on request, the reader had taken up his trusty crate opener and smacked his customer over the head. He was now being charged with an assault causing grievous bodily harm — and only for doing what he had regarded as 'reasonable', and hence in direct accordance with advice given to him by learned Counsel in a book of the law.

In particular fields of law, precedents give clues as to what a court is likely (or unlikely) to regard as 'reasonable'. But as cases, like people, are never the same, precedents can only be approximate.

So who decides what is or is not 'reasonable'?

Again, all depends on the circumstances of the case. Section 6 of the Health and Safety at Work Act says that 'manufacturers, designers, importers and suppliers' must take such steps as are 'reasonably practicable' to protect those who use their articles or substances at work. So the 'manufacturers, designers, importers and suppliers' make the first judgment. Next comes the Factory Inspector. If he prosecutes, then the decision moves to the court.

Happily, in dealing with exclusion clauses, Parliament has been a little more helpful. It has laid down criteria for reasonableness. These appear in identical terms in both the 1973 and the 1977 Acts, the former in Section 4(5), the latter in Schedule 11, which is headed: 'Guidelines for application of reasonableness test'.

'The matters to which regard is to be had in particular . . .' for the purposes of applying the reasonableness test . . . 'are any of the following which appear to be relevant –

'*(a)* the strength of the bargaining positions of the parties relative to each other, taking into account (among other things) alternative means by which the customer's requirements could have been met'. If, for instance, you buy your supplies of a particular material from a company which is in a monopoly position, the chances of an exemption clause being binding in its contract with you are low.

'(b) whether the customer received an inducement to agree to the term, or in accepting it had an opportunity of entering into a similar contract with other persons, but without having to accept a similar term.'

Suppose that you refuse to accept an exemption clause in a contract offered by certain suppliers. They say: 'Agree to the clause and we will reduce the price'. Assuming that the reduction was itself a reasonable one, the clause will probably be effective.

'(c) whether the customer knew or ought reasonably to have known of the existence and extent of the term (having regard, among other things, to any custom of the trade and to any previous course of dealing between the parties).'

The best way to ensure that a particular exemption clause is known to your customer is to draw it to his attention, in writing. Knowledge of the exemption will not of itself equal acceptance. But it is one of the circumstances to be taken into account.

'(d) where the term excludes or restricts any relevant liability if some condition is not complied with, whether it was reasonable at the time of the contract to expect that compliance with that condition would be practicable.'

You look at the time that the contract was made and ask: 'Was it reasonable to expect that compliance would be practicable?'. We shall revert fairly shortly to the time when the test is to be applied.

Finally: '(e) whether the goods were manufactured, processed or adapted to the special order of the customer'. Whether or not this would make the clause more or less reasonable would depend on the nature of the order and the circumstances in which it was given or accepted.

Those, then, are the 'guidelines'. But they do not detract from the requirement that a court should look at all the circumstances of the case.

For instance, Section 8 of the 1977 Act repeals Section 3 of *The Misrepresentation Act, 1967.* This Section provided (in effect) that a clause which seeks to exclude liability for a misrepresentation of fact (see Chapter 26) will only be enforced if it is 'reasonable'. And it seems that no court has ever held such a clause to be a 'reasonable' one. The change made in the 1967 Act by the 1977 one is simply that if you claim that such a clause is reasonable, then you must prove it. The 'onus of proof' rests on the person seeking to prove reasonableness.

Once again, this matches provisions in other legislation. Suppose that you say that you took all such steps as were 'reasonably practicable', through research or testing or otherwise, to see that your product was safe. You are prosecuted because the product proved to be unsafe? Then you must prove that you took all such steps as were 'reasonable'. The burden rests on you.

Now, Section 11(1) of the 1977 Act: 'In relation to a contract term, the requirement of reasonableness for the purpose of this part of the Act, Section 3 of *The Misrepresentation Act, 1967,* and Section 3 of *The Misrepresentation (Northern Ireland) Act, 1967,* is that the term shall have been a *fair and reasonable* one to be included having regard to the cricumstances which were, or ought reasonably to have been, known to or in the contemplation of the parties when the contract was made.' 'Fair and reasonable' are the key words: the time when the contract was made is the key moment.

The case of *Rasbora Limited* v. *J.C.L. Marine Limited* concerned an agreement for the sale of a boat which was destroyed little more than a day after delivery. An exclusion clause attempted to remove liability for engineering defects which were the responsibility of the defendants. Mr Justice Lawson decided that it would be neither 'fair nor reasonable' for the clause to be effective because otherwise the buyer would be left with no remedy at all. In that case, the Judge was entitled to look at the circumstances at the time when the alleged *breach* of contract occurred. Under the 1977 Act, the crucial moment is when the contract was made.

Section 11(2) of the 1977 Act says that: 'In determining
. . . whether a contract term satisfies the requirement of
reasonableness, regard shall be had in particular to the matters
specified in Schedule 11 to this Act; but this sub-section does
not prevent the court or arbitrator from holding, in accordance with any rule of law, that a term which purports to
exclude or restrict any relevant liability is not a term of the
contract.'

In contracts for the sale of goods; for hire purchase; or
under which ownership or possession of goods passes, the
court or arbitrator must look at all the circumstances of the
case, including those in Schedule 11. But of course (as the
Section emphasises) the exclusion clause may not be a term
of the contract at all. If you want to rely on an exclusion
clause in a contract, you must see that it is contained in the
contract and not (for instance) in some later, 'post-contractual'
document (such, perhaps, as a receipt or a delivery note).

Similarly: 'In relation to a notice (not being a notice having
contractual effect), the requirement of reasonableness under
this Act is that it should be fair and reasonable to allow
reliance on it, having regard to all the circumstances pertaining
when the liability arose or (but for the notice) would have
arisen.'

An entire Part of the 1977 Act is devoted to Scotland.
Apart from changes in terminology, there are differences in
the law of bailment between the two countries. But it seems
that the only difference in the application of the 1977 Act to
the two jurisdictions is simply this: in England and Wales,
the rules apply where exclusion clauses are in contracts *or* in
notices, but in Scotland only where they are in contracts.
However: even in Scotland, a notice may have contractual
effect; it may form part of the deal or the agreement or reflect
terms agreed. In that case, there will be no difference between
the application of the rules in the two jurisdictions.

Anyway, in the case of notices, you consider reasonableness
at the time when liability would have arisen — not when the
notice was given or put up.

Section 11(4): 'Where by reference to a contract term or
notice a person seeks to restrict liability to a specified sum of
money, the question arises (under this or any other Act)
whether the term or notice satisfies the requirement of

reasonableness, regard should be had in particular (but without prejudice to Sub-section (2) above in the case of contract terms) to

(*a*) the resources which he could expect to be available to him for the purpose of meeting the liability should it arise; and

(*b*) how far it was open to him to cover himself by insurance.'

Note that while it is well known that contracts of insurance are themselves outside the scope of the Act, we have here in Section 11(4) a very important and almost unnoticed provision. Once the doctrine of strict liability is applied to the production, distribution and sale of products, the problems of obtaining insurance — either at a sensible, reasonable price, or at all — will be upon us. They are already causing appalling difficulties in the US and, indeed, in some cases, with those who export to that country. So it is possible that an exemption clause may be held reasonable if the person seeking to rely upon it was wholly or partially unable 'to cover himself by insurance' and was therefore restricting himself to a sum which was insurable. And while the ability to pay damages is normally as irrelevant as inability to pay a fine, it may help to establish 'reasonableness' when seeking to rely on an exemption clause restricing liability to a specified sum.

Finally, under Section 11(5), it is for those claiming that a contract term or notice satisfies the requirement of reasonableness to show that it does. How far they will succeed in so doing remains to be seen.

Section 29(2): 'A contract term is to be taken . . . as satisfying the test of reasonableness . . . and to have been fair and reasonable' (in stated cases), if it is 'incorporated or approved by, or incorporated pursuant to a decision or ruling of, a competent authority acting in the exercise of any statutory jurisdiction or function and is not a term in a contract to which the competent authority is itself a party.'

It seems that at present there are no occasions when this clause would apply. But laws change and some authority — like, perhaps, the Director General of Fair Trading — may acquire competent authority, one of these eventful days.

Meanwhile: I hope that the view of 'reasonableness' held by any competent court or arbitrator will agree with your own.

Chapter 24

Fundamental breach and the end of the contract

Courts have always disliked exemption clauses and some judges have leaned over so far backwards as to fall off the Bench in their efforts to find ways round them. In the process, they have created a whole area of excruciatingly complicated and intricate law — most of which revolves round the concept of 'fundamental breach'.

Briefly, where a party smashes a contract . . . strikes at its very root . . . is in fundamental breach of the agreement . . . the other party has a choice. He may treat the breach as terminating the contract; or he may elect to treat the contract as still in being, and claim for damages as compensation.

Now suppose that one contracting party is in breach of his contract and relies upon an exclusion clause. He is saying: 'Even if I did break the contract, you have agreed to the exclusion of your rights'.

'You have destroyed the contract', retorted the courts. 'The contract has disappeared — and the exclusion clause along with it.'

The continuation of a line of cases came in *Harbutt's 'Plasticine' Limited* v. *Wayne Tank & Pump Company Limited.* Harbutt's asked Wayne's to design equipment suitable for storing and dispensing stearine at their factory. It was left to them to choose and specify a suitable material for the required piping.

On the very first night when the equipment was put into use, a fire broke out which destroyed the factory. The cause: the material for the piping was unsuitable. To rebuild the factory would have cost £146,581. The limitation of damages contained in an exclusion clause: £2,300.

Unanimously, the Court of Appeal decided that the defendants were in 'fundamental breach' of their contract. They were therefore debarred from relying on their exclusion clause.

Still, the distinction between breaches which were and those which were not 'fundamental' provided splendid employment for lawyers and for courts. Hence Section 9 of the

1977 Act: 'Where for reliance upon it a contract term has to satisfy the requirement of reasonableness, it may be found to do so and be given effect accordingly, notwithstanding that the contract has been terminated either by breach or by a party electing to treat it as repudiated'.

If an exemption clause is reasonable, then even if the contract has died, the exemption clause may be 'given effect'. Conversely, if the clause is unreasonable, it cannot be relied upon, even if the plaintiff has elected to treat the contract as still alive.

Again: 'Where on a breach the contract is nevertheless affirmed by a party entitled to treat it as repudiated, this does not of itself exclude the requirement of reasonableness in relation to any contract term.' If the plaintiff decides to require the other party to comply with the terms of the contract and to claim damages for breach, the 'requirement of reasonableness' remains effective.

All of which is eminently sensible and should reduce the area of unnecessary − and entirely unreasonable − disputes between parties to a contract, regarding the entire horrific legal area of 'fundamental breach'.

Chapter 25

Retention of title and the *Romalpa* case

Normally, only those who are parties to a contract can sue under that deal. Even if the contract was specifically made for their benefit, they must leave it to the parties to enforce their rights. One exception (as we saw in Chapter 14) has emerged in the law on collateral warranty − generally, representations made (directly or in advertisements) by manufacturers or distributors, intended to induce people to buy from others (generally, retailers or dealers).

Another and exceedingly important exception to the rule arose from the (now famous) case of *Aluminium Industrie Vaassen B.V.* v. *Romalpa Aluminium Limited* − commonly called 'the Romalpa case'. Vaassen sold aluminium foil to

Romalpa. The terms of sale included the following clause: 'Ownership of the material to be delivered will be transferred to the purchaser only when he has met all that is owing to the vendor'. The vendor sought to retain ownership of the property until he had been paid for it.

Romalpa went into liquidation and its bank appointed a receiver under the terms of a debenture, secured by a floating charge. At this stage, Romalpa still retained part of the aluminium in stock; it had sold the remainder to purchasers or to sub-purchasers.

Question one for the Court of Appeal: Was the clause effective to retain the seller's title to the goods? Must the receiver hand over the goods still in stock, as these belonged to the seller until he had received his money?

Unanimously, the three judges held that the clause (already common in other EEC countries) was effective here.

Second question: Could the vendor effectively claim the proceeds of the sale of the remainder of the aluminium (some of which, incidentally, the receiver had prudently set on one side in a separate account)?

'Yes', said the judges. The purchasers were entitled to sell on the goods, subject to their obligation to account to the vendors for the proceeds of such sale. It followed that the vendors were entitled to 'trace' those proceeds and to claw them back to Holland. And that right to recover its cash had priority over all other preferential debts, including the insolvent company's secured overdraft.

So Vaassen was entitled to sue Romalpa with whom it had a contractual relationship. But suppose that goods belonging to Vaassen (the unpaid vendor) had been sold on to purchasers or to sub-purchasers, who had not yet paid for them — or, indeed, who had paid someone less prudent than Romalpa's receiver, and the money had gone down the drain. The primary object of a Romalpa clause, of course, is to give the vendor rights against the receiver of an insolvent purchaser. But could it not also create rights against a purchaser or sub-purchaser?

The vendor would not be entitled to claim back 'his' goods, even if they had been incorporated into the purchaser's or sub-purchaser's property. *The Sale of Goods Act, 1893* [Section 12(1)] together with *The Factories Act, 1889*

(Section 9) prevent the original supplier from successfully claiming ownership, as against the ultimate buyer. But these Sections do not prevent an action to recover the proceeds of such sale or sub-sale. The right to 'trace' exists not only as against the other contracting party (or its receiver) but as against total strangers.*

It is largely for this reason that purchasers attempt to avoid 'retention of title' clauses in contracts for the purchase of goods. They themselves may have both the intention and the means to pay. But what if someone up the line becomes insolvent? In that case, they may have to pay twice — once to their supplier and once again to the original vendor.

Again, if the sub-purchaser himself wants to sell on, his customer may insist on acquiring the goods free of any liability to anyone else. Otherwise, he may find that he has 'bought' goods which still belong to the unpaid, original vendor. So those who cannot sell goods made entirely of materials or components which they themselves provably own — and with no Romalpa clause attaching to them — may find difficulty in selling at all.

So nowadays, sellers frequently attempt to introduce Romalpa clauses. Why not? At no extra expense, they retain the ownership of the goods they sell until they get the money they are owed. Equally, purchasers seek to purge these clauses from their contracts. Therein lies potential danger and expense.

Now suppose that the goods sold with a Romalpa clause attached are defective and that a sub-purchaser or a stranger suffers injury, loss or damage as a result. What are his legal rights?

The injured 'ultimate consumer' may claim damages against the manufacturer, who was himself at fault — irrespective of any contract. He will claim in a civil action for damages for the tort (or wrong) of negligence.

Equally, the original purchaser will be entitled to claim damages for breach of contract. If personal injury has been caused, no exclusion clause will have any legal force or effect (see Chapter 20). Equally, an exclusion clause in a business contract for the supply of goods may be declared void by any court if it is 'unfair or unreasonable'.

What, then, of the third party who suffers only financial

* The seller may also be able to trace the value of his product if it is incorporated by the buyer into a product manufactured by him.

loss due to a defect in the product? The owner of the product may sue him if he (the owner) is not paid the money that he is owed. But the converse does not apply. He (the ultimate consumer) cannot successfully sue the manufacturer. His rights lie against the contracting party who sold the goods to him and if that party has gone into liquidation, his rights may not be worth the paper upon which (hopefully) they were duly inscribed.

Chapter 26

Representations and puffs — about your products

How far will your liability for defects in your products be affected by statements that you made about them in order to induce your purchaser to buy? The answers lie in both the civil and the criminal law. In this chapter, we look as 're-presentations' and 'commercial puffs' which (together with the Misrepresentation Act) govern civil liabilities. Elsewhere, we consider the Trade Descriptions Act and the criminal law on misdescribing products.

*   *   *

There are two categories of statement which you may make about products or services. The first is a 'representation'; the second a 'puff'.

A 'representation' is a statement of alleged fact. In the main, if it is untrue and the buyer has been deceived, he may successfully claim damages.

A 'puff' is a mere statement of opinion. The seller engages in 'exaggerated praise of his own product'. The buyer relies upon it at his own risk.

Usually, the distinction between the two categories is clear. Sample representations: 'Made in Britain'; 'All wool'; 'Details of performance are as follows: . . .'; '24-hour maintenance service available at all times . . . .'. Each statement is provably true or false.

Examples of 'puffs': 'Splendid offer'; 'Unrepeatable bargain . . .'; 'Everyone's favourite . . .'; 'Washes whiter than white . . .'.

Unfortunately, the borderline between 'representations' and 'puffs' is not always clear. 'Beauty lies in the eye of the beholder', so you might have presumed that a statement that a car was 'beautiful' would be a 'representation'. But in a Trade Descriptions Act case, it was held to mean that the car was 'roadworthy'. The seller was not portraying a vehicle for some vintage car museum and (said the court) both meant and was taken to mean that the vehicle was roadworthy.

It was defective, so the seller had 'applied a false trade description' to the goods and the buyer was entitled to be compensated.

Nor can any exclusion clause take away the buyer's rights not to be deceived. *The Misrepresentation Act, 1967*, as amended by *The Unfair Contract Terms Act, 1977*, makes any such clause void unless a court holds it to be 'reasonable' which (it appears) has never happened.

If the buyer of a defective product relies on a 'mere commercial puff' (which is not, as one wit suggested, 'a male hustler in Soho'), he cannot lawfully complain if he suffers loss. But he who is fooled by a false statement of fact may return the goods and demand back the return of any money paid, plus damages for any loss that he has suffered as a result of the misrepresentation. Alternatively, again thanks to the Misrepresentation Act, he may retain the goods and claim damages.

At one time, the deceived buyer had to prove fraud or breach of some important contractual term (a 'condition' as opposed to a 'warranty') if he wanted to keep the goods. Today, his options are open. If, for instance, you buy plant or equipment which is alleged to have been made in 1978 but turns out to have been in service since 1976, you have clearly acquired less valuable goods than those to which you were contractually entitled. You may still want to keep them, though. You would claim the difference between the value of the goods as they are and that which they would have had, if the seller had complied with his contract.

"NO GOGGLES, NO BREAK-IN . . . !"

Part Four
CRIME

Chapter 27

Introduction

Almost any wrongful act may lead to two consequences, one civil, one criminal. The civil law gives a remedy against the wrongdoer to any individual, firm or company who suffers loss. The criminal law sets up minimum standards designed to protect the community.

You drive carelessly and cause a crash? Then you may be *sued* by the other driver or by a passenger or by another sufferer. You may also be *prosecuted* for careless or dangerous driving.

A man loses his temper and assaults you? You may claim damages for 'trespass to the person' and your assailant may be prosecuted for assault . . . assault causing actual or grievous bodily harm . . . or (at worst) manslaughter or murder.

A thief steals your property? *You* may sue for its return and *he* may be prosecuted for theft.

An employee is injured at work? He may claim damages — and those responsible for the unsafe practice may be prosecuted under *The Health and Safety at Work etc. Act, 1974.*

You produce or market a defective product? Then anyone who suffers as a result may *sue* you — in contract, if he has a contractual relationship with you, or otherwise in the tort of negligence. But you may also be *prosecuted* under Section 6 of the Health and Safety at Work Act, if the article or substance is intended or designed (respectively) for use at work.

So far, this book has been mainly concerned with the civil law. But increasingly, the public is demanding better standards from manufacturers and others. Already, the criminal law is acquiring a new grip on manufacturing processes. And just as the civil law is likely to move fast in the direction of strict liability, so the trend towards making manufacturers criminally liable is certain to advance — if not through new legislation, then by stricter enforcement of existing rules.

Chapter 28

Crime insurance and prosecution

If a customer or anyone else brings a successful action in a civil court and obtains an order for damages against you or your company, who pays? Often you or your company will have an insurance policy covering such an eventuality and therefore it will be your insurers who will pay. Naturally you will regret the events which brought about the action and your premium may rise next time around. But essentially, the insurers not only lift the financial weight but also the burden of anxiety from the shoulders of the wrongdoers.

If you are prosecuted for a criminal offence, the result is very different. Then you and not your insurers will be in the dock. If you are convicted, they will not pay your fine nor (still less) serve your time. You may pass on your civil liability to your insurers, who will step into your shoes . But it is 'contrary to public policy' for anyone to insure you against criminal responsibility.

Your insurers may take on your legal costs. After all, if you are criminally convicted, they are much more likely to have to pay out on a civil claim. But any advance agreement to pay your fine would certainly be improper, unenforceable and itself unlawful.

Your employers may tell you: 'We will pay your fine' — but it could not be held to its bargain. In practice, it may if it wishes stand behind you. There is no law to prevent your outfit meeting your obligations any more than anyone (including Hugh Scanlon, then head of the AUEW) could prevent an anonymous stranger paying that famous £60,000 fine, imposed by the (now defunct) National Industrial Relations Court, in the days of the Industrial Relations Act.

Still, the real effect of a criminal sanction is to impose a personal burden on the individual wrongdoer — a burden which he cannot shift onto anyone else. He bears a personal responsibility.

Where the individual claims damages, he sues in a civil court. In general, claims up to £2000 are brought in County Courts; claims for higher sums go to the High Court.

Criminal prosecutions always start in Magistrates Courts.

The more serious ones are usually 'committed for trial' by jury 'on indictment', before Crown Courts.

A civil court may grant damages; may grant an 'injunction' – an order forbidding the continuation of a particular practice or, on occasion, requiring specific action to be taken; and in cases in which damages would not provide an adequate remedy (such as the enforcement of contracts for the transfer of shares or of interest in land) it may order 'specific performance' of agreements. In actions concerning defective products, damages are the normal remedy sought or granted.

Criminal Courts impose sanctions . . . penalties . . . punishments . . . These range from bind-overs to absolute or conditional discharges or sometimes to imprisonment.

In the past, defective products have largely been regarded as problems for the civil courts. Increasingly, Parliament and the (Health and Safety) Inspectorate are recognising that (alas) society has to be protected from itself. Those who say: 'Why make laws and impose penalties when we should be left to set our own industrial and commercial standards' underestimate the harm which we cause each other if we are not brought into line by the criminal law.

In general, criminal liability rests on the party at fault. This may be the company, firm or authority. It may be the individual director, manager or company secretary – or even the employee concerned. But while the employer is 'vicariously liable' in civil law for the wrongful acts or omissions of his employee, committed during the course of his employment (see Chapter 12), liability in criminal law rests on the party at fault. Corporate or incorporate, group or individual, the responsibility for criminal acts rests on those who commit them.

Chapter 29

Criminal law and civil liability

The manufacturer may conveniently market his products in watertight packets, each neatly separated from the next. Not so the law. Even where you have two separate branches – civil and criminal – they interact, one on the other. So consider: if you are guilty of a criminal offence in connection with your products, how can this lead to a civil liability spin-off?

Most criminal statutes provide no civil remedies. The man who steals your property is convicted of theft? A Criminal Court has only limited power to award compensation. If you want to recover what he owes you, you may have to sue him, in a Civil Court.

If an employee is injured by defective equipment, anyone at fault may be prosecuted. Perhaps the employer did not take such steps as were 'reasonably practicable' to ensure that the equipment was in proper order? Or the manufacturer failed adequately to research or test the item? The court may convict, fine or (theoretically, at least) even imprison. But the sufferer will have to go to a civil court to claim his damages, either at common law or under the Employer's Liability (Defective Equipment) Act.

However, every simple legal rule has its exceptions. In this

First, in some cases, courts are given specific powers to compensate, as well as to punish. If you are convicted of an offence under the Trade Descriptions Acts, for instance, the court may in its discretion order you to compensate your victim by such amount as it considers appropriate.

Secondly, the fact of a criminal conviction may provide almost irrefutable evidence for civil proceedings. A maniac driver crashes into your vehicle? He is being prosecuted for dangerous driving? Then wait before you sue. If he is convicted, his insurers will almost certainly pay you without argument — which explains why, if a prosecution needs defending, the insurers of the accused will probably and properly pay his legal costs.

It is, of course, 'contrary to public policy' for insurers to enter into agreements to pay the criminal penalties of their assured. About as close as they can get to such an arrangement is the scheme which provides a car with chauffeur for a policy holder removed from vehicular circulation because of a conviction involving drink. Also, even under the Health and Safety at Work Act, insurers may pay the cost of defending a prosecution because a conviction will so inevitably lead to civil liability.

If an employee is injured at work, he will normally only get damages if he can prove that his employers were either negligent (i.e. in breach of a common law liability) or in breach of some *statutory* duty, and that the breach gave rise to the damage complained of.

For instance, the Factories Act requires (in broad terms) dangerous machinery or moving parts to be properly fenced. If a machine is not properly guarded and the employer is convicted, the employee may claim damages, to compensate him for loss suffered through this breach of *statutory* duty.

Section 6 of the Health and Safety at Work Act requires manufacturers and others to take reasonably practicable steps to ensure that products used by others at work are safe. But the Act [in Section 47(1)] specifically says that breach of any general provision under the Act shall *not* give rise to civil liability. In practice, this is a nonsense. The product manufacturer convicted of putting into circulation machinery or equipment which is inadequately researched or tested and has caused injury will be about as likely to avoid civil liability in a negligence action as the fabled snowball in legal hell.

So in practice, a criminal conviction gives rise not only to penal consequences but also to civil liabilities.

Finally, note that *The Consumer Protection Act, 1961* (Chapter 37) specifically gives a person 'affected by the contravention of or non-compliance with a Regulation made under the Act' a right to take civil proceedings. As in other legal circumstances, the tide of the law may flow through different channels, but the waters have a disconcerting habit of intermingling. So while through necessity this book (like those tides) is divided into Parts and Chapters, these must be read and understood together.

Chapter 30

Product liability and the criminal law

Section 6 of the Health and Safety at Work Act contains potential dynamite. It introduces into the realm of product liability the concept of duty not merely to an individual sufferer but to the community — a duty enforced not through a civil action for damages but by prosecution in a criminal court.

'It shall be the duty of any person who designs, manufactures, imports or supplies . . .'

So it covers those who design the product . . . produce it . . . or supply it. . . . 'Supply' is defined by Section 53 as meaning supply 'by way of sale, lease, hire or hire purchase, whether as principal or as agent for another'. Any sort of 'supply' is covered.

'Designers' of potentially lethal 'products' have long been wary of this section. The word 'design' is not defined by the Act but rather by ordinary usage, and is broad in its application.

Importers are covered because they come within the jurisdiction of our courts, whereas the manufacturers of the articles they bring into the UK are not. If an importer acts as your agent (as opposed to being a 'principal'), then you come into this category (see Chapter 12).

The word 'article' is not defined. It means a thing or product. An 'article for use at work' means '(a) any plant designed for use or operation (whether exclusively or not) by persons at work', and '(b) any article designed for use as a component in any such plant'.

It is not the use actually made of the article that matters but whether it was in practice 'designed' for use 'at work'. The statute is for health and safety *at work*. Consumers (who do not use articles 'at work') have other protection (see, for example, Chapter 37).

So what are the duties of designers, manufacturers, importers or suppliers? Each is bound

'(a) to ensure, in so far as is reasonably practicable, that the article is so designed and constructed as to be safe and without risks to health when properly used.'

You are not required to guard against improper use but (as we shall see in a moment) you must provide sufficient instructions or information to enable the user to be able to protect himself.

Next duty: '(b) to carry out or to arrange for the carrying out of such *testing* and *examination* as may be necessary for the performance of the duty imposed on him by the preceding paragraph'. Either he must carry out the research and testing himself or make sure that someone else has done so.

Note: Whilst the person or company must do what is 'reasonably practicable' to see that the 'design and construction' is safe, there is no such proviso in connection with research or examination. He must take such steps as are reasonably practicable to see that the article is 'designed and constructed so as to be safe and without risk to health when properly used'; and he must (without any proviso as to reasonableness) ensure adequate testing and examination.

Finally, he must 'take such steps as are necessary to secure that there will be available in connection with the use of the article at work adequate information about the use for which it is designed and has been tested, and about any conditions necessary to ensure that, when put to that use, it will be safe and without risk to health'.

Section 6(2): 'It shall be the duty of any person who undertakes the design or manufacture of any article for use at work to carry out or to arrange the carrying out of any necessary research with a view to the discovery and, in so far as is reasonably practicable, elimination or minimisation of any risks to health or safety to which the design or article may give rise'.

Again: Research. And an absolute duty.

Section 6(3): 'It shall be the duty of any person who erects or instals any article for use at work or any premises where that article is to be used by persons at work, to ensure — in so far as is reasonably practicable — that nothing about the way in which it is erected or installed makes it unsafe or a risk to health when properly used.'

So 'erectors and installers' join 'designers, manufacturers, importers and suppliers'. They must erect and instal plant or equipment in so far as is reasonably practicable — so as to minimise danger to life or limb.

Section 6(4) applies almost identical rules to those who 'manufacture, import or supply' any 'substance' for use at work. Substances are not 'designed', so the wording is slightly different.

The word 'substance' is defined by Section 53 as meaning 'any natural or artificial substance, whether in solid or liquid form or in the form of a gas or vapour'. Question, unanswered:

What about electricity? This would not appear to be a 'substance'.

A 'substance for use at work' means 'any substance intended for use (whether exclusively or not) by persons at work'. With 'articles' the question is: For what purpose were they *designed*? With substances: For what purpose were they *intended*?

Section 6(6): 'Nothing in the preceding provisions of this section shall be taken to require a person to repeat any testing, examination or research which has been carried out otherwise than by him or at his instance, in so far as it is reasonable for him to rely on the results thereof for the purposes of these provisions'.

If someone else has done the 'testing, examination or research', then you only have to repeat it if it would not be reasonable for you to rely upon the testing already done.

This helpful exception can only apply, though, if you knew of previous work done on the product. So you should en-quire . . . satisfy yourself that the testing, research and ex-amination is adequate for safety purposes . . . and then, if it turns out that the product is dangerous and that the hazards would have been discovered through adequate research, testing or examination, you must be prepared to prove that you reasonably relied on work done by others, ahead of you in the line of production or circulation.

'Impossible', you say. 'A politician's counsel of perfection, offered without regard to the realities of business life. How can we conceivably do as you suggest?'

Fine. Then do not do it. But recognise that you will have removed about your only likely defence if you are prosecuted. You may not like the statute, but − unless and until it is amended or repealed − it contains the law.

You may, of course, simply ignore these suggestions and hope for the best. All being well, there will be no complaint, no accident, no disaster, no prosecution and no civil claim. Indeed, so far Section 6 has largely been held in reserve as a weapon for future use. But at least you now know the risks.

The Section offers you one other potential defence: '(8) Where a person designs, manufactures, imports or supplies an article for or to another on the basis of a *written* undertaking by that other to take specified steps sufficient to ensure, in so far as is reasonably practicable, that the article will be safe and without risks to health when properly used, the undertaking shall have the effect of relieving the first mentioned person from the duty imposed by sub-section 1(a) above to such extent as is reasonable having regard to the terms of the undertaking.'

In other (and more ordinary) words — if you design, manufacture, import or supply an article (but *not* a substance) for a customer and he gives you his *written* undertaking that he will carry out any necessary research, examination or testing to see that the article will be safe and without risks to health, then you may rely on that undertaking. Note: the undertaking must be in writing — an oral promise is not good enough.

Suppose, for instance, that you quote for the production of certain equipment. Your customer demands a decrease in price. You say: 'We have to quote high because we must carry out any necessary research, testing and examination, to ensure safety and absence of risk to health'. Your customer replies: 'We will undertake to carry out the research, inspection and examination . . . So on that basis, kindly reduce your price . . .'.

Make sure that you get the customer's undertaking in writing and you may then proceed, without worries under Section 6. If it turns out that your customer does not comply with that undertaking, then he may be criminally liable, if he has either incorporated your product into one which he is marketing for use at work or even if he simply puts it on the market in an unsafe condition.

The civil consequences of the transaction are also clear. Your customer is extremely unlikely to have any claim against you because of any defect in your product which would have been revealed by inspection, research or examination which you would have carried out, were it *not* for his undertaking. If the 'ultimate consumer' is injured and sues you, you would deny negligence and in any event claim an indemnity from your customer. If in due course the rules of strict liability are applied, then you would be liable to that ultimate consumer because your product was defective, but (once again) you would have a good claim over as against your customer (see Chapter 44 for 'third-party proceedings').

Section 6(9) applies similar rules to the supply of articles
for use at work under hire purchase, conditional sale or
credit sale agreements. And Section 6(10) repeats: 'An article
or substance is not to be regarded as properly used where it
is used without regard to any relevant information or advice
relating to its use which has been made available by a person
by whom it was designed, manufactured, imported or
supplied.' So be careful to inform and to advise – and be
prepared to prove not only that you have done so but to give
details of the advice or information supplied. You may have to
do so one day to a court.

*   *   *

When this Section first appeared on the statute books,
troops of cats leapt around the pigeonries of our industry and
commerce. Here indeed was a sharp sword, ready to smite the
careless designer, manufacturer, importer, supplier, erector,
installer . . . . Civil liability for creating or circulating a
dangerous article or substance is bad enough – but criminal
liability as well?

So far, then, the Section 6 sword has largely been resting
in its sheath. One day, though . . . .

Chapter 31

Who is the criminal?

There are no private prosecutions under the Health and
Safety at Work Act. Theoretically, a private individual or
company may obtain the consent of the Director of Public
Prosecutions to proceed. In practice, his consent has rarely
been sought and has never been given. The Inspector decides
whom to put into the dock. So how is that decision made?
Who is criminally liable, where a defective product leads to
potential prosecution?

A few years ago, an elderly man went into a Tesco Super-
market in Northwich; selected a packet of detergent from a
shelf marked with a cut-price offer; took it to the pay-out

desk; and was required to pay the full price. 'Sorry, Sir', said the girl by the till, 'but we have run out of the cut-price packets'.

The customer reported Tesco's to the local Consumer Protection Authorities who prosecuted. The Trade Descriptions Act makes it an offence to offer goods for sale at a price lower than that at which you are in fact prepared to sell them.

Tesco's proved to the magistrates that they had given firm and adequate instructions to their managers. Goods on shelves marked with a special offer were to be sold at the lower price until the advertising material was removed. Unfortunately, the manager had failed to pass on the instructions to the pay-out girl.

The magistrates convicted. An employer, after all, obtains the benefit of what his employee does correctly and must bear the blame if he makes a mistake or does wrong. The Court of Appeal upheld the conviction. Tesco's took their case to the House of Lords.

Unanimously, the Law Lords decided that Tesco's had complied with their obligations. In civil law, of course, they could be held 'vicariously liable' for the wrongful acts of their employees. Had the customer sued in a civil court for damages for misrepresentation the company could not have avoided its responsibilities by saying: 'Blame the manager, not us'.

However, in a criminal prosecution, the accused is only guilty if he has done something wrong. Tesco's had come up to the standard required by law and by society. The prosecution should have been brought against the manager.

The same principle applies under the Health and Safety at Work Act. Every 'director, manager or secretary' is personally liable if the default has occurred with his consent or connivance or as a result of his 'neglect'.

Worse, if the accused maintains that he 'took all reasonably practicable steps' to avoid the commission of the offence, he must prove his innocence. Usually, the prosecution must prove guilt beyond all reasonable doubt. But in Health and Safety at Work Act cases, once a wrongful act has been committed, the accused must show that the fault was not his.

If, then, you are prosecuted because of a defect in a product marketed by your company, you may maintain that the fault was not yours. You may prove that you did all that was 'reasonably practicable' to avoid the offence. And you may also show that the fault was that of some other person. The law allows you to pass the legal buck, if you can.

Candidates for promotion in the Navy were once faced with the question: 'Correct the following: "It were me what done it".' One bright spark wrote: "It were NOT me what done it'. He was allegedly promoted forthwith to Rear Admiral.

Anyway, the 'It weren't me what done it' principle is one worth promoting. But be prepared to prove your case. Can you show that you (like Tesco's) gave appropriate instructions to your juniors? Or maybe you recommended additional research or testing to your board, who turned it down? Have you got copies of memoranda or letters, to back up your recollection? If not, you may be in difficulty.

When product liability becomes a criminal matter, the law applies the same principles, then, as in other criminal cases. You are not criminally liable merely because your company is guilty of an offence. After all, you may have had no control over the circumstances. There may be no 'consent, connivance or neglect' on your part.

Equally, if the fault was yours, the company may properly put the blame against you.

Or perhaps the Inspector considers that your company (or firm or authority) was at fault, but so were you. He may then prosecute you as well as your company — and, incidentally, either as well as or in substitution for the person or people on whom you seek to heap criminal blame.

Chapter 32

Criminal liability of the designer

Accidents often begin on the drawing board. So what is the liability of the designer, in criminal and in civil law?

*   *   *

A Director of Roads was prosecuted and convicted of an

offence under the Health and Safety at Work Act. The Factory Inspector alleged that the death of an employee on the road was due to the 'neglect' of the executive at the head of the Department. The Director was convicted and fined. He appealed — and lost.

The Appeal Court held, in effect, that while the Director was not expected personally to inspect and supervise the individual operation, the chain of responsibility led straight back to him. His duty was to set up and to maintain in operation as best as he reasonably could a safe system of working. He must take such steps as are reasonably practicable to protect those who work under him, both personally and through prudent and careful delegation.

So the criminal law, which sets up minimum standards for the protection of the community, looks along the chain of causation to see who was really responsible for the dangerous act. To misquote President Truman, the American 'buck' may 'stop' in the White House; the safety 'buck' is thrown back to the person at fault.

Section 6 of the Act recognises that this guilty individual may be the 'designer, manufacturer, importer or supplier' of an 'article' designed for use at work or of a 'substance' intended for use at work. Each must take such steps as are 'reasonably practicable' to protect those affected by their work.

If, then, a product is dangerous, the criminal court will ask: Whose fault was it? Was it the eventual user, who had failed to follow proper instructions? Was it the assembler, erector, or installer who had failed to take ordinary, proper care? Was it the manufacturer, within the UK, or the company or firm which had imported the dangerous object from abroad, without proper testing or research? Or was the designer really to blame? Was he careless in his calculations? Did he fail to take adequate precautions, to ensure, in so far as he reasonably could, that the product would be safe?

There is no absolute duty placed on the designer or on anyone else. 'Strict' (or 'no fault') liability is already imposed on employers who provide equipment for employees which causes personal injury or death. *The Employer's Liability (Defective Equipment) Act, 1969*, says that an employer is 'deemed' to have been negligent, if an employee is injured through the use of such equipment. He (or his insurers) must compensate the employee and then look for his indemnity against his supplier or against the manufacturer or designer concerned. But this is civil law. In the law of crime, you will only be held responsible if you are at fault.

Equally, in civil law, the employer may be held 'vicariously liable' for the wrongdoings of his employee. If the designer makes a mistake which causes injury, loss or damage, the employer will have to pay. In criminal law, the designer must bear his own responsibility and pay his own penalty. Today, the maximum penalties are: in a Magistrates Court, up to £400 fine; in a Crown Court, unlimited fine and/or two years' imprisonment.

As we saw (in Chapter 31), in *Tesco Supermarkets Ltd* v. *Nattrass*, the House of Lords held that a company or other employer is only liable in criminal law if it has itself been guilty of some fault. Tesco's had given full, proper, written (and hence provable) instructions to its managers, which one of them had failed to follow. He, not the company, should have been prosecuted. He, not his employer, was responsible in criminal law for adhering to the minimum standards needed to protect the public.

So the designer bears a personal responsibility under Section 6. He may be prosecuted, whether or not his employers (or, for that matter, any fellow employees) are put in the dock.

At this stage (as we saw in Chapter 31) the Act imposes a very heavy burden on the accused. If there is an unsafe practice and he says: 'Don't blame me . . . I took such steps as were reasonably practicable in the circumstances . . .' the Act says 'Prove it'. 'It shall be for the accused to show . . .' his innocence, and not for the prosecution to prove his guilt. So the designer must be prepared to produce his calculations, his records, his work sheets, his drawings, to show that he in fact took those precautions which should have been taken by the ordinary, prudent, skillful designer or draughtsman, in his position.

Under Section 6, a designer, manufacturer, importer or supplier may pass off his responsibilities only if he can show that he reasonably relied on research or testing done by others or that his customer gave a written undertaking that he would research or test the product. Otherwise, he retains the blame.

Chapter 33

Testing and quality control

The larger the operation and the smaller the product, the greater the problems of testing and quality control. When 'strict liability' arrives, it will be no excuse to say: 'It wasn't our fault . . . we couldn't have done any greater testing than we did . . .'. If the product is defective, its maker will be legally liable. But even then, the court will have to ponder problems of real fault, when deciding how to allocate blame between various potential defendants. So consider the duty of care imposed by law on a manufacturer to ensure that his product is properly tested.

As we saw in Chapter 30, Section 6 of the Health and Safety at Work Act imposes a criminal duty on all designers, manufacturers, importers and suppliers. In broad terms, they must take such steps as are 'reasonably practicable' to ensure the safety of any article or substance to be used by others at work. This must be done through research and testing. They do not have to retrace steps which they reasonably believe were properly taken by others for the purpose. And a written undertaking from a customer that he will control quality and safety will suffice.

In civil law, the manufacturer must exercise 'reasonable care'. He is not under any absolute duty to ensure that his product is safe but he must take such steps as are reasonable to see that his products are safe. Naturally, he must keep up with current research and knowledge. He may have to engage in original research or development. The greater the risk involved, the higher the degree of care imposed upon him.

To what extent, then, will a court impose standards of testing, inspection or quality control?

In *Grant* v. *Australian Knitting Mill Ltd** the plaintiff proved that he had contracted dermatitis due to the presence of an irritant chemical in underwear manufactured by the defendants. They pleaded that although they had produced nearly 5 million of the same garments by the same methods, they had received no complaints. Unfortunately, many of the best accidents occur in undertakings or operations with fine safety records.

* See Chapter 2.

The Privy Council agreed that the method of manufacture was correct and the danger of excess chemicals being left in the garments was both 'recognised and guarded against'. The process was intended to be foolproof and if excess chemicals were left in that particular garment, someone must have been at fault.

A more hilarious example of failure to spot defects appeared in the renowned House of Lords decision in *Smedleys Ltd. v. Breed.* Smedleys, of course, process food — including millions of peas. Obviously, they cannot inspect each pea. So they installed what the House of Lords described as a 'satisfactory system' for spot checks, which included a mechanical screening process to eliminate waste matter of markedly higher or lower specific gravity than the peas themselves plus visual inspection of all peas on their way along the conveyor belt towards what the Law Report charmingly calls 'their final destination'. Trained and experienced women sorters inspect and remove extraneous material.

During the 1971 canning season, some 3½ million tins of peas emerged from the factory and Smedleys received only four complaints of extraneous matter in the tins. One was made by a customer that in addition to the peas the tin contained a caterpillar.

The company argued that because the caterpillar was of a similar density, diameter and weight to the peas, it had escaped the mechanical screening process. And because it was pea green, it had escaped the eagle eyes of the inspectors.

Smedleys were prosecuted under *The Food and Drugs Act, 1955.* It was alleged that the food was not 'of the nature or substance or quality demanded by the customer' and that the Inspectorate were 'reasonably satisfied' that the offence was due to 'the act or default of the defendants'. Smedleys maintained that they had 'taken all reasonable care to avoid the presence of extraneous matter in the food', and that they were therefore protected by Section 3(3) of the Act.

Viscount Dilhorne rejoiced at the justices' finding that the caterpillar was 'sterile, harmless and would not have constituted a danger to health if it had been consumed'. Better still the caterpillar 'did not affect the substance of the peas'. However: had Smedleys 'taken all reasonable care'? Was 'the presence of the extraneous matter . . . the *unavoidable*

consequence of the process'? The presence of the caterpillar
was not 'unavoidable' because if it had been noticed, its
presence could have been avoided and it would have been
taken out. Commenting, in effect, that the prosecution had
wasted public time and money, Viscount Dilhorne nevertheless dismissed the appeal.

Lord Hailsham agreed. Smedleys could not establish the
absence of negligence on the part of their own inspectorate.
The caterpillar had 'achieved a sort of posthumous apotheosis
. . . . A housewife who orders peas is entitled to complain if,
instead of peas, she gets a mixture of peas and caterpillars. . . .
She is not bound to treat the caterpillar as a kind of un-
covenanted blessing . . .'. The presence of the beast was not
'unavoidable'.

Now, this was of course a criminal prosecution. How would
these rules be applied in the 'tort' of negligence? It might be
argued that the presence of the caterpillar 'spoke for itself'
(see page 208 on *res ipsa loquitur*). More likely, though, a
court might infer negligence from the presence of the extraneous matter.

So much for defects which could have been spotted with
the human eye. What of those damages which research might
have revealed? This problem was considered in the case of
Vacwell Engineering Co. Ltd. v. *B.D.H. Chemicals Ltd* (see
also Chapter 2). The judge held that the manufacturers owed
a 'duty to take reasonable care to ascertain major industrial
hazards of chemicals marketed by them and to give warning of
such hazards to their customers'. Had the manufacturers
'carried out adequate research into the scientific literature
available to them in order to discover the industrial hazards
of a new or little known chemical . . . the explosion hazard
. . . would have come to light and a suitable warning been
given . . .'. No warning was given; an explosion occurred; a
man died; and negligence was established. None of the four
books which the defendants had referred to had noted the
danger of an explosion. But this was not enough to free them
from the burden placed upon them by the law of negligence.

Chapter 34

Defective manufacture — and defences to a criminal charge

If you are prosecuted under Section 6 of the Health and Safety at Work Act because of an alleged failure as 'designers, manufacturers, importers or suppliers' of an article or substance intended or designed for use at work, what possible defences are open to you? Here is a checklist:

1   That you did all that was 'reasonably practicable' to ensure that the design or construction of the article (or that the substance itself) was safe and without danger to health or safety. Problem: The burden of proving that you did what was 'reasonably practicable' will rest on you.

2   That you in fact (a) carried out or alternatively (b) arranged for the carrying out of such testing and examination as was necessary to ensure safety as above.

3   That you took all necessary steps to ensure that adequate information was supplied concerning the design, etc., so as to facilitate proper (and hence safe) use of the article or substance

4   That any failure on your part to test, examine or research was due to reliance upon testing, examination or research which you reasonably relied upon others to carry out.

5   That you obtained, in the case of an article, a written undertaking from your customer that he would take steps specified to ensure safety.

6   That the offence was due to the act or default of some other person who may be one of the following:
a   The person who should have carried out the testing, research or examination (see 4 above).
b   The customer, who gave the written undertaking (5 above).
c   Your superior, whom you had advised and recommended to set aside appropriate funds, facilities or equipment to

carry out the necessary research, testing or examination but who had lamentably failed to follow your recommendations.

d   Your subordinate, to whom you had provided proper and adequate instructions, which he had failed to follow.

Chapter 35

Delegated legislation

Like so many of our modern statutes, the Health and Safety at Work Act is an 'enabling Act'. Parliament enables others to make rules which have the same force as if they were made by the legislature itself. It delegates its powers.

This process is inevitable in a complicated society with a Parliament which has insufficient time for its work, even before it assumed some responsibility for overseeing appropriate EEC legislation.

Regulations have precisely the same force as if they were contained in the mother statute. They are spawned by the hundred in areas which every businessman will recognise — not least, in those affecting safety.

For instance, since 1 October 1978 new Regulations created by the Health and Safety Commission have required employers to take two steps:

1   To consult with safety representatives appointed by independent, recognised trade unions.
2   To set up and to operate safety committees, at the written request of two or more safety representatives.

These committees will inevitably and primarily be concerned with the safety of employees. But they could and should also keep an eye on product safety.

The Regulations contain no details of the functions of a safety committee. Nor is there any Code of Practice concerning committees, breach of which may be used in any relevant proceedings, civil or criminal. Instead, the Commission has merely given guidance, which at present ignores the area of product liability. One day, concern with the dangers of products to those who manufacture them will spread to perils for consumers.

Much more important, though, is Schedule 3 of the Act, reproduced in full as part of Appendix 6. Regulations may be made by the Commission (as opposed to Parliament) covering almost any health or safety aspect of the manufacturing or distribution process. Design, construction, examination, testing, inspection . . . manufacture, supply, use . . . testing, labelling, examination . . . research in connection with any (appropriate) activity . . . provisions for registration and licensing . . . for monitoring atmospheric or other working conditions . . . keeping and preservation of records . . . or even 'restricting, prohibiting or requiring the doing of any specified thing where any accident or other occurrence of a specified kind has occured'. By all means beware of the Act. But do not ignore Regulations.

Remember, Regulations of any sort have the same force as the statute under which they are made and breach of the Regulations (except where otherwise stated) renders the offender liable to precisely the same penalties as those available for offences under the Act itself. Codes of Practice (like the Highway Code) should be followed where possible because breach is likely to mean the losing of a relevant legal action, civil or criminal. And even Guidance Notes are intended to provide a sensible framework which should not be ignored without careful thought.

Chapter 36

Consumer protection

Governments protect. Some have particular regard for sections of the population which they consider to be especiall in need of that protection.

Take employees, who were covered (among other recent statutes) by *The Redundancy Payments Act, 1965; The Contracts of Employment Act, 1972; The Trade Union and Labour Relations Act, 1974; The Employment Protection Act, 1975* – and other statutes giving personal protection, the provisions of which are now happily brought together in *The Employment Protection (Consolidation) Act, 1978.*

Then there are trade unions — organised, independent workers' organisations and especially those 'recognised' to any extent for collective bargaining purposes. They and their members are covered by many of the statutes already listed. Corporate protection is likely to be consolidated in a statute expected to be unfurled in 1979.

Or take women or employees who belong to ethnic minorities. *The Equal Pay Act, 1970; The Sex Discrimination Act, 1975; The Race Relations Act, 1975* — all apply to them.

The Health and Safety at Work etc. Act, 1974, is a criminal statute. Different sections of the Act protect different sections of the community: Section 2, employees; Section 3, non-employees, affected by the employer's 'undertaking'; Section 6, anyone who suffers through defective design or manufacture, construction, erection or installation or sale or supply of articles or substances designed or intended for use at work.

The crucial sections of *The Sale of Goods Act, 1893,* cover all sales — private and business. A term is normally implied into any contract of sale, no matter who makes it, that the goods will be 'of merchantable quality' and 'reasonably fit for the purpose supplied'.

Still, a mass of modern legislation, actual and in contemplation, is designed to protect the private individual. Rightly or on occasion wrongly, he is regarded as less able to take care of himself than is the business or professional man who supplies him with goods or services. The government . . . the state . . . the family in the national sense . . . must therefore step in and protect him, usually against others but sometimes even against himself.

Hence (as we have seen in Part 3), *The Supply of Goods (Implied Terms), Act 1973,* and *The Unfair Contract Terms Act, 1977,* both provide different criteria to contracts made with 'consumers'. The 1893 Act protects both business and private buyers, but only as against a business seller. Product liability law is really designed to provide Lord Atkin's 'ultimate consumer' (first introduced in *Donoghue* v. *Stephenson* — the case of the snail in the bottle — Chapter 2) with much wider cover. Until now, the 'consumer' has either had to prove a breach of contract or breach of a duty of care, i.e. negligence, in order to recover damages. When strict liability emerges, he will have much the same rights as a contracting party, even though he is a stranger to the people sued.

Meanwhile, Parliament has passed a series of statutes designed in the main to protect 'consumers' against unsafe industrial and commercial practices. The latest is *The Consumer Safety Act, 1978,* and upon that Act and upon the Fair Trading Act, we shall now briefly concentrate.

Chapter 37

The Consumer Safety Act, 1978

The Consumer Safety Act, 1978, came into force on 1 November 1978 (except for certain repeal provisions). It repeals *The Consumer Protection Act, 1961* (and its Northern Ireland equivalent) and *The Consumer Protection Act, 1971* and gives the Secretary of State for Prices and Consumer Protection far wider powers than previously. It enables him not only to make prohibition orders and notices to prevent the supply of dangerous goods but to require goods to be marked with warnings or instructions and to include additional markings such as first aid advice or warning symbols.

Extending to the whole of the United Kingdom, the Act has much the same twin effect as most other statutes which apparently impose criminal duties. Anyone who is in breach of Regulations made under the Act is not only guilty of a criminal offence but also of what is sometimes called 'negligence *per se*' — it will of itself be negligent not to attain the standards created by Parliament as necessary for the protection of the public.

The 1978 Act has six main functions:

1   It widens ministerial powers to make regulations.
2   It enables the Minister to take rapid action to ban the sale of dangerous goods.
3   It gives power to require distributors of potentially dangerous goods to publish warnings about the hazards they present.
4   It enables the Minister to serve notices requiring the furnishing to him of information that he needs so as to exercise his functions under the Act.

5   It confers an enforcement duty on local Trading
     Standards authorities.
6   It widens the powers of enforcement already held by
     Trading Standards authorities.

The Minister retains previously existing powers to prescribe
requirements as to 'the composition or content, design, construction, finish or packing of goods . . .'. Existing powers to
require warning or instructions to be marked on or to accompany goods remain. These are now widened to include 'other
information'. So new regulations may require goods to bear
the name and the address of the manufacturer or supplier;
warning symbols; names of ingredients; or first aid instructions.

Goods may have to be approved by a specified body.
Certification of compliance with a standard created by that
body may also become obligatory.

The Minister is given power to approve standards for
any purpose, or any safety regulations. For instance, he may
regulate that compliance with an approved standard which
shall be deemed to satisfy the requirements of the Regulations
for the purposes of criminal liability. And Regulations may
contain supplementary provisions to require the prior approval
of goods, as well as fees chargeable and appeals against refusal.

Regulations may require testing or inspection of goods,
together with standards for test or inspection. The government may now lay down standards for quality control
procedure relevant to safety, at the point of manufacture.

Regulations may prohibit the supply of goods which are
considered unsafe or others (such as inefficient safety
equipment) which do not adequately reduce the risk of death
or personal injury in the circumstances in which the goods
may be used. Regulations may also restrict the supply of
goods to people below a specified age.

The government now has power to take urgent action to
prohibit unsafe goods. It may make prohibition 'orders' or
prohibition 'notices'. As with the Health and Safety at Work
Act, a 'prohibition order' prohibits anyone from continuing
to supply in the course of his business, goods that the Minister
considers unsafe. Such orders may last up to twelve months.

A prohibition notice is a notice which the Minister may
serve on a person, prohibiting him from continuing to supply
goods which are considered to be unsafe and which are

described in the notice. There is no limit on the duration of these notices.

Procedures for both types of notice are set out in the First Schedule to the Act. In either case advance notice should be given so that the person concerned may make representations. But if the risk of danger calls for immediate prohibition on the supply of goods, then warning may be dispensed with.

The Minister may now serve a warning notice on any trader who has supplied goods which in some respects were unsafe and represented a risk to users of the goods. He must then himself publish suitable warnings about risk from the goods.

Local Trading Standards authorities will enforce the rules, unless and until the Minister transfers this function to some other body. The enforcement powers are similar to those in the Trade Descriptions Acts and other consumer protection legislation. Maximum penalty: £1000 fine.

*   *   *

This important new statute resulted from a Conservative Private Member's Bill, passed with Labour Governmental support. Regulations formerly in force governing (for instance) nightdresses, oil heaters, electric blankets, toys and cooking utensils, remain in force, subject to the new penalties and procedures. And future Regulations will continue to be made, piecemeal and as the government reacts to injuries and pressures. But at last it may ban the sale of dangerous goods and take steps which are both swift and effective to take them off the market.

One object of the law is to enable the person injured to obtain recompense. But it is far preferable to head off that injury. The promotion of safety and the prevention of accident is far preferable to cure and compensation.

"SUBJECT TO CONTRACT AND TO SURVEY —
WILL YOU MARRY ME?"

Part Five

FAULT AND ENFORCING JUDGMENTS — AT HOME AND ABROAD

Chapter 38

Parts and components

Each person in the chain of production, distribution and supply bears his own legal responsibilities. When an accident occurs, courts have to sort out who should pay the bill.

The manufacturer of the finished product and the producer of the parts and components which go into it both owe duties in contract, in tort and in criminal law, in connection with the manufacturing process. But the carriers and the storage and warehouse contractors must not cause a defect through bungling their jobs. And goods which are not defective when they reach the retailer may sometimes be sold to the public in a dangerous condition.

If food is poisoned, whose fault was it? If a windscreen shatters, was it the fault of the manufacturers of the vehicle or the producers of the windscreen, or did someone cause the danger by the way that he screwed the windscreen into place? Or was it maybe the shared fault of all concerned? Perhaps the windscreen was not sufficiently supple to take the kind of strains which would be imposed by the installers? Or did the manufacturers of the windscreen give adequate instructions to others who would be handling or installing it as to how to avoid dangerous strain? These problems were canvassed in *Evans* v. *Triplex Safety Glass Co.* in which the unfortunate Mrs Evans lost her case against the glass manufacturers but might have won it had she sued those who installed the windscreen.

At present, the injured plaintiff must prove fault — with the sole exception of cases covered by *The Employer's Liability (Defective Equipment) Act, 1969*, where the employer is 'deemed' to have been negligent if his employee is killed or injured through a defect in equipment supplied. So the well known case of *Taylor* v. *Rover Co. Ltd,** as well as that of *Davie* v. *New Merton Board Mills Ltd* (in which the employee failed in an action arising out of eye damage caused through a defectively manufactured drift would have been decided differently. Nevertheless, a statement of the law by the judge in Taylor's case is now frequently quoted as setting out neatly and accurately a manufacturer's liability for components.

'A manufacturer's duty', said Mr Justice Baker, 'is not limited to those parts of his products which he makes himself. It extends to component parts, supplied by his sub-manufacturers or by others, which he uses in the manufacture of his products. He must take reasonable care, by inspection or otherwise, to see that those parts can properly be used or put his product in a condition in which it can safely be used or consumed in the contemplated manner by the ultimate consumer or user.'

The manufacturer may receive parts or components which he ought to test (see Chapter 5 on 'intermediate examination'). Anyway, he must ensure that he uses, instals or incorporates the parts or components, carefully and in accordance with appropriate instructions.

Equally, the manufacturer of those parts and components 'owes a duty of care' — in contract and in tort.

At present, all these duties, other than those owed to employees by their employers not to supply them with defective equipment, depend upon breach of contract or breach of duty. When the day of strict liability arrives, the sufferer will still have to prove the defect, but not the negligence. Courts will then decide whether and to what extent the manufacturer of the finished product will be held liable for all components in it, subject to his rights in appropriate cases to claim contribution of indemnity from those who supplied defective parts or components. Meanwhile, the best assurance will certainly lie in adequate insurance — if you can get it, at a price that is reasonable.

Chapter 39

The meaning of 'defective'

Whether a manufacturer or other 'circulator' of defective goods is liable with or without fault still begs one crucial question: When are goods 'defective'? *The Sale of Goods Act, 1893,* does not use the term 'defective'. Instead it says 'unmerchantable' or 'not of merchantable quality'. So when are goods 'unmerchantable'?

Perfection is an attribute of some other world. Minor blemishes in a major product do not make it such that a 'merchant' would not sell it. But a major breach in a minor product would destroy its saleability. Naturally, the grey area comes in between.

Section 62(1A) of the Act [implanted by *The Supply of Goods (Implied Terms) Act, 1973*] reads: 'Goods of any kind are of merchantable quality . . . if they are fit for the purpose or purposes for which goods of that kind are commonly bought as it is reasonable to expect having regard to any description applied to them, to the price (if relevant) and to all the other relevant circumstances; and any reference on this Act to unmerchantable goods shall be construed accordingly'.*

So we start once again with that ubiquitous word: 'Reasonable' (see Chapter 23). Would the reasonable buyer or seller regard the goods as 'fit for the purpose . . . for which goods of that kind are commonly bought'?

Next, what description, if any, was 'applied' to the goods? Although in law most goods are 'sold by description', that does not necessarily mean that something special was said about them. If it was, then the words used will help determine 'merchantability'. For instance, were the goods described as 'new' or 'reconditioned', 'manufactured to your order' or 'second-hand'?

You attach the description to 'fitness for purpose' and read the two together. In the past, the test of 'merchantability' was 'saleability'. You asked: 'Were the goods reasonably saleable'? Today the question is: 'Are they reasonably fit for the purpose, having regard to the description used for them?'

A product may, of course, be unmerchantable even though it does its job properly. A vehicle may perform with distinction but the buyer will certainly be entitled to complain if the paintwork has peeled, flaked or bubbled. The distinction between the two portions of Section 14 of the Act remains. The goods must be both 'reasonably fit for the purpose' and 'of merchantable quality' but Section 62(1A) has gone a long way to amalgamating the tests for compliance.

The leading case in this area of law is still *Henry Kendal & Sons v. William Lillico & Sons Ltd & Others*. In a massive and complicated judgment, the House of Lords held, in effect,

---

* Article 4 of the Strasbourg Convention says much the same. 'A product is defective when it does not provide for persons or property the safety which a person is entitled to expect' (see Appendix 14).

that even though the groundnuts in question were contaminated, they could still be fed to cattle; therefore they were fit
for one purpose, if not for another; and they were therefore
not 'unmerchantable'. The fact that the feed would kill
pheasants did not make it 'unmerchantable' in a particular
case when it was to be sold for cattle.

If you run into difficulty over this problem, you should
take legal advice because Kendal's case has been considered,
followed, applied, distinguished, praised and criticised in a
great stream of later litigation. The most important:
Ashington Piggeries Ltd v. *Christopher Hill Ltd.,* which
occupied two weeks of House of Lords' arguing time in 1971.

Ashington Piggeries wished to market 'king-sized mink
food' according to a formula prepared by their Mr Udall.
Christopher Hill were well known animal feeding stuff com-
pounders and they agreed to supply ingredients to the best
quality available, and to supply the mink food either to
Ashington or to their customers.

After about a year, Mr Udall's herd of mink and other
animals all over the country who had been fed 'king size'
suffered severe liver disease. The mink food was held
responsible. Ashington withheld payment and Christopher
Hill sued for the price of goods sold and delivered. Ashington
retorted that the goods were worthless; and alleged that
Norwegian herring meal included in the food was the cause
of the toxin which killed the mink. In due course, it became
clear that the herring meal was indeed responsible for the
disaster.

At the time the mink food was made up, the possibility of
the chemical reaction caused through the use of the pre-
servative in question was 'unthought of. In the existing state
of scientific and commercial knowledge, no deliberate
exercise of human skill or judgment could have prevented the
meal from having its toxic, and lethal, effect on mink.' Ashington counter-claimed for damages, to compensate them for
the loss they had suffered through death and injury to the
mink. They alleged that the goods were neither fit for the
purpose supplied nor of merchantable quality.

The House of Lords decided as follows:

1   Ashington relied at least partially on the skill and judg-
     ment of Christopher Hill to see that the ingredients

were of a quality suitable for compounding animal feeding stuffs, therefore Section 14(1) of the Sale of Goods Act applied and a condition of fitness was implied into the contract between the parties.

2   As it was proved that the herring meal was lethal to mink, the burden lay on Christopher Hill to show that it was otherwise of a quality suitable for use in compounding feeding stuffs for domestic animals and poultry generally; and as they had failed to discharge this burden by showing that the meal could have been fed with impunity to all other types of livestock, so they were in breach of contract.

3   By a majority, the Lords held that Christopher Hill must compensate Ashington. As they 'dealt in' goods of that description (i.e. of that kind) they had supplied goods which were defective and not of merchantable quality.

4   Note: It was held by a majority that although the meal was poisonous to minks, there was no breach of the implied condition that the goods shall 'correspond with their description'. Lord Hodson said: "The herring meal was contaminated but no poisonous substance was added to it so as to make the description 'herring meal' erroneous."

Luckily for Christopher Hill, they were able to show that they received the defective herring meal from a third party, who was in breach of his contract with them. The real fault and liability lay with that third party.

Where the law depends on fault, the courts try to see where the fault lies and to lay the expense along with the blame. Even when strict liability arrives, 'third parties' will remain firmly attached to the legal hook. Meanwhile, the sort of questions worrying the drug industry include, amongst others: If a patient takes more than one drug . . . or if a doctor prescribes by a generic name . . . or if a chemist cannot state by whom a prescribed drug is made . . . or if a doctor deliberately and for the patient's own sake does not warn of possible side-effects — who then (if anyone) will be responsible for subsequent injury? Is one or more product 'defective' — and who will be able to prove what and against whom?

Chapter 40

Retailers and product liability

If an article or substance is defective and causes personal injury or death, it is generally the manufacturer who bears at least the initial moral and legal responsibility. But there are occasions when the retailer may be held liable to the sufferer, even if that victim is not his own customer. As those occasions will inevitably increase when the day of strict-liability reckoning arrives, consider the rules.

If you sell dangerous products, the law places three main responsibilities upon you. You must: (1) take reasonable steps not to sell goods which you know or ought to know are in a dangerous condition; (2) warn your customers of dangers which are intrinsic or inevitable; (3) take care not to place dangerous products into irresponsible hands.

Of course, if a product is designed to your own specification, you may acquire an additional responsibility for the results of design deficiencies. Or if you negligently repair, service, instal or label an appliance in a dangerous way, then you may yourself be held liable for the defect in the product.

A retailer's initial responsibility lies to his own customer. *The Sale of Goods Act, 1893,* states that a customer is generally entitled to a product that is 'merchantable' and 'reasonably suitable for the purpose supplied'. A defective product will probably be neither (see Chapter 39).

The Unfair Contract Terms Act, 1977 (Part 3) has ensured that no exclusion clause which seeks to reduce or remove liability for death or personal injury has any legal effect.

The Supply of Goods (Implied Terms) Act, 1973, provides that if the customer is a private buyer (or 'consumer') no other exclusion of his rights to goods which are 'merchantable' and fit for the purpose will have any effect (see Part 3).

So if you sell defective goods, your customer will have effective legal rights against you. In your turn, you can pass the contractual responsibility back to your supplier — to the distributor, wholesaler, importer or manufacturer from whom you bought goods and with whom you have a contractual relationship.

At this stage, you may run again into exclusion clauses, this time aimed at reducing or removing your rights. Remember that even though such a clause is in a business (as opposed to a consumer) contract, a court may still declare it void if it is 'unfair or unreasonable', in the particular circumstances of your case. Challenge the clause and you will probably find that your supplier will cease to rely on it.

So far, the question of fault has scarcely arisen. You will have to recompense your customer, even if the fault lay with the goods and not with you. And the same is likely to apply as between you and your supplier. But you will have additional liabilities in the civil wrong of 'negligence'.

First, do you sell dangerous products? In the case of *Burfitt* v. *Kille,* a shop sold a pistol and blank cartridges to a 12-year-old lad, without warning him of the need to clean the barrel. He fired into the air and shot a small piece of copper into the eye of a younger friend, standing nearby. The friend's eye was blinded.

The High Court held that the pistol and ammunition 'constituted something dangerous in themselves'; and they should 'never have been put into the hands of one so young'. So mind what you sell to children.

This rule was followed in the important Privy Council case of *Yachuk* v. *Oliver Blais.* A 9-year-old boy called at a garage together with his 7-year-old brother. They asked for petrol, telling a lie in order to get it. In spite of his doubts, the attendant sold him a small quantity, which the children then used for a Red Indian game. Result: explosion and injury.

The Privy Council held that the boy's story was 'such as to arouse rather than to allay suspicion in the mind of a reasonable man'. So they could not avoid liability because the lad had not told the truth. They were negligent in putting an explosive substance into the hands of a lad who had limited knowledge of the likelihood of an explosion. He did 'something which a child of his age might be expected to do'. Therefore they were liable because of the inherent danger of the product which they sold into the wrong hands.

So you must do your best to sell products which are safe; but if inevitably you retail goods which have inherent dangers, you must take reasonable steps not to place them into irresponsible hands or at least to give adequate warnings of dangers or defects of which you know or ought to know and which would make the goods dangerous.

You may, of course, know of dangers through having received previous complaints about a product. Or if you were negligent in the way in which you assembled or repaired, stored or installed or labelled a product, you might find unexpected liability shifted onto you.

An interesting case was decided in 1937 by the then Lord Chief Justice. A school teacher provided chemicals for an experiment which caused injury. The people who supplied the chemicals to the school 'had ample and repeated opportunity of intermediate examination and if they had taken the simple precautions which the invoice warned them to take, no mischief would have followed'. They were therefore held liable to the injured child.

In *Watson* v. *Buckley and Others**, the man who suffered injury after having had his hair dyed recovered damages from the hairdresser (for breach of contract) and also from the distributors. The product itself was dangerous; an 'unusual standard of care was required'; the distributors owed a duty to the customer in tort; and as they were in breach of that duty, he had a good claim against them for damages for breach of contract.

So is the retailer bound to carry out an inspection or to test products to look for defects, which they have no cause to suspect? Bearing in mind that he (like his customer) is normally entitled to expect that goods supplied to him will be 'merchantable' and 'reasonably fit' for the purpose, he is normally entitled to sell them without inspection.

Still, even a retailer must take care to see that goods manufactured by others are properly labelled when sold on to his customers — as appeared from the sad case of *Devilez* v. *Boots Pure Drug Co. Ltd and Another* (see Chapter 4).

In that case the court said that there was 'a duty on the defendant to give some warning and to secure the bottle in some better way than with a cork'. The judge added: 'Whether or not that would have made any difference in this case is difficult to say, but the defendants were in breach of their common law duty.'

Incidentally, that case also illustrates the fact that even though Boots had sold some 20 million bottles of the preparation without mishap, the fact that there had been no

* See Chapter 43.

previous misery did not free them from liability when disaster struck. Both the manufacturers and the retailers were liable to the unfortunate sufferer.

Of course, Boots were not expected to test the corn solvent. But the seller of a second-hand car must certainly test it to ensure that it is roadworthy and does not suffer from (for instance) defective brakes or steering. In *Andrews* v. *Hopkinson* the court held that the car sellers were negligent. They had delivered to Mr Andrews a car which they knew he would use on the road and which was in a dangerous condition. The defect could have been discovered by the exercise of reasonable diligence. The dealer had failed either to have the car examined or even to warn the plaintiff that no examination had been carried out.

Finally, the well known saga of *Godley* v. *Perry & Others* — the case of the defective catapult. A newsagent sold a toy catapult to a 6-year-old child, Nigel Godley. It broke; it injured his left eye which had to be removed; and he then sued the newsagent who sought an indemnity from the wholesaler who, in his turn, sued the personal representative of the importer of the catapults from Hong Kong (the importer himself having died).

The Judge held that although the catapult was 'a most dangerous toy to be let loose on the juvenile market', the defect was not one that would have been apparent on reasonable examination of the samples shown to the retailer. So while he was liable for the defective product, because he was in breach of contract with his customer, he would *not* have been responsible had the person injured *not* been the customer. Both he and the distributor were entitled 'to regard without suspicion the samples shown'. They had previously done business with the ultimate supplier and were entitled to rely upon him. Therefore the ultimate responsibility was his.

So responsibility passed right down the line. There was judgment against the retailer, in contract; he obtained his indemnity from the distributor who, in his turn, passed the liability and the expense (including the legal costs) back to those who had placed the defective product onto the market. How lucky, though, for the retailer that those higher up the line were both available to be sued and sufficiently solvent to bear the weight of the damages and of the costs.

Chapter 41

The Fair Trading Act, 1973

The Fair Trading Act, 1973, established a whole new legal framework for consumer protection. Successive governments have scarcely used their new powers with manifest energy. Successive Director-Generals of Fair Trading have been men of personality and energy, but have used their statutory powers with discretion — preferring to leave major acts of protective wisdom (such as those on exclusion clauses, detailed in Part 3) to Parliament, rather than achieving similar results through regulation. The Consumer Protection Advisory Committee has scarcely been permanently in the headlines.

Still, every business and industry is either actually or potentially affected by the Act. So here is a breakdown of the rules.

*   *   *

The Director General of Fair Trading, who may hold office for up to five years and then be re-appointed, is a very powerful man. It is his duty 'so far as appears to him to be practicable from time to time' to 'keep under review the carrying on of commercial activities in the United Kingdom which relate to goods . . . or to services . . . supplied to or for consumers in the United Kingdom'. He must collect information with regard to both the activities of the people by whom they are carried on 'with a view to his becoming aware of and ascertaining the circumstances relating to practices which may adversely affect the economic interest of consumers in the United Kingdom'. If it may 'adversely affect the interest . . . economic . . . or with respect to health, safety or other matters . . . of consumers in the United Kingdom', then he will 'collate' all available evidence.

In addition, it is the Director's duty to keep under review 'the carrying on of commercial activities in the United Kingdom and to collect information with respect to those activities and the persons by whom they are carried on, with a view to his becoming aware of and ascertaining the circumstances relating to monopoly situations or uncompetitive practices'.

So the Director has two main areas of duty — the collection, collation and review of evidence concerning consumer practices; and the collection of information and review of 'monopoly situations or uncompetitive practices' — his job, in two words, is to deal with 'unfair trading' on any scale.

Once the Director has information, then — on his own initiative or that of the appropriate Minister — he will supply the information to the government — and to the new Consumer Protection Advisory Committee, as well as to the Monopolies and Mergers Commission (formerly the Monopolies Commission). He may refer 'an unfair consumer trade practice' to the Consumer Protection Advisory Committee for its consideration. The term 'consumer trade practice' is carefully defined. It includes 'any practice which is for the time being carried on in connection with the supply of goods (whether by way of sale or otherwise) or in connection with the supply of services to or for consumers'. But it must be a practice which relates —

'(a) to the terms or conditions (whether as to price or otherwise) on or subject to which goods or services are or are sought to be supplied' — so that includes terms as to credit, discounts or deliveries; or

'(b) to the manner in which those terms or conditions are communicated to persons to whom goods or services are or are sought to be supplied' — so he may (and on occasion does) examine the contents of order forms and other contractual documents; or

'(c) to promotion (by advertising, labelling or marking of goods, canvassing or otherwise) of the supply of goods or of services or to methods of salesmanship employed in dealing with consumers' — advertising, salesmanship, promotions — all are covered — ranging from double pricing to misleading advertisements; or

'(d) to the way in which goods are packed or otherwise got up for the purpose of being supplied'. What will happen to those apparently large cartons, with vast but invisible indentations at the bottom, carefully designed to make the buyer think that he is getting far more of the substance than is in fact the case? Or;

'(e) to methods of demanding or securing payment for goods or services supplied'. Add this to the recent rules forbidding 'harassment of debtors' and the creditor must watch his legal step.

Of course, the only practices covered are those involving people who do not seek or buy the goods 'in the course of a business carried on by them', but who do buy them from businessmen. Sales by private individuals or to businessmen are not the concern of this part of the Act.

Where it appears to the Director that a consumer trade practice has particularly unfortunate effects, then he may also include proposals for recommending to the Secretary of State that he should exercise his powers to produce a statutory instrument which would either ban or curb the practice concerned. The 'practices' are set out in Section 17. They are those which have or are likely to have the following effects:

'(a) misleading consumers as to, or withholding from them adequate information as to, or an adequate record of, their rights and obligations under relevant consumer transactions, or

'(b) of otherwise misleading or confusing consumers with respect to any matter in connection with relevant consumer transactions, or

'(c) of subjecting consumers to undue pressure to enter into relevant consumer transactions, or

'(d) of causing the terms of conditions on or subject to which consumers enter into relevant consumer transactions to be so adverse to them as to be inequitable.'

Any misleading or confusing practices are covered; undue pressure may be curbed; and almost any aspect of consumer rights may result in governmental action. The Director and the Committee are given an enormous area of potential power. But it can only be exercised through the Secretary of State.

Suppose that a business practice is referred to the Committee either via the Director or, perhaps through an MP or by the Minister himself. After examination, it must decide whether the practice 'adversely affects the economic interests of consumers in the UK'. The Committee will already have taken into consideration representations by people appearing to them to have a 'substantial interest' or by bodies representing such persons — and, in most cases, they will have heard all the evidence if such persons sought to give it. It will have done its best to exclude the publication of anything relating to 'the private affairs of an individual' where the individual might be 'seriously and prejudicially affected' — and except where necessary, even company affairs will not be publicised. But the report of the Committee will be laid before Parliament and duly published.

Section 22(2) then gives the Secretary of State power to make a statutory instrument, a draft of which must be laid before Parliament and approved by resolution of both Lords and Commons, 'giving effect to the proposals set out in the reference'. In other words, he may make such order as he sees fit, to deal with the 'unfair consumer practice'.

At this stage, Parliament has one power only — and this is theoretical. It may reject the order. It has no power to amend it. As in practice Parliament is likely to approve of the major proposals and as in any event a government usually has a sufficient majority to ram it through both Houses, the Minister has even more delegated power by the Act than most traders realise — and Parliament has even less power to curb the Minister's efforts. If the Director, the Committee and the Minister are all agreed that a practice must be discontinued or modified, then the laying of the draft before Parliament — probably producing an hour's debate, late at night — will be no more than a necessary formality.

The Act, of course, provides penalties for those who infringe its rules. These may be as high as a fine of unlimited amount of imprisonment for up to two years or both. This Act is not intended to be flouted.

The Act fills some 130 pages. It created new rules for everything from monopolies and mergers to the Restrictive Trade Practices Acts (repealed). But if you understand its main outline and watch how the Director and the Committee combine with the government to put it into action, you will find much future food for both anxiety and action. The Act is designed to protect clients and customers — and it may do so with a legal vengeance previously unknown.

Chapter 42

A repairer's liability

What are a repairer's liabilities? For instance, if a garage carries out a repair on a vehicle, how far is it responsible in law to a person who is injured if that repair was done incorrectly. Will it make a difference if the customer was a trader who himself had the opportunity to inspect the vehicle after it had been fixed?

* * *

A repairer has two legal duties, one in contract and one in the 'tort' (or civil wrong) of negligence. He owes a contractual duty to his customer to do the job in a proper and workman-like manner and with reasonably suitable materials. And he is also bound to take reasonable care to avoid acts or omissions which he ought reasonably to contemplate would be likely to cause injury to a third party. This 'tortious liability' in negligence extends to complete strangers.

Suppose, then, that a repairer messes up a job. This may be through no real fault of his. But if he or his employee has been careless, his customer will almost certainly be entitled to have the job put right. The repairer is in breach of his contractual obligation. Equally, if anyone is injured as a result of that carelessness, he — the innocent, injured third party — will be entitled to damages. The fact that someone in between might have carried out an inspection will be irrelevant.

This rule was laid down in the case of *Stennett* v. *Hancock & Peters*. Miss Stennett was walking along the pavement, with a lorry approaching from the opposite direction. Suddenly, the flange which kept the tyre on one of the wheels of the lorry became detached and, bowling along the road, mounted the pavement and struck Miss Stennett's leg. She was severely injured.

The court found that the owners of the vehicle had entrusted its repair to 'a competent repairer'. Having done so, they were not liable to a person who suffered injury on the road because the 'competent repairer' had been negligent. Nor was he under a duty 'to ascertain for himself, in so far as his capability has allowed him to do so, whether the competent repairer had competently repaired the lorry'.

On the other hand (said the court) the repairer was liable to the injured party. 'He was in the same position as that of the manufacturer of an article sold by a distributor in circumstances which prevented the distributor or ultimate purchaser or consumer from discovering by inspection any defect in the article.'

The fact that the customer might have found the defect was irrelevant. The repairer must have realised that there was no real possibility that his customer would carry out an inspection. Therefore he was liable to compensate 'the ultimate sufferer'.

A court came to a similar decision in the case of *Herschthal* v. *Stewart & Ardern Ltd.* Stewart and Ardern supplied a car to another (associated) company, so that it might be hired out on hire purchase terms to U.P. Ltd. They knew that the car was going to be used — and used immediately — chiefly by Mr Herschthal.

On the same day as the car was delivered and after it had been driven only a few miles by Mr Herschthal, the nearside rear wheel came off. Mr Herschthal was injured. There was no suggestion that anything had been done to the vehicle between the time when it was delivered and the moment of the accident.

The judge held that although Mr Herschthal had an opportunity to examine the car for the purpose of discovering any defects, Stewart & Ardern had never anticipated that there would in fact be any such examination. It is not enough that the buyer or hirer has the opportunity to examine. To remove the responsibility from the supplier, you would have to show that he reasonably anticipated that such examination would take place.

Chapter 43

A distributor's liability

Legal responsibility generally depends upon fault; and if a product is faulty, the responsibility usually lies with the manufacturer. However, both under the law of contract and that of negligence, the distributor (agent, wholesaler or other) may be held liable.

The distributor, after all, must comply with his contractual obligations to his customer. If he supplies a defective product, he will be in breach of that obligation and (subject to exclusion clauses), he may be successfully sued for damages for breach of contract.

In addition, the distributor owes a duty of care to those who are likely to be affected by any negligent act or omission on his part. If he is careless (perhaps in the storage or handling of the goods or substances concerned) and as a result a stranger suffers injury, loss or damage, then he may be liable in tort. The 'ultimate consumer' is his 'neighbour' (see Chapter 2).

In addition, the distributor may be held liable if he issues an advertisement which 'intentionally excludes interference with, or examination of, the article by the consumer'. He brings himself 'into a direct relationship' with the consumer, in contract — and the consumer may sue for 'breach of collateral warranty'. This was the effect of the decision in *Watson* v. *Buckley Osborne, Garrett & Co. Ltd.*

The distributors of a hair preparation which contained acid advertised the product as 'absolutely safe and harmless and . . . needing no preliminary tests before use'. Just as the distributor may be liable if he has failed to carry out intermediate examination (where appropriate), so he may acquire an additional responsibility in contract by placing himself in a position that he warrants to users that products are safe without such examination which might otherwise have been made.

Finally, the problems of 'collateral warranties' are intricate and important, practical and intriguing and are analysed in Chapter 14 (falling as they do into the realm of contract law).

Chapter 44

Third-party proceedings — and passing the blame

If an employee is injured through defective equipment you supplied, then you are strictly liable in law and he may sue you for damages. But you may pass the blame back to your suppliers, if they were really at fault.

If you supply defective goods to your customers, they may successfully sue you for damages for breach of contract. But if you can show that someone else was the real culprit, you can make him liable.

You may be manufacturers incorporating a sealed part into a final product without the possibility of intermediate examination — so if that part is defective, why blame you? Or you may be distributors or retailers, landed into contractual trouble through your suppliers' default.

How, in practice, though do you bring the true blame home to rest on the party who was really at fault? What are the legal procedures?

* * *

If you are sued, you may 'issue third-party proceedings' against those whom you say are really responsible for the default. You may bring that company or firm or individual into the action as 'third party', seeking an appropriate contribution towards any damages which you may have to pay or (better still) a total indemnity. If the other party was partially to blame, then he will have to make a contribution; if the fault was totally his, then you should get an indemnity.

The third party may try to pass the blame further up the line. You sell to the public and are sued by your customer because you sold him defective goods? Then you may bring the wholesaler into the action as third party and he may join the manufacturer who sold the goods to him as a 'fourth party'.

Precisely the same procedure applies in safety cases. A boiler or vessel exploded killing a workman. His widow sued

his employers, alleging that they had supplied him with faulty
equipment or alternatively had failed to train or supervise him
adequately or at all. The employers claimed contribution or
indemnity from the erectors or installers who (they said) put
up the machine without unsealing the safety valves, properly
or at all or (alternatively) without adequately informing their
(the defendants') employees as to how the job could and
should be done safely.

The erectors and installers then joined the manufacturers,
claiming that the machine was faulty in the first place.
Ultimately, the three lots of insurers split the agreed damages.

These, of course, are the rules in civil law. Similar principles
apply to crime. You are prosecuted under Section 6 of the
Health and Safety at Work Act for failing to take such steps
as were reasonably practicable not to make it a dangerous
product? Then you may blame the consultants who advised
you . . . those who supplied you with your parts or accessories
. . . or anyone else whom you say was really responsible. The
inspector may then prosecute them — together with you or in
your place.

Strict liability law is a largely a civil concept, designed to
give the sufferer the right to direct legal access to the bank
account of (usually) the manufacturer. It in no way prevents
that unhappy defendant from seeking contribution or indemnity from someone else, if he was not at fault. Unfortunately,
that 'someone else' may be insolvent or in some far off land
. . . which is a matter for regret, but one which the manufacture
should have foreseen and (through insurance) guraded against.

A businessman once owed £100,000, payable the following
day. Knowing that he could not find the money, he tossed
and turned, sleepless in his bed. Finally, he arose, dressed and
drove to his creditors' house.

'Joe', he called out, as he knocked at the window. 'I want
to speak to you'.

'What is it?'

'You know I owe you £100,000 which I am due to pay
tomorrow morning?'

'That's right.'

'Well, I am sorry to tell you that I won't be able to pay.
Until now, I've not been able to sleep. Now you can stay
awake and worry. . . .'

To some extent at least, product liability law concerns who should stay awake at night and worry. That person should not, at any rate, be the innocent individual who suffers because someone has — for his profit — put a defective product into circulation.

Chapter 45

Suing the foreigner

If you buy or sell products overseas, you may need to enforce your rights against your foreign customer or supplier. Whether or not you can do so in the UK courts — and, if so, which law will be applied by those courts — will depend upon some complicated rules — which you should know, at least in outline.

If you wish to bring a foreigner before our courts, you have to serve him with the appropriate writ or summons. A private individual who is physically in the UK is just as subject to our laws as he is entitled to their protection. Equally, if you deal with an overseas company which has a registered place of business in the UK, you will be able to serve your process on the company at its business address. Otherwise, you will have to serve your writ 'out of the jurisdiction'. To do so, you will need the leave of the court.

Order 11 of the Rules of the Supreme Court lays down detailed rules, the operation of which depends upon the nature of the 'cause of action'.

If the action is founded on negligence (see Chapter 2), the question is: Was the wrongful act or omission 'committed within the jurisdiction' of our courts? 'The jurisdiction' means England and Wales, but not Scotland, where the rules are different. It would appear to include territorial waters up to the three-mile limit.

Next question: If a product is negligently manufactured and causes damage, is the negligence committed within or outside the jurisdiction?

American Cyanamid & Chemical Corporation manufactured Cyanogas gas, used for destroying rats. George Monro Ltd imported Cyanogas gas and sold it to a local authority which supplied it to a farmer for 'de-ratting'. The farmer sued the local authority, claiming that he had suffered loss through a defect in the gas and the authority, in its turn, sought and obtained an indemnity from George Monro, who applied for leave to sue American Cyanamid in New York.

Clearly, the damage (if any) caused by the negligence was suffered in the UK. But the Court of Appeal unanimously agreed that any negligence occurred in the production process which was carried out in the USA; there was therefore no wrongful act committeed within the jurisdiction; and while the manufacturers owed a duty to 'the ultimate consumer' in the UK, there was no breach of that duty in this country. So George Monro (or, hopefully, their insurers) had to bear the blame.

The place of the wrongdoing is technically called the *locus delicti*. Two other important decisions have shown how the courts fix it.

In one of the Thalidomide cases, a child in Australia attempted to apply an equivalent rule to serve the manufacturers in the UK. The Privy Council held that the court must ask the question: Where was the wrongful act committed? The plaintiff complained of a manufacturing defect? Then where did the breach of duty of care arise?

Second: In the *Cordoba Land Co.* v. *Black Diamond Steamship Corporation* the plaintiffs sued shippers, alleging that they fraudulently issued clean bills of lading. The trial judge held that if (as the plaintiff contended) a fraudulent misrepresentation had been made in Massachusetts, that was the *locus delicti*. The wrongful act did not occur in Britain, where the plaintiff had relied on the defendant's statements or (again in Britain) where he suffered his loss.

This approach might create difficulty for people in the UK seeking product liability damages based on the negligence of a manufacturer in some far-off land. In the Thalidomide case, the plaintiff attacked the distributors, alleging that they should have issued due warnings. And in criminal law (Section 6 of the Health and Safety at Work Act), a specific responsibility is placed on importers (as well as on designers, manufacturers and suppliers – see Chapter 30).

So negligence must be established within the UK. What, the of product liability cases founded on breaches of contract.

Chapter 46

Enforcing contracts

Order 11 , Rule 1(f) of the Rules of the Supreme Court states that 'If the action begun by the Writ is brought against a defendant not domiciled or ordinarily resident in Scotland to enforce, rescind, dissolve, annul or otherwise affect a contract, or to recover damages or obtain other relief in respect of the breach of a contract, being (in either case) a contract which:

1   Was made within the jurisdiction, or
2   Was made by or through an agent trading or residing within the jurisdiction on behalf of a principal trading or residing out of the jurisdiction, or
3   Is by its terms, or by implication, governed by English law',

then the court may give leave to serve out of the jurisdiction.

So we first exclude defendants 'domiciled or ordinarily resident in Scotland'. To sue them, you go to the Scottish courts — unless (as explained in the previous chapter) they have a presence within the jurisdiction.

Much of the law which applies in England and Wales is also effective in Scotland. But some is not; and the administration of justice in these parts of the UK frequently differs. Anyway, you cannot get leave to serve English or Welsh process against a defendant 'domiciled or ordinarily resident' in Scotland.

In broad terms, a person (which includes a company) is 'domiciled' where he has his permanent residence; he may at one time have more than one residence; but an individual may be permanently domiciled (either as a result of origin or choice) somewhere other than in the country in which he 'ordinarily resides'. If you run into difficulties over these definitions, consult your lawyer.

Now assume that the proposed defendant is not domiciled or ordinarily resident in Scotland. You wish to sue for damages for breach of contract. Maybe your supplier has failed to deliver the correct quality or quantity of goods . . . or your customer has refused to pay . . .

First question: Was the contract 'made within the jurisdiction' of our courts?

If your customer comes to your factory and makes a deal on the spot, then the contract is made within the jurisdiction. But if you go abroad and place your order in someone else's country, it is made outside the jurisdiction. The main complications come where the deal is made by telephone or correspondence — whether by letter, cable or telex. The normal rule is that if a deal is done by cable or letter, the contract is 'made' where the offer is *accepted* by the posting of a letter or the dispatching of a cable of acceptance. But a telexed contract is 'made' where the offeror *receives* the notification of the offeree's acceptance.

In the recent case of *B.P. Exploration (Libya) Ltd* v. *Hunt*, it was held that if you make a contract within the jurisdiction and then amend it outside, unless the amendment has the effect of substituting a new agreement for the old one, the amended contract is still taken to have been made within the jurisdiction. Whether or not a new contract has been substituted for the old is a matter of immense complication — as, indeed, is much of the law in these chapters.

Now suppose that the contract was made outside the jurisdiction. Question two: Was it made 'by or through an agent trading or residing within the jurisdiction, on behalf of a principal trading or residing out of the jurisdiction'? The person (or the company or firm) acting for the defendant must have 'made' the contract — or have negotiated it (so that it was made 'through' him), even if the principal abroad actually concluded the deal.

Finally: Question three: Was the contract wherever made, 'by its terms, or by implication, governed by English law'?

Parties to a contract may decide which law applies. They may (and, if wise, they probably will) say: 'This contract is governed by English law'. In that case, English courts will assume jurisdiction and will normally give leave for the process to be served outside that jurisdiction.

Conversely, recognising that foreigners sometimes have a peculiar preference for their own laws or customs, the contract may expressly provide that it be governed by the law of (say) the USA or France or anywhere else 'outside the jurisdiction'. In that case, Order 11, Rule 1 (f)(3) will not help.

Difficulties arise in deciding whether a contract is 'by implication' governed 'by English law. We shall look at the problems of 'choice of law' in the next chapter. But unless the parties expressly agree as to 'the proper law' governing the contract, there may be real difficulties. It seems from the cases of *Compagnie Tunisienne de Navigation S.A.* v. *Compagnie D'Armement Maritime S.A.* and of *Coastlines Ltd* v. *Hudig Chartering* that the ultimate test should be: 'What is the system of law with which the transaction has the closest and the most real connection?'

Finally, Order 11, Rule 1(g), which once again applies where the defendant is neither domiciled nor ordinarily resident in Scotland — but this time, the exclusion also applies where the defendant is domiciled or ordinarily resident in Northern Ireland.

This rule applies 'in respect of a breach committed within the jurisdiction of a contract made within or out of the jurisdiction'. The court has power to give leave to serve out of the jurisdiction, even if 'the breach was preceded or accompanied by a breach committed out of the jurisdiction that rendered impossible the performance of so much of the contract as ought to have been performed within the jurisdiction'. For this rule to apply, the breach must have occurred 'within the jurisdiction'. Ask: 'Where was the contract broken?'

Once again, the law is exceedingly complicated. The chances are that in a contract for the sale of a product the breach occurs when the goods are sold and not when the defect comes to light. In the case of *Crowther* v. *Shannon Motors,* for instance, it was held that the contract was broken at the time of the sale and not when the vehicle broke down.

Where does a breach occur? Probably at the place of shipment — especially if that is the time when ownership of the goods was transferred. But when we talk of transfer of ownership, that is also a legal quagmire (see Chapter 25, for instance, on the *Romalpa* case). So this area is yet another in which you should take all relevant documents and a statement of the facts to your solicitor, to sort out the rule most likely to apply in your particular case.

*   *   *

The fact that a judge has power to give leave to serve

process out of the jurisdiction does not mean that he will necessarily do so. He must exercise his discretion in accordance with the rules, or risk having his decision overturned by an Appeal Court. However, this discretion is wide. So if you are involved in a product liability case involving an overseas defendant, you must consider on what basis a court is likely to give you permission to serve your Writ or Summons outside its jurisdiction.

The application must come not only within 'the letter of the Rule' but also within its spirit. Would it be right for the court to order before it the foreigner who owes no allegiance to it? Is there a good arguable case, made out on the facts and on the law? Has there been an 'inordinate delay' in seeking leave to serve the Writ? Do the interests of justice demand that leave be granted?

One important factor: Which is the most convenient forum for the consideration of the dispute? In legal terms, what is the *forum conveniens* for the trial of the matter? What would be the 'comparative cost and convenience' of hearing the matter in England or Wales, as opposed to the trial taking place elsewhere?

As in the case of the assessment of 'reasonableness', so here in the exercise of a court's discretion — in each case, all will depend upon the view taken by the particular judge who hears the application.

Still, if you can bring yourself within the rules set out in the previous chapters; if you have a *prima facie* case, a good, arguable case on the facts made apparent to the judge; and if it is apparently convenient that the hearing be held here — then leave is likely to be given.

Chapter 47

Enforcing foreign judgments

A barren judgment is one which cannot be enforced. To sue a 'man of straw' is to throw good money after bad. Equally, to obtain a judgment against a foreign defendant is useless if it goes unsatisfied. Conversely, if a foreign customer obtains judgment against you because of a defect in a product which you have sold abroad, you can laugh all the way to the factory if that judgment cannot be enforced against your assets. So consider: When is a foreign judgment enforceable here — or your judgment in some foreign land?

The first place to look for the defendant's money is within the jurisdiction of our courts. Even if the defendant is overseas, if he has assets here you may use the resources of our courts to enforce your rights. You may, for instance, 'levy equitable execution' on his property, i.e. obtain an order for the sale of all buildings belonging to him, so that the judgment debt may be satisfied. Indeed, you may even send in the Sheriffs, to take hold of his movables.

Equally, if you have assets in (say) the United States and an American court gives judgment against you, then the resources and methods of the US enforcement processes may be used to snatch up your property, real or personal, to obtain satisfaction of the judgment debt.

If, as is more likely, the judgment must be enforced against you in the UK or against the other party in his own country, you must look to see whether there are arrangements with that country for the reciprocal enforcement of judgments. It is unthinkable, for instance, that the judgment of a court of that country would be enforceable here against you, while you remained unable to enforce your rights through the courts of that country.

So in each case you must look to see whether one of the various Acts of Parliament which provide for the reciprocal enforcement of judgments apply as between the UK and the country with which you are concerned. If so, then you would be able to register your judgment in the court of that country, which would then enforce your judgment as if it were its own. Conversely, if the successful foreign plaintiff is able to register his judgment with our courts, you had better prepare for payment.

The Administration of Justice Act, 1970, provides for the reciprocal enforcement of judgments by superior courts in many parts of the Commonwealth. *The Foreign Judgments (Reciprocal Enforcement) Act, 1933,* has been applied to Austria, Belgium, France, the Federal Republic of Germany, Guernsey, the Isle of Man, Israel, Italy, Jersey, the Netherlands and Norway — and also to certain Commonwealth and former Commonwealth countries not covered by the 1930 Act (including India and Pakistan). Judgments obtained in Scotland or Northern Ireland are, of course, mutually enforceable — in this case, through *The Judgments Extension Act, 1868*. Finally, it is possible on occasion to sue on the foreign judgment in our Courts, recommencing the proceedings on the basis of the foreign judgment.

European Community judgments are covered by *The European Communities (Enforcement of Community Judgments) Order, 1972*. And the entire area of reciprocal enforcement is dealt with in Order 71 of the Rules of the Supreme Court.

If any question of the enforcement of a foreign judgment against you should arise, you should at once consult your solicitors. The rules are complicated and there are even some useful wrinkles in the enforcement procedures.

For instance, if a foreign judgment is registered against you in the High Court here, there are grounds upon which you may be able to set it aside. Examples:

1   Would the enforcement of a judgment be contrary to public policy in this country?
2   Was the judgment obtained by fraud?
3   Is the wrong person applying to enforce the judgment? Are the rights in the judgment vested in someone else?
4   Did the courts of the country of the original court have jurisdiction, in the circumstances of the particular case?
5   Was the judgment registered in contravention of the provisions of the Act concerned?

Note: You cannot get the registration set aside merely because the claim would not have succeeded had it been brought in our courts. If, for instance, the overseas plaintiff obtains judgment against you on the basis of strict liability for your product, when you would not have been held liable in Britian, you will still have to meet the judgment here, if we have the appropriate reciprocal arrangements for the enforcements of judgments, with the country in question.

Unfortunately for the British judgment debtor in a foreign court, though, it may be possible for the judgment creditor to bring a new action in the UK, based on the foreign judgment. He may sue in our courts, claiming the amount judged due abroad. He would not then have to show the original 'cause of action' but he may win his money by a roundabout but well tried route. If you face this problem, your first step should be a swift one in the direction of your solicitors.

Chapter 48

Enforcement of American judgments

An American customer has obtained a judgment against us in a local court. He alleges — we believe, incorrectly — that the product we sold to him was defective. Because of the cost and the distance involved, we were not able to fight the case. But we would now like to know whether a United States' judgment is enforceable in the UK?

* * *

Not at the moment, although there is a treaty being negotiated to bring this about. However, if damages are awarded in the United States, then the judgment creditor can bring an action in the UK for enforcement of that judgment.

For example, suppose that X Company is ordered to pay $1000 to Y Company. Then if X has assets in the UK, Y could bring an action for the $1000 and would not have to prove the reason why X should pay them, but merely show that there is such a judgment in existence.

Chapter 49

Damages

The object of product liability law is to give the sufferer the right to a remedy. Hopefully, the party who is at fault will have to pay. The concept of 'fault' which applies in the absence of strict liability is fairer for the supplier than the 'no fault' liability which is likely to replace it. But the difficulty in 'the proof of fact' frequently leaves the innocent sufferer carrying the burden of hardship.

Anyway, suppose that the sufferer wins his case. What remedies can the law provide?

According to the law of contract, if the defect in the goods is a serious one and is a 'breach of condition' (as opposed to a mere 'breach of warranty'), the customer may return the goods and claim damages. Otherwise, he may have to retain the product and sue for financial recompense.

Either way, just as almost any product has its price, so damages are normally an adequate remedy for a breach of contract. (That explains, incidentally, why you cannot get an order for 'specific performance' of the contract for the sale of goods. That remedy is only given in cases, such as contracts for the sale of land or for the transfer of shares, in which damages are not regarded as a sufficient remedy for the wrong done.)

How are damages for breach of contract assessed? They normally represent the difference between the value of the goods as they should have been and their actual value. Ask yourself: What has the innocent party lost as a result of the contractual breach?

You sell defective goods? Your customer has to spend money on remedying the defects? Then the cost of repair or replacement or reinstatement of the defective parts or goods is likely to be the proper measure of damage.

You buy goods which would perform a particular task were they in accordance with contract? In practice, their performance is less than satisfactory? Then ask yourself (or an independent expert, perhaps): 'What is the difference between the value of the goods as they are and their value as warranted, represented or contracted for?'

Now go further and ask: 'What other loss has resulted from the breach?' The innocent contracting party is entitled to be compensated for other damage which ought reasonably to have been in your contemplation as flowing naturally from the breach, if you applied your mind to the problem.

You supply defective goods to a retailer? His customers return those goods? Then he has bought useless goods from you and is entitled to the return of his money, but he has also (as should have been expected) lost his profit. That, too, is claimable.

The usual rules in negligence cases are very similar. A

defective product causes the 'ultimate consumer' physical injury or damage to his property? Then he may claim damages which are intended as compensation to him and not as a penalty against the wrongdoer. Compensation means putting him so far as possible into the same financial position as he would have been, had the goods not been defective.

Some damages can be calculated with precision. These come under the head of so-called 'special damage'. You sell a defective car? Result: an accident? Then the special damage will include the cost of repair to the vehicle. If someone is injured, then he can also list such other special damage as: loss of remuneration when recovering from his injuries, convalescent expenses; replacement of torn clothing or broken spectacles and other items for which he can produce bills.

The non-special damage — referred to in law as 'general damage' — is far more difficult to assess and provides the usual reason why lawyers hedge when asked by an accident victim: 'How much will I get?' Just as no two people and no two accidents are the same, so no two judges take the same notice of the same injury. Provided that an award comes within the general area of damages awarded for that sort of injury, no appeal court will interfere.

If a lawyer has to work out the likely award for, say, a lost limb or even for severe nervous shock leading to depressive or other psychiatric illness, he goes to his books. He checks law reports and whole tomes, devoted to details of awards made by particular judges for specified injuries, and he emerges with what he *thinks* is likely to be the result.

If a claim for damages for personal injuries comes to Counsel's Chambers — to a set of rooms, shared by barristers, each of whom operates individually but who together employ staff — the case is likely to be 'hawked around'. Members of Chambers are asked for their view and by the exchange of opinion, the *probable* result emerges. Still, the key word is 'probable'.

After all, you can state what it would cost you to repair your machine, but not the value of your lost leg. Indeed, your leg may be worth less to you in financial terms than the limb of a labourer, while loss of your power of speech could destroy your livelihood, while it is less likely that the loss of the power of speech would destroy the labourer's livelihood.

Or what of 'loss of expectation of life', caused by an accident? Or who can place a precise value on loss of future earnings, when no one really knows how speedy or how full the patient's recovery is likely to be? A court must come to a conclusion.

Anyway, you can reckon that either a contractual breach or a negligent act which causes damage will allow the sufferer to obtain compensation (or 'damages') for two types of loss. First: there is the direct and immediate result of the wrongful act. Second: there is 'consequential loss' — which must be 'foreseeable' and hence not 'too remote' from the act itself.

In Britain, damages tend to be moderate. In the United States, their extent is terrifying.

Those UK businesses which only trade in this country are in some ways fortunate. But are you sure that the accessories which you sell here will not be sold in the United States, so that if they prove to be defective, you may face a claim from across the Atlantic? Do not count on the damages being assessed on our conservative basis.

Some British manufacturers are so horrified by the huge damages awarded by American courts and by the massive cost of insuring against such claims that they have moved out of the American market altogether. Have you checked on the amount of cover which you require for your overseas deals? What percentage of the selling price will you have to find, to provide the insurance which you will need because strict liability has already arrived on the American scene and because it is combined with awards of damages so massive that they even boggle the mind of a banker or of a car manu-facturer?

Finally, do take advice if you run into specific damage problems. For instance, there is much academic discussion as to whether there is any real difference between the proper measure of damages in a claim based on contract as opposed to one founded on negligence.

Your lawyers will no doubt refer to the famous case of *Hadley* v. *Baxendale*, decided in 1854, which said that you are entitled to damages if the loss is of a nature which would arise 'according to the usual course of things' or if there were special circumstances which the seller knew would make the loss likely on the facts of the particular case.

Almost a hundred years later, this principle was largely upheld in the case of *Victoria Laundry (Windsor) Ltd* v. *Newman Industries Ltd.* But these contortions can safely be left to the lawyers, whose minds are trained to be acrobatic. It should be enough for the business or professional person to know that damages for a defective product are normally based on loss which is occasioned by or as a natural and foreseeable result of the defect.

" I WONDER IF HE'S TAKEN OUT AN INDEMNITY POLICY. "

Part Six
INSURANCE

Chapter 50

Insurance law

All manufacturers and other businessmen carry insurance.
Some is compulsory: car insurance, for instance and insurance
against liability for death or personal injury caused to employees
[under *The Employers' Liability (Compulsory Insurance) Act,
1969*]. Most is as voluntary as it is necessary. Either way,
problems are inevitable.

Here, then, is your quick guide to some of the most crucial
areas of insurance law.

*　　*　　*

You get what you buy

Are you covered against a particular risk? What are your rights
against your insurers? All depends upon the terms of your
contract. Look at the policy document and you will discover
what you have bought in return for your premium.

'All risks' and 'Comprehensive'

Be careful of the names that insurers give to their contracts.
An 'All Risks' policy covers those risks included and not
those which are excluded. A 'Comprehensive' policy 'com-
prehends' that cover which is stated and paid for.

As in the case of all other contracts, the purchaser should
decide what cover he wishes to acquire and should then shop
around to see the best terms that he can acquire. Comparison
between policies and terms is often difficult and a broker can
frequently help. However if you do employ a broker, make
sure that he is well established and well recommended.

Claims

To benefit from your insurance contract, you must comply

with its terms. Notification of a likely claim must normally be made within a specified time or at least as swiftly as is reasonably possible. Delay may well be fatal. Even if you decide in the event not to claim — perhaps, as in the case of a motor insurance contract, because you do not wish to lose your no claims bonus — you should still notify the insurance company of an accident.

Duty to disclose

Insurance contracts are said to be 'of the utmost good faith' (or, to use the Latin expression, they are contracts *uberrimae fidei*). Therefore the assured is bound to reveal all information 'which would be likely to affect the mind of the reasonable assurer' — and he must do so whether or not he is asked for it. If previous claims have been made against other insurers in respect of the same sort of loss, they would clearly be relevant. So would any criminal convictions of the assured or, indeed, of people of his board.

   If there has been a failure to disclose, the insurers will almost certainly be entitled to repudiate liability; to refuse to pay; and merely to hand back the assured's premium.

Exclusions

Insurance contracts are not covered by *The Unfair Contract Terms Act, 1977*. So it is up to the assured to have the exclusions removed if he wishes. If the exclusions are decreased, then both the cover and the premium will be increased.

Product liability insurance

Insurance against strict liability for injury, loss or damage caused by goods is comparatively new. An analysis, by courtesy of Oliver Prior, of the new and practical problems facing those who wish to take out this form of cover now follows in Chapters 51 and 52.

Chapter 51

Insuring against product liability at home and overseas

By Oliver Prior, Executive Director of Bland Payne

History and development of product liability

The very first product liability insurance was written in England in 1840. The insurance was known as 'Poison Insurance' and was bought by bakers who required coverage against roach powder accidentally entering the dough mixture. The records unfortunately do not tell us the name of the insurer of this type of risk or indeed the premium charged. The first statute to arrive on the scene was *The Sale of Goods Act, 1893*, which ruled that a contract of sale in the course of business normally implies that the goods sold are fit for the purpose for which goods of that kind are usually bought. If the article purchased is defective and, as a result of the defect, injury results from its use in the manner in which it was intended to be used, then the Act deems that it is unfit for the purpose for which it was bought. In these circumstances whether or not the seller has been negligent the buyer can sue for damages. The problem with this statute is, however, that firstly it is only available against the seller and secondly only injuries sustained by the buyer will result in a successful claim. The next milestone in the development of product liability was the decision in the case of *Donoghue* v. *Stevenson* (1932) which established the liability of manufacturers of defective products in the tort of negligence in English law. This case established that the following four points had to be satisfied in order for a product liability action to succeed:

1   The defect must be such that it may result in injury to the consumer.
2   The defect must exist at the time the manufacturer parted with the possession of the product.
3   The defect must not be one that the manufacturer could reasonably have expected the consumer or some third party to notice and correct before it could do harm.

4   The existence of the defect must be attributed to lack
     of reasonable care on the part of the manufacturer.
These rules stood the test of time until the late 1960s when
various factors began to bring pressure upon them. The first
of these was the Thalidomide tragedy where no legal decision
was reached since the case was settled out of court, but it is
generally accepted that the company might not have been
liable at law for the injuries. The second point was that the
United States courts have moved towards strict liability in
fact and in practice. The third factor was the rise in 'con-
sumerism' in the 1960s, spearheaded by such gentlemen as
Mr Ralph Nader who gained a great deal of publicity and
success in his attacks on the manufacturing giants.

There is little doubt that the demand for a change in the
basis of liability for defective products is growing daily. This
can easily be justified when one considers that in the early
days of product liability products were normally handmade
or individually made and of a relatively simple nature and the
doctrine of *caveat emptor* seemed perfectly reasonable in that
climate. However with the advent of mass production, the
internal combustion engine, synthetic chemicals and the computer, products have now become far too complex to enable
the average purchaser to understand their intricacies and
methods of operation. There is therefore a growing demand
for consumer protection, but this cannot be achieved by
imposing absolute 'no fault' on the manufacturer since such
action could set manufacturing techniques and development
back at a critical time in their growth.

In 1970 a Special Commission of the International Court
at the Hague recommended a move to strict liability in the
field of products. In 1972 the Council of Europe convened
a committee of legal experts to study the subject. They, too,
were unanimous in their support of a move to strict liability
and this study culminated in the Convention at Strasbourg
in 1976 which is open for signature. Whilst this was going on,
in 1974 the EEC Commission under instruction from the
Council of Ministers began a study of liability resulting from
defective products. The result of their study is a draft
Directive, the objective of which is to harmonise the laws of
the Member States to the extent required for the proper
functioning of the Common Market. Thus the two important

works on the subject are the EEC Directive and the Strasbourg Convention. They both agree in the following areas:

1 Both require proof of a defect in a product and require that a causal link should be established before liability can attach.

2 Both base their notion of defect on the criterion of objective safety, i.e. the safety which a person is entitled to expect as a member of the public.

3 Both relate to all types of victims including the innocent bystander.

4 Both channel liability to the producer (or certain deemed producers such as importers).

5 Both introduce the system of strict liability which is neither absolute (as it permits the producer certain defences), nor wholly removed from fault, (since it demands proof of the defectiveness of the product).

6 Both include the development risk, making the producer responsible for his products regardless of the state of Art existing when the product was put into circulation.

7 Both permit the producer to escape liability by proving there was no defect in the product when it was put into circulation by them, or that the producer did not put the product into circulation.

8 Both introduce a limitation feature whereby a producer is only liable for his product for a period of ten years from the date of putting it into circulation (this means the introduction of the product into the stream of commerce).

There are, however, three differences between the Strasbourg Convention and the EEC Directive which concern insurers and these are as follows:

a The Convention concerned itself only with personal injury whereas the Directive contained an additional feature of private property damage with small monetary limits. It is argued by insurers that it is unnecessary to include property damage within the area of strict liability since full coverage is available on a first-party basis and the purchase of the same by all persons should be encouraged. This statement, of course, is fundamentally correct. Nevertheless there are many insurers in this country who still resist issuing insurance policies on an

'All Risks' basis and whose policies contain a minefield
of exclusions and conditions which could leave the
insured with no cover and with the onus of proving the
tort of negligence prior to recovering costs for, say,
clothing damaged by a defective product, when he may
have already collected under strict liability adequate
compensation for personal injury.

b   The Convention recognises contributory negligence in its
text but there is no such recognition in the Directive.
Insurers are particularly anxious to retain the defence of
contributory negligence for obvious reasons.

c   The Convention does not stipulate a monetary limit of
liability but permits signing nations to impose such a
limit if they so desire. The Directive limits strict liability
with a monetary ceiling. The ceiling they propose is 25
million units of account (approximately £15 million at
the time of writing) and it is argued that this limit should
cater for most catastrophes. Many insurers claim that
the limit is totally unnecessary since it could well have
the effect of becoming a 'target' for a plaintiff or group
of plaintiffs who have suffered what may unquestionably
be a catastrophic loss (as, for example, in the Thalidomide
case) and this could result in awards on the scale of those
currently made by US courts. The limit, in addition,
places many manufacturers of innocuous articles such as
pencils, paper-clips and the like in a position of having
to buy the limit of liability specified which could increase their insurance costs enormously, whereas the
companies in the more hazardous areas such as aircraft
manufacture and pharmaceuticals, may well breathe a
sigh of relief since the limit is well below their current
policy limit. However, the most convincing argument is
that when the limit of liability had been exhausted by
claims in respect of one product, then persons injured
by that product, who have not yet registered their claim,
must resort to the tort of negligence for compensation.
This could mean that there will be cases where one
plaintiff will be reimbursed for injuries received under
strict liability and another will receive no compensation
because of his inability to prove negligence on the part
of the manufacturer.

Most recently the Law Commissions and a Royal Commission chaired by Lord Pearson have both endorsed the Strasbourg Convention as being the most suitable means of introducing strict liability for products into the United Kingdom, in preference to the Directive, and it is hoped that the former will be adopted.

Insurance coverage

In theory a product liability insurance policy should simply indemnify the insured for all sums that he shall be required to pay at law by way of settlement of claims made against him by third parties for bodily injury or property damage, including consequential losses arising therefrom, caused by defective goods sold by the insured. The policy should contain a definition of a product in accordance with the statutory or case law definition of the same and the policy should only contain exclusions of 'product guarantee', 'product recall' (both of which are insurable separately) and the standard accepted non-marine insurance exclusions such as nuclear risks and war risks. Most insurers define the three separate categories of insurable product risks as follows:

1 *Product liability*   The legal liability of a manufacturer to third parties for personal injury and/or property damage (including consequential loss arising therefrom).
2 *Product guarantee*   The expenses incurred by a manufacturer or a third party arising out of the repair, replacement, treatment, etc., of the defective product itself.
3 *Product recall*   Any expenses incurred by the insured when recalling a defective product. These may be the cost of advertising, labour, etc., and may include the transportation of the defective product to the factory for repair.

Of these three areas of coverage in the product field, the best known by far is product liability and the other two do not fall within the field of this book. As stated above, the standard product liability should provide full coverage against legal liability arising out of the sale of goods. Nevertheless, in many policies issued today this is not the case. Some of the problem areas are as follows:

1   Many policies will only indemnify the insured for accidental bodily injury and/or property damage (including consequential loss arising therefrom). This means that the insured, in order to claim under the policy, must demonstrate that the originating cause of the loss was accidental. Most policies should now have been converted to cover losses howsoever occurring and not just losses of an accidental nature. Nevertheless there are still some policies left which only provide indemnity for accidental losses.

2   Many of the standard policies issued today still contain 'design, formula exclusions'. These exclusions can take two forms. The first being an absolute exclusion of all losses resulting from errors in designs, formulas, plans or specifications, the second being losses arising out of errors in design, formulas, plans or specifications supplied to third parties for use in their own products. The former exclusion obviously restricts the coverage to a great extent since many product liability losses arise from this cause. The latter is obviously not so onerous since the policy will provide coverage for errors in design, etc., when the design is incorporated into the insured's product but when a licence is given for a third party to manufacture products on the basis of the insured's design then no indemnity will be provided. Insurers will argue that both these exclusions can be deleted for an additional premium, thus coverage is freely available but only on request.

If we are to see a new statute in the United Kingdom relating to product liability, it is hoped that insurers will construct their policies to respond more closely to the statute. I believe that it is reasonable to assume that an insured, having purchased employer's liability insurance and automobile liability insurance where the policies provide coverage in accordance with the law, has every reason to believe that his product liability insurance will provide similar protection without him having to read the small print.

The reforms proposed in the law in the area of product

liability are sufficiently major to warrant a complete review
of practice and coverage by insurers in order that they too
can be prepared to face the future.

There are three other points that should be taken into
account when studying the coverage provided by a product
liability insurance policy and they are as follows:

*1   There are two main fundamental methods of constructing
a policy*, the first being 'losses occurring', the second being
'claims made'. A 'losses occurring' policy provides indemnity
for losses occurring during the policy period and this means
that if a claim is made against the insured company, then
insurers indemnify from the policy year of account in which
the loss occurred. This may mean that a claim can occur in
1975 but not be made against the insured until 1978, in
which case the insurers would look to the 1975 policy to pay
the claim. A 'claims made' policy operates in the opposite
fashion and irrespective of when the loss occurred the policy
that will pay the claim is the one during which period it was
made against the insured. Thus, to take the same case, if a
loss occurred in 1975 but no claim was made against the
insured until 1978, then it would be the 1978 policy that
paid the claim.

Both bases are acceptable to most insurers but the 'claims
made' basis is normally imposed where the trade of the insured
is particularly hazardous (such as pharmaceuticals). There are
advantages and disadvantages to both methods and the main
points are as follows:

a   Losses occurring   The advantage of a 'losses occurring'
policy is that, irrespective of what happens and even in
the event of a catastrophic claim, the coverage remains
in force until all claims are paid up to the policy aggregate limit. One disadvantage, however, is that since all
claims whenever they are made revert back to the year
in which the loss occurred and the losses from one
catastrophic cause tend to occur within one policy year,
the insured is only able to collect indemnity up to the
aggregate limit for the year in which the loss occurred.
Another major disadvantage of a 'losses occurring' policy
is that the insured is buying cover today for claims which
may not be made or become apparent until many years

in the future. Thus he is having to decide on the policy limit he should purchase for perhaps the next few years today. This, of course, has proved a particular problem in the last few years of inflation and will prove even more of a problem should the proposal to introduce index-linked periodic payments be taken up since this could cause awards to rise more rapidly. The same would also apply if strict liability were introduced since the number of claims that will be made against certain producers will be greater than the ones being made at the present moment. At this stage of course it is too early to say how the legislation for product liability will be introduced and from what date and on what basis strict liability will attach in respect of existing products already in circulation.

b   *Claims made*   With a 'claims made' policy, at the inception of the policy the insured only has to make a decision relating to the limit of indemnity that will be required to cover claims made during the policy period. This means that the insured is able to assess the effects of inflation fairly quickly and a 'claims made' policy is good protection in times of inflation or changes in the law. With a 'claims made' policy if an insured knows that strict liability is to be introduced and this will have an effect on the number of claims that will be made against him, he is able to purchase a higher limit of indemnity at the next renewal and this automatically applies to all claims made thereafter irrespective of the year in which they occurred. The major disadvantage of a 'claims made' policy is that, in theory, if an insured has a major claim made against him two days before the renewal of his policy and it is clear from the nature of the claim that there will be others to follow, then insurers are in a position of being able to decline the renewal of the policy totally, leaving the insured with only two days' cover and no means of extending the policy. Whilst, of course, in theory, this is correct, in practice I have never known it to happen and unless insurers considered that in some way the insured had caused the loss deliberately, or it was a morally hazardous risk, I do not believe that they would refuse insurance to a company faced with this problem. They could, of course, be seeking an increase in premium, but then there is nothing to stop an underwriter with a 'losses occurring' policy seeking an increase in premium as soon as he becomes aware of any claims. So this latter point does not carry much weight.

There is little doubt that from the insured's point of view the 'claims made' format is the best and if the current policies could be amended slightly to allow the insured time to think in the event of a catastrophic claim being advised two days prior to his expiry, then I believe this method would ultimately replace the 'losses occurring' format. It is interesting to note that all of the major insurances written for professional negligence in respect of solicitors, accountants, insurance brokers, etc., are on a 'claims made' basis and have been for several years and I have never found any injustice being applied or had any problems arising from this.

2   *Limit of indemnity*   It was argued in the early days of product liability that it was impossible to have any idea of how many people may be injured by a product sold and thus in theory, even though an insurer may limit the amount of any one claim, he could be exposed to an unlimited number of claims. This, of course, is a different situation from that which occurs in most other classes of insurance. With employer's liability and automobile liability one can reasonably estimate the maximum number of persons who could be involved in a catastrophe. For this reason insurers insisted that an aggregate limit should be applied and in this country it was decided that the limit would be equal to the amount of any one claim. Thus, if a manufacturer in the pharmaceutical field considers that he could be exposed to a number of fairly large claims, then he would have to buy an aggregate limit of indemnity large enough to satisfy the total number of claims. This practice is not the same in all countries in Europe since, for example, it is common, in Germany and Holland, for policies to be issued with an 'any one claim' limit and an 'annual aggregate' limit of twice the amount of any one claim. Thus it is not necessary for an insured to arrange high cover for any one claim. I do not envisage that insurers in the

UK will ever move away from the concept of aggregate limit of indemnity.

3 Jurisdiction   There are two parts to the jurisdiction question. The first is the jurisdiction between the insured and the person making the claim against him and the second is between the insured and his insurers in the event of a dispute in the policy conditions. In the early days of product liability, worldwide coverage was freely given provided that the exports to the United States (other countries were not restricted) did not exceed 10 or 15 per cent, or in other word were incidental. Where the exports were greater, coverage wa still available but one could expect a slight increase in premium. However, in the early 1970s insurers started to receive frightening reports about product liability claims in US court particularly arising out of the court's willingness to 'rewrite' the policy to suit the circumstances of the claim. Insurers therefore maintained the UK jurisdiction clause in the policy (which governed jurisdiction between the insured and the underwriters in the event of any dispute concerning the policy) and continued to give worldwide coverage, but still providing that United States sales where incidental. The situation, however, developed at a pace and, as far as UK insurers were concerned, became impossible. About two year ago they completely ceased to insure any UK company with regard to their US sales and this left many companies uninsured for what was an extremely dangerous exposure. At the time many insurers were heard to say that this was an American problem and they should solve it and not look to us for a solution. Fortunately, common sense and some stron pressure by certain groups in the industry prevailed and insurers softened their attitude slightly. Coverage is now available for a company that exports products to the US but need less to say the cost is extremely high and the excess (the amount of any loss which must be borne by the insured) is also very high. This means that for a UK company with relatively small sales to the USA, the premium will in many cases exceed the total profit that they make from such sales. Continuing to trade on this basis is most unsatisfactory. I personally considered that when no coverage at all was available to UK-based companies exporting to the USA, the insurers were behaving in a most unjust manner. However the insurers have now modified their thinking. They will now provide coverage at a price. This price they justify by saying that it is less than that charged to US companies for product liability by US insurers. There is thus not a great deal to object to and many manufacturers who are still pressing this issue strongly should now cease to do so.

Although, however, I believe there is an obligation on UK insurers to provide this coverage, I do not believe that there is any obligation upon them to subsidise UK companies wishing to export to the USA. The product liability insurance premium that a US company has to pay is taken into account when pricing its product and, by creating an anomaly with lower insurance rates available in the UK, we would in effect be 'dumping'. If a company wishes to export to the USA. they must take into account the insurance problem and include this in their selling price when preparing their sales figures.

The foregoing points all relate to coverage or lack of it provided by insurers in their product liability policies. It is worth noting however that apart from Lloyd's and a few London-based insurance companies, insurers normally do not insure product liability as a separate class of business, nor as a result do they have available separate underwriting statistics. The current practice is to issue a combined liability policy which contains three sections, i.e. employer's liability, public liability and product liability, and the premium charged will be one amount across all three categories. When the product liability 'crisis' in the US blew up, the Federal Interagency Task Force report stated that one of the factors that aggravated the situation was that US insurers had developed 'package' policies which covered automobile, general, employer's and product liability and that insurers could not isolate product liability as a class of insurance either in premium or loss terms. Whenever a class of insurance goes wrong it is essential to have a comprehensive statistical analysis of past results so that future trends can be established. The figures themselves are the 'bricks' and the underwriter is the 'architect' who shapes in his mind a future pattern using the 'bricks'. However, without the building material, the 'architect' cannot do his job.

I hope that the UK insurance market will learn by the mistakes of the US insurance market and will at least develop or maintain separate product liability statistics in the future. Otherwise I am sure that, as has happened so often in the past, what is occurring in the US today will be happening in the UK in ten year's time.

Other factors which could affect product liability insurance

Index-linked periodic payments

Lord Pearson and the Royal Commission that he chaired have recommended the introduction of index-linked periodic payments for long-term disability claims. This is a factor that could considerably affect the insurance market were it to take effect. The British Insurers' Association gave evidence to the Royal Commission in which they stated that index-linked periodic payments should present them with no problem provided that an inflation-proof ceiling could be applied by some means. The idea proposed was that insurers would agree to pay up to a certain percentage increase each year due to inflation and that a government fund would reimburse them for any amount paid in excess of the agreed percentage. Many Lloyd's underwriters have already stated that they are strongly against index-linked periodic payment and it would be extremely difficult for them to comply with this proposal since it directly conflicts with the existing Lloyd's accounting system. There is little doubt that the major insurers would be able to handle index-linked periodic payment claims after making certain adjustments internally. However, the administration involved would increase premiums. Particularly worrying, however, is the large number of approved, small to medium sized UK insurers who would not have the resources or the inclination to insure the areas where this will be a possible form of claim. This means that the capacity of the market could well fall quite drastically since many of these medium and small companies provide the necessary capacity on the larger risks. When periodic payments were introduced in France and Germany a number of insurers withdrew totally from writing this business for fear of becoming involved in such claims. They could, of course, react differently when faced with a situation in their own country, but I somehow do not believe that this will be the case. There is also no doubt that index-linked periodic payments will ultimately result in a larger settlement figure and will certainly require the insured to buy larger limits of indemnity. The requests for larger limits of indemnity coinciding with a reduction in the market could result in a fairly dramatic increase in premiums and a potential monopoly situation developing. This would certainly not be to the insured's advantage. Rather than index-linked periodic payments being introduced I would like to see the existing lump-sum system maintained and government assistance provided in the investment field with, perhaps, guaranteed inflation-proof bonds provided for individual victims or surviving family, etc., this ensuring that their capital remained intact and guaranteeing them a reasonable income for the rest of their lives. I do not believe that this latter scheme differs greatly since the government would merely be protecting the victim against inflation directly as opposed to protecting the insurance company who would in turn be protecting the victim against inflation. The nett result is the same, namely the government would be protecting against excessive inflation.

Punitive and exemplary damages

It is now common practice for US courts to award, in addition to normal damages, punitive or exemplary damages designed to penalise the defendant for gross negligence and to ensure that he will take greater care in the future. Many of these awards have related to cases concerning defective products since these are particularly suited to the circumstances surrounding such awards. The amounts involved grow larger and larger and in a recent case involving the Ford Motor Company the punitive damages element for one individual was in excess of $100,000,000. This award was subsequently reduced on appeal to a much smaller amount but nevertheless it indicates the manner in which punitive or exemplary damages are being used by US courts. Insurers are not quite certain where they stand on this issue. Some believe that it is immoral to insure punitive or exemplary damages since these are effectively fines or penalties and the latter two forms of 'damages' would not normally be met by a policy of insurance. On the other hand some insurers regard the punitive or exemplary damage element of any award as merely being an aggravation which leads to larger claims which can still be met by insurers but which will ultimately result in higher premiums. There has been much discussion amongst US insurers on this issue and they are rapidly drawing towards the conclusion that punitive and exemplary damages should be excluded from their standard policies and that insurers would then have the discretion to provide coverage for these items if they so wished. As far as a UK exporter to the USA is concerned he will fare worse. The majority of insurers in the UK will seek to exclude punitive damages from the policy since they believe that to insure these items is not correct.

Reciprocal Judgments Convention

There has been a great deal of discussion during the last three years about the UK signing a reciprocal judgments convention with the USA. The text of the Convention was initialled by representatives of the Foreign Office and the Lord Chancellor' Department in October 1976. The outcome of any reciprocal judgments convention that is finally ratified will be very far-reaching indeed and will result in a situation whereby judgments in any court in the USA will be virtually rubber-stamped by a court in the UK. Up to now, many manufacturers who export to the USA have been successful in defending suits that have been threatened against them by American citizens by demonstrating that the US courts do not have jurisdiction over them. This, of course, would no longer be possible if the Convention were ratified. The effects on availability of coverage and premium for product liability insurance could be very dramatic for companies who sell to American citizens or who export to that country.

Underwriting product liability risks, present and future

At the present moment the underwriting of any form of
liability risk is based on obtaining as much information as
possible from the insured at the outset by means of
questionnaires and by studying the documents issued by the
insured such as annual reports and brochures relating to their
products. The important questions concerning product
liability are as follows:

1   What products are made by the insured?
2   How many of each in quantity and monetary terms does
     he sell in a year?
3   What quantity of each product manufactured is exported
     and to which countries?
4   Are there any past losses or incidents which may give
     rise to a claim in the future?

Given answers to the above four questions and assuming that
the product or products manufactured are known to the
insurer, then the underwriter should be able to develop a rate
for the limit of indemnity required. Unlike most other classes
of insurance, in most cases no survey or risk management
service will be provided or required and the insured is unlikely
to be asked to supply evidence of his quality control methods,
inspection or test methods, or indeed supply any fact concerning his method of production, research, etc. It has been
said that if the recommendations of the Pearson Commission
relating to product liability take effect then there could be
some dramatic changes in both insurance coverage and
premiums. Obviously it is too early to tell how insurers will
react. Nevertheless they believe, and so do several other
people in the insurance industry, that provided that the
insured currently purchases adequate limits of indemnity and
the correct type of coverage, the conversion to strict liability
should not increase his premium by more than 100 per cent.
This is obviously an average figure and there are bound to be
exceptions. At one end of the scale one has the manufacturers
of fairly hazardous articles who are already subjected to high
premiums since many decisions in recent years have been
close to strict liability. At the other end of the scale one has
organisations such as caterers and mining companies who at
the present moment have little or no product liability exposure

but will be particularly vulnerable under strict liability. The latter class, namely people handling agricultural produce, food or raw materials, will be subjected to fairly dramatic increases in their premium since many pay very small premiums at the moment, if indeed they insure at all.

Loss prevention and risk management

As I have stated above, product liability at present is insured as part of a combined policy, embracing public liability and employer's liability, in most cases. In the area of employer's liability, insurers carry out frequent inspections with a view to ensuring that the statutory duties imposed on the employer are being observed and that the possibility of loss is reduced as much as possible by good management and good housekeeping. To a much lesser degree public liability insurers inspect premises with a view to ascertaining the degree of exposure to third-party liability, but this is by no means a normal or regular undertaking. In many cases no inspection or survey will be carried out with this particular area of insurance in mind and it is usually only the major or prestigious risks that are surveyed. I may be maligning some insurers who are aware of the value of loss prevention and risk management in this field, but in the main insurers do not carry out surveys or inspections with regard to product liability risks. Indeed, a manufacturer can obtain product liability insurance by simply completing a questionnaire and answering the relevant questions correctly. It is unlikely that a representative of his insurance company will visit him to verify the facts contained in the questionnaire or give him any advice concerning quality control or loss prevention. Product liability is one of the few fields left in insurance where risk management and loss prevention techniques are not pursued as a normal course of events.

By risk management and loss prevention techniques I do not mean that insurers should seek to impose restrictions or tell the insured how to manufacture his products. Nevertheless the insurer, with his wide knowledge and experience of international losses, can advise a manufacturer on problem areas that have arisen with similar manufacturers in other countries, which, hopefully, will lead to a reduction in the number of losses. Another important way in which the insurer can assist is in helping the insured to draft his contracts and set up his business to avoid, wherever possible, unnecessary liability attaching. A classic case for this would be assisting an insured to decide whether he should export to the United States or not. Many small products manufacturers in this country would not be facing the problems that they currently face with their exports to the USA if they had consulted with their insurers before deciding the method with which they should approach this difficult market. A typical example would be that an insurer would amost certainly advise an insured contemplating entering the US market to make sure that he had no fixed assets in the form of an office in that country and to make sure that any agreements that he may have with a marketing representative in that country should protect the UK manufacturer's rights. Over the last two or three years I have met with many manufacturers who have chosen the wrong way to enter that market and, having done so, find themselves faced with a considerable premium bill for many years even if they make the decision today to withdraw totally on the grounds of unprofitability.

Conclusions

As I have endeavoured to point out in the foregoing text there are many different methods of handling product liability insurance in force in the UK at the moment. I would like to see a greater harmonisation of policy coverage and conditions so that each manufacturer could be assured that when he purchases a policy it will reasonably indemnify him for all insurable losses. What I think the insurance industry needs at the present moment is the incentive that strict liability *is* to become a reality in order that all parts of the industry can join together to strive for uniformity. I believe that the Pearson Commission's virtual endorsement of the Strasbourg Convention's proposals should be sufficient evidence to the insurance industry as a whole of the fact that strict liability is now destined to become a reality. The form that any statute will take is reasonably obvious and I hope that the insurance

industry will take every opportunity in the next two or three
years' breathing space before strict liability becomes a statutory
provision to put its house in order and to think of ways in
which they can be of greater service to the host of manufacturers in this country. Many manufacturers believe and have
publicly stated that the government should take a hand in
product liability insurance in order to ensure that the burden
of premium does not become so onerous on our industry that
it becomes non-competitive. Having seen our insurance industry
in practice over the last few years I would emphatically disagree with that proposal. This country is the home of creative
insurance and we have been the leaders in many areas and the
sole insurers of the world in others because of the ability of
the underwriters at Lloyd's and in the British insurance
companies. Our system of insurance has, furthermore, proved
profitable and has a reputation for honouring claims and, more
importantly, adhering more to the intent of the policy than
abiding strictly by its text and I do not think that any government intervention could improve the system. Over the years
a market has built up in the City of London which specialises
in product liability and insures manufacturers all over the
world. This country would not have achieved the status it
currently has in world insurance terms without having been
competitive. This point alone is sufficient evidence in support
of the continued involvement of the private insurance sector
in the product liability field.

Chapter 52

Questions of insurance

*Which insurers provide cover for product liability and what is
the best way to approach them?*

There are over 100 organisations in the UK alone who
undertake insurance and the majority of them will issue
policies in respect of product liability. These organisations
break down into four main categories:

1 Lloyd's This organisation is unique in the world of insurance. It is made up of syndicates which are financed by individuals placing their personal wealth 'at risk'. Over the three centuries it has been operating, Lloyd's name has become synonymous with flair, innovation and fair trading. As far as product liability is concerned many syndicates transact this type of business. Lloyd's syndicates have built their reputation in creating special covers for the majority of the 'heavy' risks such as pharmaceutical manufacturers and new technology groups. It is only possible to approach Lloyd's through a Lloyd's Broker and these brokers work very closely with the syndicates with whom they effect the insurance. The result is normally a 'tailor-made' policy which provides wide cover, which by its very nature commands a higher premium than that charged by alternative markets providing standard coverage. Lloyd's also provides valuable capacity for the organisations that require large limits even though their policy may not have been originated by Lloyd's.

2 'Accident Offices Association' companies This is a group of companies who have joined together to form the Accident Offices Association and this Association is designed to pool the ideas of the companies involved and ensure a uniform approach to certain fundamental principles relating to accident insurance, including product liability. A large number of the policies issued by these companies are of a composite nature and provide liability coverage in the three main areas, namely: Employers' Liability, Public Liability, Product Liability. These companies tend to have offices situated all over the UK and are able to give a complete insurance service ranging across all categories. The standard product liability policy that they provide contains several exclusions which they are prepared to withdraw during negotiations but this point should be watched by any prospective organisation approaching them for insurance and some of the defects in their standard coverage are explained in more detail at a later stage in this chapter.

3 British insurance companies who are not members of the Accident Offices Association There are many companies within this group and they all tend to work independently.

Some of them are situated in the City of London and either underwrite policies 100 per cent or participate in larger policies. The policies that they provide vary from one company to another and again should be studied carefully during the negotiation stage since they are also flexible on various aspects of cover. Many of these organisations are now spreading into other regions of the UK and are offering realistic competition to companies who are members of the Accident Officers Association.

4   Foreign insurance companies   There are a large number of highly reputable foreign insurance companies resident in the UK and authorised by the Department of Trade & Industry to underwrite insurance in the UK. In addition some of the foreign insurance companies choose to reside abroad (in Brussels for example) and offer their capacity in the main for UK risks to insurance brokers situated in the City of London. Certain of these companies have excellent worldwide networks which enable them to offer policies in each of the countries in which an insured may be resident, backed by a 'master policy' in the UK. This method of coverage is extremely useful to multinational companies who desire to insure with one company but at the same time wish to comply with the laws of the country in which they are operating. In certain instances the standard product liability policies provided by these companies give wider coverage than those issued by companies subscribing to the Accident Offices Association and they can be extremely competitive in their premium quotations where they are satisfied that the insured is of above average quality.

The choice of which company one should approach and how one should approach them is daunting. With the enormous variances in attitude towards product liability insurance and the large number of organisations transacting this type of business many insureds are seeking professional advice from insurance brokers. An insurance broker should be capable of giving impartial advice to the insured, and analysing the risks that the insured faces, and seeking out the best market for him. It is important that the insurance broker chosen by the insured should have access to all of the four markets stated above and that he should be fully conversant with the ever changing scene surrounding product liability in the UK. Whilst an insurance broker can be of great assistance there are many insureds who have chosen not to avail themselves of this service and have either trained their own staff to the best of their ability in this area or alternatively have hired specialist insurance staff to advise. The important point to bear in mind is that there are a large number of insurance companies who transact product liability in the UK and that very few of them produce standard policies that will provide full coverage without some alteration. As a result it is always advisable to seek the views of more than one company and to select the policy which provides the widest possible coverage at the most equitable premium.

Does the standard insurance policy for product liability provide full cover?

As has been stated in the previous paragraph the majority of standard insurance policies in respect of product liability do not provide the full coverage that is required. In theory, a product liability policy should indemnify the insured for all legal liability that he incurs arising out of the sale of 'goods'. The policy should only exclude risks which are the subject of other insurance policies or such items as war or nuclear energy risks which are excluded from all non-marine insurance policies. Regrettably, most standard insurance policies contain more exclusions which restrict the cover and which in some instances can be deleted for additional premium. Owing to the large number of insurance companies who transact product liability insurance the competiton for business in the past has been fierce. In order to trim the premium in certain instances companies have deleted essential parts of coverage resulting in policies that do not provide cover against full legal liability in the 'product' area. Unlike motor vehicle and employer's liability insurance there is no statute to regulate the minimum permitted coverage and as a result many insureds currently purchase restrictive policies without being aware of this fact.

It would be extremely difficult to legislate for compulsory product liability insurance. Thus it is hoped that in the future insurers and their insurance brokers will concentrate more on providing wide coverage and better service and less on 'rate cutting' to obtain new business.

How can the standard policy be improved to provide greater protection?

It is extremely difficult to generalise in this area since each policy will vary slightly and these differences can be important. Nevertheless, as a general rule the following points should be carefully studied:

1   The policy should indemnify the insured against liability at law for damages and claimant's costs and expenses in respect of injury to any person and/or damage to property (including any loss consequent upon such damage) occurring during the period of insurance. Many policies however still insert the word 'accidental' and amend the foregoing to read '. . . accidental injury to any person and/or accidental damage to property (including any loss consequent upon such damage)' By doing this the insurer in effect reverses the onus of proof since the insured must at all times prove loss under the policy and with the word 'accidental' inserted the onus is upon the insured to prove that the circumstances causing the loss were indeed accidental. If these words are omitted the insured merely has to prove that the circumstances leading to the legal liability actually occurred. If he can do this he can substantiate a claim under the policy and it is then necessary for insurers to demonstrate that the claim is not covered by the policy, if that is the case.

2   Many product liability policies contain an exclusion of any liability which attaches because of an agreement but which would not have attached in the absence of that agreement. In simple language this means that if an insured enters into a contract which contains conditions which go beyond the legal liability that would normally attach to the insured without such conditions applying, then any liability arising out of that contract which is beyond normal legal liability will be excluded. The majority of products are sold or distributed under contract and in many instances the manufacturer of a product is required to provide an absolute indemnity arising out of the

sale, by third parties, of that product. An example of a problem which can occur would be Company X who manufacture cameras and then supply them to Company Y who alter the cameras slightly and distribute them in their own name. The contract between the two companies states that Company X will indemnify Company Y for all claims made against them arising out of the cameras in question. If, due to the alteration, injury occurs to the ultimate purchaser and Company Y is proved legally liable for this injury, then Company Y can still call upon the contractual indemnity provided by Company X and seek reimbursement from them. Company X's insurers in the circumstances, with a contractual liability exclusion of the form outlined previously, would not pay since in the absence of negligence, Company X could not be held liable for the subsequent alterations to the product made by Company Y. This is a simple example and the problem becomes very much more complex when several parties are involved and an exchange of counter-indemnities is accepted. It is important therefore to ensure that contractual liability is covered by a product liability policy where the insured transacts business under contract conditions.

3   Many product liability policies exclude any form of liability arising from defective design or formulation of any goods. This means that if the originating design, formula or specifications used for the manufacture of a product are faulty, and this results in injury or damage to the subsequent purchaser or his property, then such claims will not be met by the policy. Practically all insurers who have this exclusion in their standard product liability policies will agree to delete it for an additional premium. It is essential to ensure that there is no exclusion relating to defective design or formulation of any goods in a product liability policy since many of the losses under such policies will arise from design errors and indeed it could be argued that all major catastrophes will result from a design error rather than a mechanical fault in the product.

4   It is essential to ensure that the policy does not restrict in any way the use of the goods after their sale. Some policies absolutely exclude any goods installed in an aircraft. It may

be that a manufacturer of nuts and bolts or rubber hosing is not aware of the ultimate use of his product and such an exclusion could mean that if an aircraft crashes as a result of a defect in one of his products, he will not be covered by his policy even though he was not aware that his goods were installed in aircraft.

The above examples are a few of the common restrictions applied by insurers to a product liability policy but they are by no means all of the problem. If you are at all concerned about the coverage provided by your policy I suggest that you consult an expert. The fact that you purchase a product liability policy does not necessarily mean that you are fully protected against your legal liability in this area.

Does the standard policy provide coverage in respect of products exported to other countries?

Most policies will provide full coverage for all exports to countries other than the USA or Canada. It is advisable to appraise your insurers of the fact that you will be exporting your products and provide them with a list of the countries to which you export with the approximate percentages show for each. In this manner your insurer will be obliged to provide the export coverage or demonstrate where the policy is defective for such coverage. The question of exports to the USA are a completely different matter. Over the past five years the rash of product liability claims in the USA has resulted in insurers having to review their whole attitude to the export risk where it involves products sold in this countr At the present moment if a product is manufactured by a UF company and bought by a citizen of the USA who then take it home with him, if he is subsequently injured he cannot bri the action in his own courts against the UK company unless they have assets in the USA to which he can attach a law sui This situation could, of course, change if the proposed Reciprocal Judgment Convention between the UK and the USA is signed, but since this document at the moment is on) in draft form we shall proceed as though it was not in existence.

If however, a UK company consciously decides to export to the USA it will take one of two main courses of action. I

Part Seven

IN CONCLUSION

Chapter 53

Philosophy and practice

As drivers, we deplore the habits of pedestrians; as pedestrians, who loves drivers?

As employers or managers, we may find the unfair dismissal rules and other employment protection legislation irksome, unreasonable and expensive; as employees (however mighty) we may be extremely grateful for that same protection.

As a manufacturer, distributor or retailer — or other person, firm or company who puts products into circulation — you may deeply resent the trend of the law. But if you or any member of your family happens to be injured through a defective product, you may be exceedingly grateful to the Law Commissions, the Pearson Commission, The Council of Europe, the EEC and above all to our own Parliament for enacting and for our courts for interpreting those very same rules.

If you do not like what is coming, then it is your democratic privilege to fight it — now. Just as no vote is counted until it is in the ballot box, so no law is effective until it has received the Royal Assent.

You may decide that the whole concept of strict liability is not only contrary to your interests but repugnant to your philosophical concepts. Britain is a free country; you are entitled to be wrong; and if you can convince enough people that your error is commendable, you may deflect the direction of the law.

Or you may find that political as well as philosophical good sense suggests that you should accept the inevitability of change but attempt to mould the legislative future to the self-interest of your business and its proprietors. Then do not wait until you are faced with certainty. Action is preferable to reaction — and inaction is fatal. So mobilise your own individual, corporate, trade or industrial resources and have a go. Do so and fail and you can blame the system. Fail to do so and: *volenti non fit injuria.*

You may, of course, accept the concept that those who
make money through putting defective goods onto the
market should, in fairness, be held liable to strangers as they
are already, in contract, to those with whom they have
made an agreement. But (you may say) the cost will be too
high . . . the consumer will eventually pay . . . or maybe you
will have to go out of business because you cannot get (or
afford) the necessary insurance. Maybe — but United States'
experience suggests that however hideous the possibilities the
likelihoods are rather less awful.

Anyway, in the days when some of us campaigned for a
ban on those odious and deceitful 'guarantees' and 'warranties'
(see Part 3), we were told: 'Remove the exclusion clauses and
the price of the product will rocket . . .'.

Then there were the car park people who used to charge
plenty, require you to leave your key in the ignition in case
your car had to be moved, and then say: 'If we damage your
car through our negligence or otherwise, you will pay for the
repair — or lose your no claims bonus . . . We shall not be
responsible for loss or damage howsoever caused, whether by
the negligence of our employees or otherwise . . .'. When it
was suggested that these rules were repugnant and disgraceful,
they replied: 'Take them away and every lorry driver will
maintain that the damage to his vehicle was done in our car
park . . .'.

Well, the exclusion clause legislation has settled into our
industrial and commercial scene and neither the manufacturers of the 'guaranteed' or 'warranted' products nor the car
park manufacturers seem to have gone out of lucrative
business and certainly not for that reason.

Gradually, then, the concept of strict liability for products
is spreading across the Western World. Britain is unlikely to
stand Canute-like on the shores of what you may not regard
as progress, commanding the waves of legislation to halt. Nor
is this type of law the prerogative of any particular political
party. The Conservatives introduced the Fair Trading Act and
the Supply of Goods (Implied Terms) Act; the Labour
Government the Health and Safety at Work Act and the
Unfair Contract Terms Act; and Queen Victoria's Whigs the
Sale of Goods Act.

So, he who puts defective goods into circulation for his

profit must also bear loss.

The concept of strict liability may spread to road traffic accidents. Is it not ludicrous that the difference between a financially secure future for a person disabled in a road accident may hang upon the thread of human judgment as to what did or did not happen in a split second of unrecorded time?

Industrial Injuries Benefit does not depend upon proof of fault. The state — or the public or family of the nation or however else you wish to call it or regard it — accepts the burden of the duty of caring for a person disabled at work. So why should the employer, who employed the injured person for a financial benefit of his business, not carry — by adding to the weight of his insurance premium — the burden of damages? A contracting party may be morally thoughtless but he is still normally liable if his product is defective. So why should this concept not spread out from an employer's liability for defective equipment into employer's liability generally . . . from strict liability in contract to strict liability in negligence. . . ?

Some lawyers may suffer. Those who specialise in fighting actions rising out of traffic accidents ('running down' specialists, as they are often called in the profession) will no doubt move across into the associated areas of the assessment and apportionment of damages.

The insurance industry will brace itself for the shock of increased responsibilities and premiums. In Britain at least, it is likely to behave in a largely responsible manner, if only because of the recurrent threat of public ownership. When insurance companies collapsed, colleagues in the industry stepped into the breach, not through pure altruism but out of enlightened self-interest.

Most of this book, then, has been concerned with law and practice, actual and potential — with the realities of the legislation, UK, European and International . . . with reports and recommendations of commissions, legal and Royal . . . with recorded decisions of established courts . . . with known and binding precedents and interpretations, statutes and regulations . . . .

Still, Industry proposes and Parliament disposes. Politicians create laws; lawyers become judges; and ethics and morality are not necessarily the same as laws and regulations. But politics, philosophy and the law are inter-tangled. In the fascinating area of product liability, we can behold the law as it stands — and beware the law that cometh. The only certainty in life is death — and in product liability law — profound and momentous change.

"YOU'RE A CLEVER LAD — THESE NICE MEN WANT
YOU TO HELP WITH THEIR ENQUIRIES . . . ! "

Part Eight

QUESTIONS ANSWERED

Questions answered

Introduction

Hopefully, this book will introduce businessmen to intricate
areas of the law with the maximum of practical impact and
the minimum of jargon. But at the end of the day — and of
the book — there will still be questions left unanswered.

So, in this final section, I have collected some of the most
common and crucial questions on product liability, together
with their answers. Some of the material is fresh; some has
already appeared earlier in the book; but all is relevant and
topical.

Development costs and product liability

*Our company does intricate research, part of it concerned
with chemicals and drugs. Surely the strict liability rules will
make our work much more financially hazardous? Does strict
liability not discourage research and development?*

To some extent, you are right. A much heavier burden is
placed on those who carry out research and development. In
criminal law (Section 6 of the Health and Safety at Work Act)
they are only liable if they fail to take such steps as are
'reasonably practicable' to avoid hazards. Strict liability means
absolute liability, even without fault — liability, that is, to
compensate the sufferers if the product is defective and causes
harm.

However, companies such as yours will have to take the
extra expense into account when pricing products. And do
you not think that you have what Lord Denning called in
another context 'a humanitarian as well as a legal duty' to
protect those who use your pioneering product and then

suffer as a result of a defect — whether or not you knew or should have known of that defect? The Thalidomide disaster will not easily be forgotten — least of all by the individuals or their families whose lives have been blighted by that apparent so beneficent drug.

The Thalidomide case and liability for drugs

What indication did the Thalidomide tragedy give as to the likelihood of drug manufacturers being held strictly liable to those who suffer through unexpected after-effects of drugs they market?

The Thalidomide drug was produced by Distillers Co. (Bayer Chemicals) Ltd. The company was sued by many of the children who suffered, but after much negotiation all or nearly all the cases have been settled. So we will probably never know whether the plaintiffs would have established breach by the defendants of their duty of care.

If strict liability is introduced into our system, breach of duty is likely to be presumed and drug companies argue that they should be exempted from such legislation because:

1   In the main their products are beneficial to mankind.
2   That the imposition of strict liability upon them would throttle innovation and development.
3   The precautions which are already required by various Regulations provide as firm protection for the community as could reasonably be expected.

Nevertheless, strict liability would be likely to include the manufacture, distribution and supply of drugs — and there may be some interesting 'concertina' litigation, in which the manufacturers seek to pass on their liability to those (pharmacists, hospitals or doctors, perhaps) who failed sufficiently to heed warnings of possible dangers, direct or by side-effect, or who failed to pass them on.

Congenital disabilities and strict liability

To what extent does The Congenital Disabilities (Civil Liability) Act, 1976, *impose strict liability on the manu-*

were liable because they had left the lift in a dangerous condition and without any reasonable possibility of 'intermediate examination' by someone who could and should have spotted the defect and had it fixed.

Cranes — and manufacturers' liability

We are construction engineers and we operate cranes. If a crane drops its load and kills or injures someone underneath, in what circumstances are we likely to be held liable in law?

You will be liable if the accident occurred through any negligence or breach of statutory duty on your part or on the part of your 'servants or agents'. For instance, did a steel girder drop because it was carelessly slung? Was the crane operator or the slinger negligent in carrying out his duties?

It may be, though, that the fault lay in the way in which the crane was manufactured. That was the allegation in the case of *Dooley* v. *Cammell Laird & Co. Ltd.* The question in this and all other similar cases is far easier to state than to answer: Whose fault was it that the accident occurred? Alternatively, if the product was defective, did the defect cause the accident? Or was it an obvious, patent defect which should have been spotted and dealt with by the operator? Or should the fault (and hence the damage) be divided?

So, eventually, we come back to problems of proof. If you can show that your employees used normal, proper and careful methods in the slinging operation, but that the sling itself failed, then you will probably win. The shorter the period since you acquired the machine from the makers or (if appropriate) from those who maintained or repaired it, the more likely it is that the fault will be theirs and the less likely that the real responsibility was yours for failing to inspect, test or repair the object.

In *Stennett* v. *Hancock & Peters,* for instance, the defendant garage had little joy in denying liability when they repaired and reassembled a wheel and a flange flew off it only an hour later.

Again, Stewart & Ardern failed to resist a claim by Mr Herschthal, injured because a wheel flew off a car, only the day after it had been delivered and without any proof that anyone had loosened the nuts in the meantime.

Conversely, a Mr Evans lost his case against Triplex Safety Glass when a windscreen shattered thirteen months after it was fitted by Vauxhalls and without any evidence of negligence on the part of Triplex.

Firework law

A child was injured by a firework. It is now said that we should compensate him because we sold it to him. Now, we do our best not to sell fireworks to anyone under the age of 16 — but you can make mistakes. You can't ask a customer for his birth certificate, can you? What is the legal position please?

Some years ago, an 8-year-old bought a firework from a shop and lit it; when nothing happened, he held it up to his eye — then, when the firework caught ablaze, it blinded him. He sued for damages — and won. The judge held that a shopkeeper had been negligent in selling a firework to so young a child.

Thanks to *The Explosives (Age of Purchase, etc). Act, 1976*, it is a criminal offence to sell a firework to someone under the age of 16. But to recover damages, the youngster in your case would have to show first that he bought the firework from you and second that it was your negligence that caused the accident — and not his own stupidity.

Anyway, you should report the matter to your insurers immediately.

Whose liability in a contract for hire?

We hire out mainly heavy plant to the construction and engineering industries. How do the product liability rules apply to us? If a defect in equipment hired causes personal injury, what rules apply to us?

First, you owe duties under your contract with your clients. Some terms will be express, others implied.

The parties to a hire contract frequently allocate responsibilities and duties as between themselves and these will

often vary depending on whether or not an operator is
supplied along with the equipment. You and your clients
remain free to make your own arrangements, except that
The Unfair Contract Terms Act, 1977, will apply to your
transaction. Exclusion clauses are likely only to bite if they
'satisfy the test of reasonableness'. However, liability for death
or personal injury resulting from negligence cannot be
excluded.

Some terms may be implied into your contract. Maybe you
supplied the plant as a matter of urgency, without having the
time to put anything in writing? But did your clients know
that you always contract on certain terms, one of which
involves exclusions of liability? Then the law may imply that
into the deal for you.

Again: in the absence of some enforceable agreement to
the contrary, your clients would normally be entitled to plant
reasonably fit to do the job required. And anyway, did you
not make some representation about fitness, to induce your
clients to hire from you?

The Reed family hired a motor launch from Dean & Co.
for a river holiday. Two hours after their happy departure,
a fire broke out. They grabbed the extinguisher thoughtfully
provided by Deans. It was out of order. Down went the
blazing launch with the Reed family's possessions, and the
hirers also suffered from burns and shock.

Ruling that a term is implied into a contract of hire that
the goods hired should be 'as fit for the purpose as reasonable
care and skill can make them', the judge awarded the plaintiffs the damages they sought.

Those who hire out goods owe a duty of care not only to
those with whom they contract but also to the 'ultimate
consumer' whom they ought reasonably to contemplate
would suffer through a defect in the product. After all, if
your equipment explodes or collapses, it is far more likely
that a stranger to the contract will be hurt than your clients
themselves.

Finally, Section 3 of the Health and Safety at Work Act
applies. You must take such steps as are reasonably practicable not to cause hazards to the health and safety of persons
whom you do not employ but who are 'affected by your
undertaking'. Your undertaking consists in the hire of plant

and equipment? Then you may be prosecuted if they are defective.

A hirer of small-scale power tools was prosecuted because a client who used his equipment while standing knee-deep in water was electrocuted and died. He was under a duty to give adequate warning of the dangers of the equipment hired. He was acquitted because the box in which the power tool was supplied bore an adequate warning in large red letters.

Can we pass the blame?

A customer returned an article purchased from us, complaining that it was defective. We think that he is probably right and offered to give him a credit note or his money back, provided that our suppliers accept the return of the goods. After all, we bought them in and any defect is not due to our default, is it? Were we right?

No. *You* made your contract with your customer and he is entitled to look to *you* to honour your bargain. If the goods are defective, then *you* could be required to accept them back or to pay to have them put into proper order.

You would have rights against your supplier. You could claim an indemnity from the distributor or manufacturer (as the case may be) from whom you bought the goods. And if you had to return your customer's money, your loss would not be just what you paid your supplier but would include your loss of profit on the deal that went wrong through no fault of yours.

So the customer has rights against you and you against your supplier.

The only circumstances in which your customer could jump the contractual queue and sue the suppliers direct would be if he suffered personal injury through a defect in the product. He would then bring his claim for damages for negligence and not for breach of contract. As the 'ultimate consumer' of the goods, he would be entitled to his remedy — which would be worthwhile having if you had gone out of business.

'Reasonable care' and breach of contract

If we are sued for damages for breach of contract arising out of a defect in goods we supply, will it provide us with a defence if we can show that we took reasonable care in connection with the item?

No. In this sense, liability in contract law is 'strict'. You may have been extremely careful . . . you may have taken all reasonably practicable steps to avoid the defect . . . but if you have failed to honour your bargain and to supply the goods 'in accordance with contract', you are legally to blame.

It is this aspect of 'strict liability' which gives a person who is party to a contract a great advantage over those strangers (or 'ultimate consumers') who have to bring their claims in negligence. Unlike plaintiffs in actions for damages for breach of contract, they have to prove negligence — at present. When the concept of 'strict liability' is applied to negligence actions, then the rights of strangers will start approximating much closer to those of contracting parties.

The contrast between the two liabilities in the law at present is well illustrated by the cases of *Donoghue* v. *Stephenson* and *Wren* v. *Holt*. In the former, a woman was poisoned by ginger beer which was clearly contaminated. Suing in negligence as the 'ultimate consumer', she proved breach of duty and won her case.

In *Wren* v. *Holt*, a man became ill after drinking beer in a pub. The drink apparently contained a minute amount of arsenic, which the unfortunate seller could not conceivably have discovered. Only an expert's analysis could do that. But the publican was held liable because — without any provable negligence whatever — he had failed to comply with his contract by selling beer which was not 'merchantable'.

Volenti non fit injuria

If an employee, a visitor or anyone else is hurt due to an accident in our works, in what circumstances will it provide us with an answer to say that he knew of the risks that he was taking and cannot therefore complain of their consequences?

It is sometimes said that a volunteer has no right to damages if he suffers injury due to a risk which he 'voluntarily, freely and with full knowledge of its nature' impliedly agreed to incur. It is not enough, then, that the sufferer knew of the danger. He must have 'full knowledge of its nature and extent'. Only then can he be said to have waived his right to take action.

If one of your employees works on a dangerous machine, that in no way frees you from your responsibility to take care for his safety. The fact that both you and he are aware of the danger imposes a greater than normal duty on both of you to take all reasonably practicable steps to minimise the risk. Even payment of 'danger money' in no way lessens your duty. There is every difference between a rugby footballer or speedway rider injured through one of the normal and accepted risks of their sport and the person who works in dangerous surroundings or circumstances and who is hurt because of inadequate training, supervision, information or precautions. The courts have been highly reluctant to permit the defence of *volenti non fit injuria* in industrial injury claims.

Res ipsa loquitur — when the producer is presumed guilty

We have heard that there are cases in which the producer of a defective product is even today presumed to have been negligent. Is this correct?

Some negligence is so obvious that it 'speaks for itself'. Contrary to the general rule that the plaintiff must prove his case, the burden of proof is thrust onto the defendant. If he wishes to show that he took all reasonable care, then let him do so. *Res ipsa loquitur* — the negligence is self-explanatory.

A barrel of flour fell off a roof. It was conceivable (said the court) that this outrage occurred without negligence on the part of the people who should have been in control of the barrel. Then let them prove their innocence.

A surgeon sewed up a patient's stomach, leaving a swab inside. Result: a further and painful and otherwise unnecessary operation for the removal of the swab. Someone had not counted the number put in and the number removed. *Res ipsa loquitur.*

A car mounted a pavement. Vehicles generally keep to

roads. The driver maintained that it was not his fault but that of a defect in the vehicle which existed in spite of all reasonable efforts to maintain it. Then let him prove his case.

There may also be cases in which defects in products are so obvious that there is an almost irresistable conclusion of negligence on the part of the manufacturer. A bottle explodes; a child who opens a refrigerator door suffers severe electric shock; . . . .

In most cases, though, the facts may be as consistent with carelessness on the part of the user or negligence on that of the operator as with a defect in the manufacture. In those cases, the burden of proving negligence rests where it normally belongs — on the shoulders of those who wish to prove it.

Liability for pranks

We are in the drinks processing business and every now and again an object turns up in one of our bottles, obviously placed there by an employee with an odd sense of alleged humour. Clearly, we are responsible if we do not clean our bottles properly or if (as in Donoghue v. Stephenson*) a dead snail causes contamination. But what is our responsibility if the object concerned is offensive but harmless — like a contraceptive for instance?*

You get the benefit of your employees' good deeds at work? Then you must take the blame in civil law for their misdeeds, committed in the course of their employment. So an employee causing your product to be defective, whether he does so carelessly or deliberately, will affect his relationship towards you, but not yours towards your customer. In other words, it will be no answer for you to meet a claim with the statement: 'Blame my mad employee . . .'. You should not have employed him.

On the other hand, the cost of the prank is likely to be very low because while 'the ultimate consumer' may become seriously ill through drinking ginger ale polluted by a dead snail, the sight of a floating prophylactic is unlikely to cause 'damage'. And the rule in civil actions for damages is, and is likely to remain, no damage suffered, no damages recoverable.

Incidentally, it is possible that a peculiarly sensitive customer might suffer personal injury through the shock of seeing the foreign substance in the food. Decisions on damages for shock are complicated and to some extent conflicting, but in the unlikely event of nervous shock provably causing personal injury to the plaintiff, then he would not have to establish actual physical poisoning in order to win damages.

Liability for low-cost products

Does the law take no account of the value of a product which causes an injury? Is it true that even a tiny part of accessory may lead to a damages claim stretching into a huge sum?

The size of the disaster is not regulated by the size of the object causing it — nor are damages in any way limited by the cost of the defective item.

A man bought a carriage with a defective pole which broke and his horse was severely injured. He was awarded £3 for replacing the pole and fifty times that sum for the injuries which were the natural consequence of the defect.

The same rule applies in other legal directions. For instance, the fact that it would drive your company into liquidation if you had to pay the amount awarded against you by a court will not prevent the court from making that award.

Is the damage too remote?

If we as wholesalers or retailers sell a product which turns out to be defective, we know that we can claim back from our supplier the cost of the product, plus our loss of profits on the abortive sale. But if we lose a customer because he feels that he can no longer rely on us to provide products which are not defective, can we successfully claim damages for the loss of that customer's future business?

Unfortunately for you — though fortunately for your supplier — damages claimable in this sort of case must not be 'too remote'. Could you prove that the loss of a particular customer should have been reasonably foreseeable to your supplier as flowing as a natural and probable consequence from his breach of his contract with you? And anyway, could you prove how much you have lost? You could show what orders that customer placed with you in previous years. But what business would you have got from him in the future?

You should discuss this problem with your lawyers in the light of the particular facts of your case. They will probably advise that it would be worth claiming for this loss but that a court would be unlikely to award damages under this head.

Strict liability and the rule in Rylands v. Fletcher

Is it correct that if you have under your control an article or substance that is inherently dangerous, courts may even now impose strict liability on you if it causes harm?

No. Under the so-called rule in *Rylands* v. *Fletcher*, when water escaped from a man-made reservoir, those who had accumulated the water were held liable even without proof of negligence. But the possibility of this rule extending to product liability is exceedingly academic.

Of course, if you do have control of dangerous articles or substances, and they cause injury, you may have difficulty in showing that you took such care as was reasonable in the circumstances. Did you personally (or through instructions and warnings given to others) take such steps as were reasonable to ensure the avoidance of unnecessary risk in, perhaps, the handling or storage of the article or substance concerned? If so, then why did the accident occur? Did you appreciate the existence or extent of the danger and take adequate steps to guard against it? Or was the accident entirely due to the act or default of someone else — perhaps the plaintiff himself?

Does strict liability mean inevitable payment?

We understand that if an employee is injured by defective equipment which we have provided, then we are presumed to have been negligent. So are we right in thinking that in those circumstances the employee will inevitably obtain compensation from our insurers? And does this mean that when the concept of strict liability is introduced in other areas of our law, anyone who is injured by a defective pro-

duct will inevitably obtain recompense from the manufacturer or other party who put it into circulation?

To obtain damages in a negligence action, the plaintiff must prove three things:

1   *A duty of care*   No problem here, so far as your injured employee is concerned. An employer must take care for the safety of his employee. Equally, the manufacturer of a product owes a duty to take care for the safety of the 'ultimate consumer'.

2   *Breach of duty*   If your equipment was defective, breach of duty will be presumed. And if liability is 'strict', then it will exist even in the absence of fault. So (here again) breach of duty will be presumed. But that leaves

3   *Damage* arising from the breach.

So the damage which the plaintiff suffered must result from the act or default of the employer or manufacturer or other defaulter. If the sole effective cause of the disaster was the behaviour of the plaintiff himself, he will get no damages.

Suppose, for instance, that the employee who is injured by the defective equipment knew of the defect; had been warned not to use the equipment until it had been fixed; had been adequately trained, supervised and instructed; and had ignored instructions, used the equipment and suffered his injury as a result. A court might well say that he was the sole author of his own misfortune.

Or suppose that you sell defective goods to a customer, pointing out the defect and warning him of the risk involved in its use (or misuse). The customer fails to heed your warning or to follow your instructions. He may well have voluntarily undertaken the risks — and a court may well dismiss his case.

Those, then, are the rules which already apply to strict liability for defective equipment. How they will apply to future arrangements depends upon Parliament. Sufficient unto the day is the liability thereof.

Product liability — New Zealand

Is it correct that no-fault rules have been introduced in

New Zealand? How do they operate there?

Yes. A state agency operates a central fund from which compensation is paid.

We have a similar sort of arrangement to provide compensation for people who suffer injury as a result of a criminal act. The Criminal Injuries Compensation Board pays out compensation, which is assessed in relation to the personal injuries actually received. However, the amount of compensation will take into account any damages awarded by a court.

What is 'movable'?

Does product liability law apply only to movable property? Is there any relationship to law governing land, buildings or other immovables?

Just as parts form the whole of a machine, so bricks and pipes join in creating a building. The building as such is in the main subject to different legal rules; but if the structure collapses due to a defect in a part, future product liability rules may well apply to the whole, as they will do to that part.*

Also, the line of demarcation between movable or immovable, a fixture or a non-fixture, is often narrow. Oil rigs and swing-bridges, lifts, cranes, sheds and a multitude of other semi-movables occupy a grey area.

As a matter of broad generalisation, items which 'adhere to the freehold' form part of the land but little part of this book. Conversely, items which lack that sufficient degree of 'annexation to the soil' are 'movable', 'non-fixtures' and better described as 'products', rather than as land, buildings or 'immovables'.

Can we insure?

We are alarmed at the incredibly high awards of damages made in the United States against people in our industry. To what extent is it possible to insure against liability of this kind?

When people talk about 'product liability' they normally mean *civil* liability, i.e. liability to pay damages to a person

* The English and Scottish Law Commissions disagreed on the question whether strict liability should continue after the incorporation of materials into a building (see Appendix 8). The Pearson Commission favoured the continuation of strict liability (see Appendix 7).

who suffers injury to his person or property through a defect in a product. The only UK problem in obtaining insurance against this sort of risk is normally the premium. While a plaintiff still has to prove fault on the part of the manufacturer, premiums are generally comparatively light. But they may be prohibitive. And if the risk is sufficiently large, the cost of insurance may drive you out of the market.

It is, of course, unlawful for anyone to insure you against criminal liability which may arise — probably under Section 6 of the Health and Safety at Work Act — for marketing dangerous goods, without taking such steps as are reasonably practicable to reduce or to remove the hazards. Your insurers may cover you against the legal costs of a prosecution, but nothing more.

Who is liable on a trade-in?

If we as traders accept goods as a trade-in, what liability, if any, has the customer for the state of the item which he part-exchanges? Is this, in any event, a contract of exchange or one of sale? What rules apply?

Trade-in arrangements are not regarded as contracts for exchange but as two interconnected and separate contracts for the sale of goods.

If you accept the private customer's goods in part exchange, then he is selling his goods to you. As he does not sell 'in the course of a business', those terms implied into contracts of sale by *The Sale of Goods Act, 1893* (in broad terms, ensuring 'merchantability' and 'fitness for purpose') do not apply. It is up to you to make sure that you are getting goods worth what you are paying for them. And you will have to put them into proper shape if you sell them on to the public.

The law has emphasised this point in a curious way. A car dealer told a customer that a vehicle he wished to trade in was worthless and unsaleable. Relying on this statement, the customer accepted a nominal sum as a trade-in price. When some two weeks later the customer saw the vehicle on sale, at a hefty price, he reported the dealer to the Trading Standards officers who prosecuted him for 'applying a false trade description' to goods that he had bought.

Standing the law on its head, the court convicted. A trade-in arrangement is a contract of sale and the Trade Descriptions Act applies to the goods bought in, as well as to those sold out.

Finally, as a trade-in arrangement is a contract for the sale and purchase of goods, *The Supply of Goods (Implied Terms) Act, 1973,* applies to it. If you try to limit your liability in any way through an exclusion clause, that clause will not be enforceable if your sale is to a 'consumer', and a court may set it aside if it is 'unfair' or 'unreasonable' and contained in a business deal.

Contribution from the seller

A customer was involved in a car accident. The collision was partly due to the negligence of the other driver and partly to a defect in his own car. The customer recovered damages from the negligent driver, but we are now being threatened with an action for damages by him — or, to be precise, by his insurers. We say that as our customer had not seen fit to sue us, the insurers cannot do so because they have no contractual relationship with us. They maintain that they are entitled to rely on The Civil Liability (Contribution) Act, 1978. *Who is right?*

They are. The Act enables a person who has been found liable to pay damages to someone else to recover a contribution towards his liability from any other person who was wholly or partly responsible. So the negligent driver in your case would try to show that he had been forced to pay at least part of his damages because you were in breach of contract with your customer in selling him a defective vehicle.

Of course, the burden of proving your fault would rest on the plaintiff. You may well show that the vehicle was road-worthy when you sold it and that it had become defective for some reason entirely beyond your control. Alternatively, maybe you could bring your supplier or the manufacturers of the defective part or accessory into the action as third parties and claim an indemnity from them.

In any such case, the amount of the contribution recoverable will depend on the extent of that defendant's responsibility for the damage.

Why documentation?

What is the best way to establish a defence to a criminal charge arising out of a defective product?
Through the use of documentation. Every court knows that memory is an unreliable guide to the truth. Documents — notes, memoranda, diary entries, letters, contracts and the like — made at the time are far more likely to reveal the truth.

This rule applies not only to criminal matters but equally to civil claims of all sorts.

When the employer is both guilty and innocent

Is it correct that we may successfully be prosecuted under Section 6 of the Health and Safety at Work Act for putting out a defective product and may still avoid liability in a civil action brought by an injured party?
Yes. You may be guilty of an offence — even a criminal one — but the cause of the accident may be the behaviour of the sufferer.

The most startling safety example appeared in the Scottish case of *McWilliams* v. *Sir William Arrol & Co. Ltd*. It arose from the traditional and notorious dangers faced by employees who work high above the ground.

Scaffolders, steel erectors, painters, decorators, insulaters and a host of other agile employees are theoretically protected by statutes and regulations which require (among other niceties) the provision and wearing of a safety harness and the erection of guard-rails and the like. In practice, most scaffolder or steel erectors will tell you that it is almost impossible for them to do their job if they wear the required harness — and anyway (they maintain) it would slow them down too much.

A painter was working at a great height, without harness. He fell to his death. His employers were convicted of an offence under the Building Regulations. The widow claimed damages, alleging that her husband's death had been caused by his employer's breach of statutory duty. She lost.

Unanimously, the House of Lords held that even though there was no harness provided at the particular site at the moment of tragedy, the deceased would not have worn it even had it been handed to him by his shop steward on a silver platter. He was an experienced and skilled worker who had frequently been asked and encouraged to wear his safety harness but who had always refused. The entire cause of his death was that refusal and not his employer's (undoubted and proved) breach of their statutory duty.

Who can bind Parliament?

Is Parliament bound to follow the recommendations of the Law Commission or of an EEC Directive? If so, then when can we expect legislation imposing no fault liability?

Law Commissions recommend and Parliament is likely to be put under strong pressure to follow their recommendations. But there is no certainty whatever that it will do so, now or in the future. The same applies to a Royal Commission Report. such as that produced by the one on civil liability, headed by Lord Pearson (see Appendix 7).

Member countries of the EEC, on the other hand, must comply with Directives. At present (January 1979), the one requiring strict liability for products remains in draft (see Appendix 15). If and when it is promulgated in final form, our Parliament will have to act.

When is Parliamentary action likely? As the only reliable prophets have been dead for over 2000 years, I can only guess: 1981 or 1982.

What is the effect of an EEC Directive?

What is the legal effect of an EEC Directive on product liability?

When an EEC Directive is still in draft it is binding on no one. It then has to be debated by the European Parliament and approved by the Council of Ministers. Once that has happened and it becomes a fully fledged Directive, it is then binding on all member states. Each must implement its requirements, although it may choose the form and method of implementation. So this means that once the EEC Directive on product liability ceases to be a draft and is put into final form, it will be binding on us and our Parliament will be forced to take appropriate action.

What is the effect of European Conventions?

The Council of Europe Convention on product liability has already been signed by a number of European states. What is the effect of a Convention of this sort?

If a member country decides to become a party to such a Convention, it will be obliged to sign and ratify the document and to introduce legislation incorporating its provisions into its law. So if the UK decides to adhere to the Convention on product liability (The Strasbourg Convention — see Appendix 14) we will have to make our national law conform with the provisions of the Convention by whatever method we choose.

Citing foreign cases

If we have a case in an English court, can decisions of foreign courts be cited — by or against us?

Our courts are bound to follow decisions of courts of a higher level and decisions of courts of equivalent stature are of a 'persuasive nature' in our own country. They are in no way bound by, or bound even to take into consideration, decisions of foreign courts — even those of United States or Commonwealth countries which follow our 'common law' system.

Still, overseas decisions do have persuasive power and interest, especially in those cases in which there is no clear decision by our own courts. Counsel may well quote (for instance) US or Australian or Canadian cases. The higher the overseas court and the more distinguished the judges, the greater the interest which will normally be taken by our judges.

Overseas contract rules, of course, also have a profound
importance when the overseas law is the 'proper law' of the
contract. There are cases in which — probably because the
parties have so decided but sometimes for other reasons — an
English court must apply foreign law.

Judgments in foreign currency

*We are both importers and exporters of various products and
unfortunately we get involved in litigation from time to time.
Is it true that damages may be awarded for or against us by
English courts in foreign currency?*

It is. Damages may be awarded by English courts in foreign
currency, with extraordinary results. If, for example, judgment is awarded against you in Swiss Francs, rather than in £
sterling, the real effects of such a judgment may be very
different to that intended.

You should draw the attention of your lawyers to this
problem — preferably at the stage when contracts are made.
Whether you want damages to be paid in foreign or in British
currency will depend upon which side of the fence you happen
to be on.

What is a 'business'?

*Much of the protection given to buyers' products by the Sale
of Goods Act is confined to goods sold 'in the course of a
business'. How narrow is this definition and what does a
'business' constitute?*

Both the amended Section 14(ii) of the Sale of Goods Act
and a most important court decision have given the word
'business' an extremely wide meaning.

The Act provides that 'business' includes 'profession and the
activities of any Government Department . . . local authority
or statutory undertaker'. Even a businessman who acts as
agent for a private seller is included unless either the buyer
knows that the sale is a private one or the seller (personally
or via his agent) has taken reasonable steps to inform him.

In the case of *Ashington Piggeries Ltd* v. *Christopher Hill*

Ltd the Court of Appeal defined the 'business' requirement narrowly. In that case, it meant that the dealer sold goods of precise contract description which was: 'king-sized mink food', rather than mere 'animal feeding stuff'. But the House of Lords disagreed with this approach.

So today, you may take it that any goods sold by anyone in the course of his business are covered by the Act. Those sold by a private individual for his private (and non-business) purposes are not. If you sell a vehicle which belongs to your business, then yours is a 'business' sale, even though you are not in the business of selling vehicles. Conversely, if you sell your own private vehicle to a friend or to a neighbour, as a private transaction, the Act will not apply — even though in another capacity you may be in the car sales business.

Legislation is designed primarily to protect buyers from businesses. Those who purchase from private people do so without most of the protection given by *The Sale of Goods Act, 1893, The Supply of Goods (Implied Terms) Act, 1973,* or *The Unfair Contract Terms Act, 1977.* While the private seller is not free to engage in fraud or misrepresentation, his customer must otherwise 'beware'.

Problems of business sales carried out from private addresses and of private individuals engaging in a series of sales which may be sufficiently continuous to amount to a business operation come into that grey area which should be discussed with solicitors by those concerned.

What is a sale 'by description'?

We have read that the Sale of Goods Act implies a term into a contract for the sale of goods by description which states that goods will correspond with that description. Are goods sold by description when the buyer actually picks them out? If not, then when is there a sale 'by description' and what is the alternative?

Goods are sold by description when the agreement is based upon a statement of the class, kind or species to which the article belongs. As Lord Wright said in the case of the underwear which caused dermatitis: 'There is a sale by description even though the buyer is buying something displayed before him on the counter. The product is sold by description, though it is specific, so long as it is sold not merely as the specific thing but as the thing corresponding to a description.'

Trade descriptions and Trading Standards

In what circumstances can it be a false trade description to give incorrect dimensions to a product?

To apply incorrect dimensions in the description of a product may amount to a false trade description under *The Trade Descriptions Act, 1968*. General responsibility in this area rests on the Trading Standards Authorities — although the government must maintain 'primary standards', by reference to which length, capacity and weight are referred to. These are: the yard, pound, metre and kilogramme.

Faulty labelling

Please can you summarise the rules on the labelling of food?

The Food and Drugs Act, 1955, makes it an offence falsely to label food. If the label on food falsely describes it or is 'calculated (i.e. likely) to mislead as to its nature, substance or quality', the offender may be prosecuted.

Defence: that the accused did not know 'and could not with reasonable diligence have ascertained' that the label contained a false description.

If the food is advertised and described incorrectly, the advertiser will be guilty of an offence. Defence: that he did not know and 'could not with reasonable diligence have ascertained' that the advertisement was incorrect, or that he 'received the advertisement for publication in the ordinary course of business'. The Act also enables regulations to be made, imposing requirements concerning labelling, marketing and advertising of food and drugs. *The Labelling of Food Regulations, 1970,* made under this power, normally require food to bear a label with a sufficiently specific description of what is contained, so as to indicate the true nature of the food to the intending purchaser. This is known as 'the appropriate designation'.

Where 'the appropriate designation' contains the names of two or more ingredients, they must be put in order of proportion of weight in which they were used in the manufacturing process.

In addition, Regulations 'to secure the observance of sanitary and cleanliness practices in connection with the storage and packaging of food for human consumption' proliferate. For details of those that concern you, consult the Department of Agriculture, Fisheries and Food.

Prepacked food

We purchased a case of particular food and put it into our refrigerator. Some three days later, when it was partially thawed, we cut it up; wrapped it in polythene; and refroze it.

Unfortunately, when we sold the food at our delicatessen counter it turned out to be defective and hence unfit for human consumption. We are being prosecuted. What sort of defence may be open to us?

The Food and Drugs Act, 1955, makes it an offence to sell 'any food or drug which is not of the nature or substance or quality of the food or drug demanded by the purchaser'.

You would probably have great difficulty in showing that you could not have avoided the deterioration of the food. It is not enough for you to show that you had taken 'all reasonable care'. You would be more likely to rely on the defence provided by Section 115 of the Act: that the food was sold within the time of the warranty given by the manufacturer in writing and that you had 'no reason to believe that at the time of the commission of the alleged offence . . . it was otherwise' than of the appropriate substance or that it was not 'in the same state as when you purchased it'.

Your trouble here will come through the decision of the High Court in the case of *Tesco Stores* v. *Roberts*. Tescos had bought a case containing pigs liver and had treated it in much the same way as you did your purchase. They relied on Section 115 and maintained that they had no reason to believe that the liver was other than in good condition, as warranted by their supplier — and that they had sold it in the same state as when they bought it.

The judge held that when a single article is cut up into a number of separate pieces, this constitutes 'a change in the state of the article'. So it was not 'in the same state' as when you bought it.

So when you sell prepacked foods which you buy in that state with a written warranty, you are far better protected than when you cut it up and hence prepare it. So you should see your solicitor — maybe he can find some defence which is not apparent to us on the facts provided.

Is silence a representation?

If we sell a product and make some false statement about its quality or fitness, we realise that we may be held liable to compensate the buyer who relies on that misrepresentation. But are we bound to say anything *about our goods? Can silence itself amount to a misrepresentation?*

If you sell defective goods, then you are normally in breach of your contract and liable in damages, whether or not you made a misrepresentation. Equally, if you knew the purpose for which the goods were supplied and they were not reasonably fit for that purpose, you will probably be in breach of the second limb of Section 14 of *The Sale of Goods Act, 1893*. The question of misrepresentation would again be irrelevant.

However, suppose that the goods are neither defective nor unfit for the purpose supplied but that they are not what the buyer expected. If his unrequited hopes resulted from your unwarranted misrepresentation, he may claim damages under *The Misrepresentation Act, 1967*.

Now suppose that you knew that he expected that which he was not going to get. You held your tongue. Will the law hold you responsible?

Unfortunately, the question is simpler to pose than to answer. Clearly, if you state a half-truth, that may amount to a misrepresentation. If you actively conceal a defect but then say nothing about it, and the buyer is misled as a result, then it seems probable that the buyer may rely upon your silence. Again, if a true statement becomes false the maker would

appear to have a duty to disclose the truth. But there is as
yet no positive authority as to whether or not silence will of
itself amount to a misrepresentation. Some experts say:
'Yes'. My view: 'No', but it should be. Which suggests that
either Parliament or the courts should one day reduce the
apparently golden quality of a seller's silence.

Warranties and the intention of the parties

*We appreciate the difference between a statement of fact and
a representation of opinion. But if we state anything as a fact
which turns out to be incorrect, has the buyer always got a
remedy against us in law?*

If you have 'warranted' the truth of the statement, then
(in broad terms) you are bound by it; the statement amounts
to a 'warranty'; and anyone who relies on it will have a good
claim against you. As Lord Denning said in the case of *Oscar
Chess Ltd* v. *Williams*: 'When the seller states a fact which is
or should be within his own knowledge and of which the buyer
is ignorant' and when he also intends that the buyer should
act on that statement and he does so, then 'it is easy to infer
a warranty'. On the other hand, if the seller states a fact but
makes it clear that he has no knowledge of his own but has
got his information elsewhere and is merely passing it on, then
'it is not so easy to imply a warranty'.

So if you intend a potential buyer to act on a factual statement you have made, you should make sure in so far as you
can that the statement is fact and not fiction.

Note, too, that the law (and especially Section 11 of *The
Sale of Goods Act, 1893*) makes a distinction between
'warranty' and a 'condition'. A condition is a very important
part of the contract and breach of a condition gives the
innocent party the right to regard the contract as 'repudiated'
. . . smashed . . . finished . . . . In practice, this means that he
may return the goods and get his money back.

Breach of a (less important) 'warranty' will only give the
innocent buyer the right to claim damages, to put him in the
same position as he would have been in, had the statement
been accurate.

In general, whether a term is a 'condition' or a 'warranty'
generally depends on the intention of the parties. If you run

into trouble over this branch of the law, you should certainly consult your solicitor.

Advertising

To what extent is a statement made in an advertisement binding on the advertiser? Can we be made liable for a defect in a product merely because a total stranger acts upon a statement contained in an advertisement?

From the contractual viewpoint, an advertisement is a mere 'invitation to treat' and not an offer capable of acceptance. However, it is sometimes possible to put an advertisement into such a form that it amounts to an offer which any person who reads it may accept.

A Mrs Carlill read an advertisement put in *The Pall Mall Gazette* by the Carbolic Smokeball Co. Anyone who sniffed their smokeballs (they said) for three weeks in accordance with their instructions and then caught a cold would receive a reward.

Mrs Carlill duly bought, sniffed, fell ill and claimed the money. The advertisers replied: 'Sorry — it was only an invitation to treat'.

The court held that the advertisement had constituted an offer which Mrs Carlill had duly accepted and that they were therefore bound by the terms of their advertising.

Next, if you make a representation of fact in an advertisement, someone acts upon it by buying the product, and the statement was untrue, he may claim damages for misrepresentation.

Finally, if the advertisement 'applies a false trade description to goods', the advertiser may be prosecuted.

Defects 'drawn to the buyer's attention'

If we draw a defect in a product to a buyer's attention before he agrees on the price, then apparently we are not liable to him in respect of that defect. But what happens if he denies we have done so? Or suppose that he says that we did not draw the full extent of the defect to his attention and that it would cost him more to rectify the defect than he had expected? What is the legal position then?

Section 14(2) of *The Sale of Goods Act, 1893,* as amended by *The Supply of Goods (Implied Terms) Act, 1973,* says that there is no implied condition as to 'merchantable quality' as regards 'defects specifically drawn to the buyer's attention before the contract is made'. Its full extent, however, does not appear to have been explained by a court.

However, applying a decision of the Court of Appeal in 1965 in the case of *Bartlett* v. *Sidney Marcus Ltd,* it seems likely that if the fault has been pointed out to the customer, the fact that it would cost more to rectify than the customer had estimated will not be the fault of the seller.

Of course, there are bound to be borderline cases. What dealer does not know how to steer a customer gently around a defect, perhaps touching upon it gently but moving away with decent speed?

The best way to reduce doubt to a minimum is (as always) to put the proposition into writing. Otherwise, a court might have to decide whether your recollection or that of your employee was correct, or whether the customer was right in saying either that there was no mention made of the defect or that its full extent was disguised or understated. Documents win cases — especially borderline ones.

Second-hand buyers

We sell both new and second-hand goods. What distinction does the law make between the rights of the buyer in either case? Surely the person who buys second-hand goods has no right to the same excellence as one who pays a lot more for something new?

Both new and second-hand goods must be both 'reasonably fit for the purpose supplied' and 'of merchantable quality'. The fact that an article is sold as second-hand gives you no right to foist upon the buyer an article which is either unsafe or defective.

If goods suffer from defects which you specifically point out to the buyer, then he cannot complain of those defects. You may say to the man who likes to fix his own cars: 'I am selling this vehicle to you cheaply because it needs the following work done to it . . .'. Then he buys it, together with the defects specified.

The Sale of Goods Act defines, 'merchantable quality' like this: 'Goods of any kind are of merchantable quality . . . if they are as fit for the purpose or purposes for which the goods of that kind are commonly bought as it is reasonable to expect, *having regard to any description applied to them,* to the price (if relevant) and to all other relevant circumstances . . .'.

If you describe goods as 'second-hand' and if the price reflects their used nature, then it is not 'reasonable' for the buyer to expect the goods to be as splendid as if they were spanking new.

Nevertheless, a car sold as second-hand must normally be reasonably fit for driving on the road. A Mr Crowther bought a Jaguar car from the Shannon Motor Company of Southampton. The milometer read 82,000 miles.

After three weeks and 2000 miles of driving, the engine seized up. Mr Crowther sued for the cost of a replacement. He alleged that when the car was sold, it was not reasonably fit to be driven on the road.

The trial judge and the Court of Appeal agreed that the dealers had broken their contract. The car had been sold under a contract which in no way removed the buyer's right to a vehicle with a 'merchantable' motor. If the defects had appeared rather later, the situation would have been different. As it was, the customer did not get what he bargained for — a vehicle which was both second-hand and satisfactory.

How long is a 'guarantee'?

If we sell a customer a defective product we understand that he has six years within which to bring his claim. Does this mean that he has, in effect, a six-year guarantee on his product?

No. All that the law guarantees to a private and, to a lesser extent, to a business buyer is that he will have rights lasting six years if he can show that the product was defective when he originally bought it.

A Mr Evans bought a car fitted with a 'Triplex toughened

safety glass' windscreen. About a year after the purchase, he
was driving the car when 'suddenly and for no apparent
reason', the windscreen fragmented and injured the people
in the car. Mr Evans sued.

The claim failed. The judge was not satisfied that the cause
of the injuries was a defect in manufacture. The lapse of time
between the purchase of the car and the occurrence of the
accident was too great; the glass might have been strained
when it was screwed into its frame; the 'intermediate seller',
i.e. the dealer, had the chance to make an 'intermediate
examination'; and anyway (and most important) 'the breaking
of the glass might have been caused by something other than
a defect in manufacture'.

Until liability without fault is introduced into this area of
law, then, the customer who wishes to claim damages against
a manufacturer must prove that he suffered loss due to a
manufacturing defect. When 'strict liability' is introduced, the
situation will be different.

Equally, the retailer is bound to sell goods which are not
defective at the time of sale. But a car which is perfectly
'merchantable' when bought may become defective thereafter
for some reason which has nothing whatever to do with the
manufacturer or with the retailer. Overuse or misuse are the
two most obvious examples.

If, then, you receive a claim from a customer who has had
your goods over an extended period, you must judge for
yourself whether it is likely that they were defective at the
time of sale . . . whether the defect complained of would have
occurred by now, had the goods been in proper order when
they were sold . . . and the longer the customer has held the
goods, the less likely it is that his claim will succeed.

How long to sue?

*Within what period must a sufferer from a defect in a product
sue or lose his rights?*

At present, the 'periods of limitation' are as follow:
1   Claims for damages for personal injuries — 3 years from
     the date when the injury was caused or 3 years from

the date when the sufferer knew or ought to have known of its existence.

2 Other claims for damages in contract or in negligence — 6 years from the date when the 'cause' of action arose.

3 Claims arising out of defects in buildings — and possibly in 'products' — where the defect is latent — 6 years from the date when the defect became 'patent'.

Various suggestions have been made regarding periods of limitation for strict liability for products, including 10 years from the date when the product was marketed. But there will certainly be pressure for an unlimited period for (at the least) drugs, whose deleterious or dangerous effects may not become known until many years after they were first marketed.

'Estoppel' — when there's no going back

What is meant by 'estoppel'?

In certain cases, you may be prevented (or 'estopped') from denying the truth of a statement which you made. If you make a statement of fact (a 'representation') as opposed to a mere expression of opinion (a 'puff'), you presumably intend someone to rely upon that statement. If they do rely on that statement, a court will not allow you to assert that it was untrue — even if in fact it was.

Interest on claims

We have had to sue for the money we are owed for certain products that our customers are alleging are faulty simply to win them time. Is it true that we can claim interest on the money we are owed?

Yes. When considering making or settling a claim, do not forget the interest on the money you are owed. This may be fixed at about 10 per cent from the date when liability arose. Litigants frequently forget to claim interest. It can amount to a considerable sum, especially when the litigation is protracted.

Hints for the County Court

Many product liability claims are for sums of less than £2000. We know that these will normally go to a County Court. Any hints, please?

If you are suing in the County Court, you may well have the option of going to arbitration. If so, the strict rules of evidence that are found in a court will not apply so you may save the time of bringing experts to court by putting in their reports; there is rarely any appeal against the arbitrator's decision; you can probably be represented by a company officer or employee, rather than by a solicitor or counsel; and the proceedings will be held in private. You should discuss this possibility and all details of procedure with your lawyers.

Quality assurance

We manufacture components for larger products. As quality assurance manager, I am required to sign a 'contractor's certificate' which states: 'We certify that the whole of the articles listed herein conform in all respects to drawings, specifications and contract/order relative hereto. We further certify that the articles have been tested and inspected in accordance with the contractual requirements and conditions'.

Obviously, I have no time to inspect each article personally, so I am wondering — if an article is found to be defective after I have signed the certificate, or does not conform with specifications, could I personally be held liable?

In civil law, your company or firm must cover you. They are 'vicariously liable' for your mistakes.

Under Section 6 of the Health and Safety at Work Act, though, you bear your own responsibility. A 'director, manager, or secretary' is responsible for a breach of the law if it was caused with his 'consent or connivance' or as a result of his 'neglect'. And as manufacturers can pass on their liability under Section 6 if they can show that they reasonably relied upon research and testing done by others; and as it appears that the documents attempt to pass that responsibility on to your company; and as you have personal responsibility for quality assurance, you must take special care to ensure, insofar as you can, that components sold on to your customers are in fact as safe as is 'reasonably practicable', when used by their employees at work.

As yet, of course, there is no 'strict liability' resting upon your company or yourself to ensure that research and testing is adequate and that products are safe. But component manufacturers in some other countries such as the United States, West Germany and France are already having to cope with product liability problems and their insurance premiums are rising accordingly.

Who protects?

If a customer has a complaint to make about a product he buys, where should he go? We have heard talk about weights and measures authorities; consumer protection officers; trading standards officers . . . what is the difference between them?

None at all. Local authorities call people with the same jobs by a variety of names. The weights and measures departments are ancient in origin and some authorities prefer to retain that traditional brand. Consumer protection is a name preferred by some because of its helpful sound. Trading standards officers tend to be the latest in the field. In practice, though, customers may go to any and the results will depend upon the energy and initiative of the organisation and of its officers, not upon their titles. A protection officer by any other name will press as hard.

Customer rights

Finally, here are answers to some of the most common questions about a customer's legal rights.

Are there any circumstances in which a customer is not entitled to return defective goods?

Broadly, only if he knows that they are defective when he buys them. Suppose for instance, that you sell 'seconds', clearly marked as defective — then the customer knows what he is buying and no doubt hopes to get a bargain.

Can you never restrict a customer's right to return goods?

In case of a private buyer (or 'consumer'), a clause in the contract of sale which seeks to exclude or restrict his rights to goods which are 'of merchantable quality' and 'reasonably suitable for the purpose supplied' is void. And in a business contract, the buyer may ask a court to declare a particular clause 'unfair and unreasonable' and hence unenforceable.

Do these rules apply where we issue a 'special offer' or when we sell at 'special discounts'?

Certainly. You can make 'special offers' or 'discounts' as you see fit. But the Trade Descriptions Act makes it an offence to show a price on sale goods as a reduction, unless they have been on sale at the higher price for a continuous period of at least 28 days during the preceding six months.

The Prices Secretary has announced plans to make it illegal to compare the price of an article you are offering for sale with a recommended retail price which is higher, unless of course the article has been sold at the higher price in the shop — this includes advertising in the media. These are expected to come into force in June 1979.

What is the effect of a notice saying 'No returns of sale goods can be accepted'?

None in law. It is also bad business practice to suggest to customers that they do not have the right to return defective goods.

Can a customer exercise his rights whenever he wishes? Or is there some time limit in law?

The 'period of limitation' in a contract for the sale of goods is 6 years. This runs normally from the date of purchase but it may sometimes be argued that the customer has six years from the date when he knew or ought to have known of the defect. There is no 'legal six-year guarantee' — but if the customer can show that the goods were defective at the time when he bought them, then he has six years within which to return them.

If goods are defective, are we entitled to offer the customer a credit note or is he entitled to the return of his money?

The customer is free to say: 'I want my money back . . . once bitten twice shy — I'll not deal with you again'. Equally, there is nothing to prevent you from attempting to induce your customer to accept a credit note. Once he has done so, there is then a new contract 'of accord and satisfaction' and he has lost his right to demand the return of his cash, even if he later regrets his new bargain.

When is my customer entitled to the return of a deposit?

If the deal goes off through your fault. If the customer puts money down on goods in stock or as a 'consideration' for your getting in goods to his order, then you are entitled to keep his deposit if he fails to pay the balance for the goods, when they are ready for him. You are not even bound to give him credit for the sum he paid. He has lost the 'consideration' which he gave to you for the option on the goods. On the other hand, if you cannot or will not comply with your side of the contract — perhaps because you are unable to get in goods of the required quality or description — then the customer is entitled to his money back, in full. Further, if he has lost a sale because of your failure to supply him, he can sue you for damages.

If a customer decides that he does not like goods that he has bought, has he any right to return them? In those circumstances, are we bound to give him a credit note?

You have complied with the contract? You have supplied goods in accordance with your agreement? The goods are neither defective nor unfit for the purpose supplied? Then the law will not require you to accept their return. You may decide to do so, to preserve customer goodwill. In that case, it is up to you whether you return the customer's money, or give him a credit note. The law would not force you to do either.

Are we entitled to refuse to sell goods on show, perhaps because we do not wish to destroy a carefully designed window display?

Yes. You are not bound to sell goods to any individual or

at all. You may keep goods in display or under the counter. Provided that you do not discriminate against customers on grounds of sex or race, you may serve or refuse to serve any group or category of people. The law will not force you to stay in business.

Is a customer never entitled to require us to sell goods at the price marked?
In civil law, never. He cannot successfully sue you because you have erroneously marked goods at a price lower than that at which you are prepared to sell them. However, you may be prosecuted for a criminal offence. The Trade Descriptions Act bans sellers from marking goods at a price lower than that at which they are prepared to sell them. So you should honour your error if you can, or otherwise recognise that if the customer reports you to the Trading Standards Authorities, you may be successfully prosecuted.

Is a customer entitled to refuse to accept goods because they were bought for him by someone who had no authority to do so?
The rules here are exactly the same as those which apply to orders placed by your employees on your behalf. The buyer is bound by the deal if the person who made it on his behalf had either his 'actual' or his 'apparent' (or 'ostensible') authority to act on his behalf. If he 'held out' the person concerned as having his authority to buy on his behalf, then he cannot afterwards crawl out of the bargain.
On the other hand, if you knew or reasonably should have known that the person concerned would be unlikely to have the authority to buy the goods on behalf of his 'principal', then you took a chance . . . you sold the goods at your own risk . . . and the principal will be entitled to renounce the bargain.
When a wife buys on behalf of her husband, she does not necessarily have his implied authority to place the order — although she may 'pledge his credit for necessities'. Care is also essential when accepting orders by children on behalf of their parents.

Part Nine
APPENDICES

Appendix 1

Introduction

This book is written for business and professional people who have to cope with the emanations of Parliament and of the courts. So I have kept it as readable as possible and have eliminated footnotes and case references.

However, I venture to hope that my lawyer-colleagues or perhaps the students they instruct may find this book helpful. And in case they wish to track down the streams of authority to their source, Appendix 2 consists of the appropriate references to all cases quoted.

Next: I have included (in date order) those statutes to which readers and their advisers will be most likely to turn, for reference and for guidance. No statute contains an alphabetical index, though. The 'Arrangement of Sections' at the start provides chapter headings; and the 'Interpretation' sections are sometimes a useful guide. But in this book, the index also covers the statutes in the Appendices.

Then come summaries of the product liability recommendations of the English and Welsh and of the Scottish Law Commissions (respectively) and of the Royal Commission on Civil Liability (the Pearson Committee) — for which I am indebted to Mr William Sandover, LLB. These are followed by the appropriate extracts from the EEC Directive and the Council of Europe 'Strasbourg Convention' on product liability. In future editions of this work, these will no doubt be amended — meanwhile, they provide a guide to current thought on future change — for which our business and professional world must prepare. That preparation must include consideration of the current situation in the USA and in other countries which have introduced the concept of strict liability into their laws.

*　　*　　*

This book is concerned with UK law. So all references in the text are to UK decided cases. If you need details of foreign law, consult a lawyer who is expert in it. Remember, too, that one country may have many legal jurisdictions. The USA (to whose Harvard Postgraduate Law School I shall always be indebted for a year of profound educational enjoyment and interest) has one jurisdiction for each state; one for the District of Columbia; and one overall Federal jurisdiction.

For readers or their legal advisers seeking further details of overseas cases in the product liability sphere I recommend: *Product Liability* by Miller and Lovell (published by Butterworths of London). There they will find that product liability problems have been litigated abroad far more than they have in Britain, with varied and often fascinating results. Unfortunately (or otherwise, depending on the case, the decision and your particular viewpoint), the rulings of overseas judges have at the most a persuasive value in our courts. But if you operate in jurisdictions where those rulings have the weight of binding precedent behind them, then by all means consult them. Meanwhile, the avoidance of confusion and the need to keep this volume to a reasonable size, combined with my modest recognition that the wisdom of our own judges is enough to surpass the understanding of one lawyer, have encouraged me to confine illustrations to the legal results of UK disasters or the disastrous results of UK decisions.

Appendix 2

Index of cases

Appendix 3

The Sale of Goods Act, 1893 (as amended)

Sections 11-15, 55 and 62 of this Act have been amended by The Supply of Goods (Implied Terms) Act, 1973, *and* The Unfair Contract Terms Act, 1977. *Cross-references are given in the relevant place to the amending or repealing sections of these Acts, which are reproduced in full in Appendices 4 and 5.*

PART I
FORMATION OF THE CONTRACT

Contract of Sale

1.—(1) A contract of sale of goods is a contract whereby the seller transfers or agrees to transfer the property in goods to the buyer for a money consideration, called the price. There may be a contract of sale between one part owner and another.

(2) A contract of sale may be absolute or conditional.

(3) Where under a contract of sale the property in the goods is transferred from the seller to the buyer the contract is called a sale; but where the transfer of the property in the goods is to take place at a future time or subject to some condition thereafter to be fulfilled the contract is called an agreement to sell.

(4) An agreement to sell becomes a sale when the time elapses or the conditions are fulfilled subject to which the property in the goods is to be transferred.

2. Capacity to buy and sell is regulated by the general law concerning capacity to contract, and to transfer and acquire property:

Provided that where necessaries are sold and delivered to an infant, minor, or to a person who by reason of mental incapacity or drunkenness is incompetent to contract, he must pay a reasonable price therefor.

Necessaries in this section mean goods suitable to the condition in life of such infant or minor or other person, and to his actual requirements at the time of the sale and delivery.

Formalities of the Contract

3. Subject to the provisions of this Act and of any statute in that behalf, a contract of sale may be made in writing (either with or without seal), or by word of mouth, or partly in writing and partly by word of mouth, or may be implied from the conduct of the parties.

Provided that nothing in this section shall affect the law relating to corporation.

Provided that nothing in this section shall affect the law relating to corporations.

4.—(1) A contract for the sale of any goods of the value of ten pounds or upwards shall not be enforceable by action unless the buyer shall accept part of the goods so sold, and actually receive the same, or give something in earnest to bind the contract, or in part payment, or unless some note or memorandum in writing of the contract be made and signed by the party to be charged or his agent in that behalf.

(2) The provisions of this section apply to every such contract, notwithstanding that the goods may be intended to be delivered at some future time, or may not at the time of such contract be actually made, procured, or provided, or fit or ready for delivery, or some act may be requisite for the making or completing thereof, or rendering the same fit for delivery.

(3) There is an acceptance of goods within the meaning of this section when the buyer does any act in relation to the goods which recognizes a pre-existing contract of sale whether there be an acceptance in performance of the contract or not.

(4) The provisions of this section do not apply to Scotland.

Subject Matter of Contract

5.—(1) The goods which form the subject of a contract of sale may be either existing goods, owned or possessed by the seller, or goods to be manufactured or acquired by the seller after the making of the contract of sale, in this Act called 'future goods'.

(2) There may be a contract for the sale of goods, the acquisition of which by the seller depends upon a contingency which may or may not happen.

(3) Where by a contract of sale the seller purports to effect a present sale of future goods, the contract operates as an agreement to sell the goods.

6. Where there is a contract for the sale of specific goods, and the goods without the knowledge of the seller have perished at the time when the contract is made, the contract is void.

7. Where there is an agreement to sell specific goods, and subsequently the goods, without any fault on the part of the seller or buyer, perish before the risk passes to the buyer, the agreement is thereby avoided.

The Price

8.—(1) The price in a contract of sale may be fixed by the contract, or may be left to be fixed in manner thereby agreed, or may be determined by the course of dealing between the parties.

(2) Where the price is not determined in accordance with the foregoing provisions the buyer must pay a reasonable price. What is a reasonable price is a question of fact dependent on the circumstances of each particular case.

9.—(1) Where there is an agreement to sell goods on the terms that the price is to be fixed by the valuation of a third party, and such third party cannot or does not make such valuation, the agreement is avoided; provided that if the goods or any part thereof have been delivered to and appropriated by the buyer he must pay a reasonable price therefor.

(2) Where such third party is prevented from making the valuation by the fault of the seller or buyer, the party not in fault may maintain an action for damages against the party in fault.

Conditions and Warranties

10.—(1) Unless a different intention appears from the terms of the contract stipulations as to time of payment are not deemed to be of the essence of a contract of sale. Whether any other stipulation as to time is of the essence of the contract or not depends on the terms of the contract.

(2) In a contract of sale 'month' means prima facie calendar month.

* 11.—(1) In England or Ireland—

  (a) Where a contract of sale is subject to any condition to be fulfilled by the seller, the buyer may waive the condition, or may elect to treat the breach of such condition as a breach of warranty, and not as a ground for treating the contract as repudiated:

  (b) Whether a stipulation in a contract of sale is a condition, the breach of which may give rise to a right to treat the contract as repudiated, or a warranty, the breach of which may give rise to a claim for damages but not to a right to reject the goods and treat the contract as repudiated, depends in each case on the construction of the contract. A stipulation may be a condition, though called a warranty in the contract:

  (c) Where a contract of sale is not severable, and the buyer has accepted the goods, or part thereof, or where the contract is for specific goods, the property in which has passed to the buyer, the breach of any condition to be fulfilled by the seller can only be treated as a breach of warranty, and not as a ground for rejecting the goods and treating the contract as repudiated, unless there be a term of the contract, express or implied, to that effect.

*See SG(IT)A, Section 14, page 275

(2) In Scotland, failure by the seller to perform any material part of a contract of sale is a breach of contract, which entitles the buyer either within a reasonable time after delivery to reject the goods and treat the contract as repudiated, or to retain the goods and treat the failure to perform such material part as a breach which may give rise to a claim for compensation or damages.

(3) Nothing in this section shall affect the case of any condition or warranty, fulfilment of which is excused by law by reason of impossibility or otherwise.

*12. In a contract of sale, unless the circumstances of the contract are such as to show a different intention, there is—

(1) An implied condition on the part of the seller that in the case of a sale he has a right to sell the goods, and that in the case of an agreement to sell he will have a right to sell the goods at the time when the property is to pass:

(2) An implied warranty that the buyer shall have and enjoy quiet possession of the goods:

(3) An implied warranty that the goods shall be free from any charge or encumbrance in favour of any third party, not declared or known to the buyer before or at the time when the contract is made.

* 13. Where there is a contract for the sale of goods by description, there is an implied condition that the goods shall correspond with the description; and if the sale be by sample, as well as by description, it is not sufficient that the bulk of the goods corresponds with the sample if the goods do not also correspond with the description..

*14. Subject to the provisions of this Act and of any statute in that behalf, there is no implied warranty or condition as to the quality or fitness for any particular purpose of goods supplied under a contract of sale, except as follows:

(1) Where the buyer, expressly or by implication, makes known to the seller the particular purpose for which the goods are required, so as to show that the buyer relies on the seller's skill or judgment, and the goods are of a description which it is in the course of the seller's business to supply (whether he be the manufacturer or not), there is an implied condition that the goods shall be reasonably fit for such purpose, provided that in the case of a contract for the sale of a specified article under its patent or other trade name, there is no implied condition as to its fitness for any particular purpose:

(2) Where goods are bought by description from a seller who deals in goods of that description (whether he be the manufacturer or not), there is an implied condition that the goods shall be of merchantable quality; provided that if the buyer has examined the goods, there shall be no implied condition as regards defects which such examination ought to have revealed:

(3) An implied warranty or condition as to quality or fitness for a particular purpose may be annexed by the usage of trade:

(4) An express warranty or condition does not negative a warranty or condition implied by this Act unless inconsistent therewith.

*See SG(IT)A, Sections 1-4, pages 265-9.

Sale by Sample

* 15.—(1) A contract of sale is a contract for sale by sample where there is a term in the contract, express or implied, to that effect.

(2) In the case of a contract for sale by sample:

    (*a*) There is an implied condition that the bulk shall correspond with the sample in quality:

    (*b*) There is an implied condition that the buyer shall have a reasonable opportunity of comparing the bulk with the sample:

    (*c*) There is an implied condition that the goods shall be free from any defect, rendering them unmerchantable, which would not be apparent on reasonable examination of the sample.

PART II

EFFECTS OF THE CONTRACT

Transfer of Property as between Seller and Buyer

16. Where there is a contract for the sale of unascertained goods no property in the goods is transferred to the buyer unless and until the goods are ascertained.

17.—(1) Where there is a contract for the sale of specific or ascertained goods the property in them is transferred to the buyer at such time as the parties to the contract intend it to be transferred.

(2) For the purpose of ascertaining the intention of the parties regard shall be had to the terms of the contract, the conduct of the parties, and the circumstances of the case.

18. Unless a different intention appears, the following are rules for ascertaining the intention of the parties as to the time at which the property in the goods is to pass to the buyer.

Rule 1.—Where there is an unconditional contract for the sale of specific goods, in a deliverable state, the property in the goods passes to the buyer when the contract is made, and it is immaterial whether the time of payment or the time of delivery, or both, be postponed.

Rule 2.—Where there is a contract for the sale of specific goods and the seller is bound to do something to the goods, for the purpose of putting them into a deliverable state, the property does not pass until such thing be done, and the buyer has notice thereof.

Rule 3.—Where there is a contract for the sale of specific goods in a deliverable state, but the seller is bound to weigh, measure, test, or do some other act or thing with reference to the goods for the purpose of ascertaining the price, the property does not pass until such act or thing be done, and the buyer has notice thereof.

Rule 4.—When goods are delivered to the buyer on approval or 'on sale or return' or other similar terms the property therein passes to the buyer:—

    (*a*) When he signifies his approval or acceptance to the seller or does any other act adopting the transaction:

*See UCTA, Section 6, page 283.

(*b*) If he does not signify his approval or acceptance to the seller but retains the goods without giving notice of rejection, then, if a time has been fixed for the return of the goods, on the expiration of such time, and, if no time has been fixed, on the expiration of a reasonable time. What is a reasonable time is a question of fact.

Rule 5.—(1) Where there is a contract for the sale of unascertained or future goods by description, and goods of that description and in a deliverable state are unconditionally appropriated to the contract, either by the seller with the assent of the buyer, or by the buyer with the assent of the seller, the property in the goods thereupon passes to the buyer. Such assent may be express or implied, and may be given either before or after the appropriation is made.

(2) Where, in pursuance of the contract, the seller delivers the goods to the buyer or to a carrier or other bailee or custodier (whether named by the buyer or not) for the purpose of transmission to the buyer, and does not reserve the right of disposal, he is deemed to have unconditionally appropriated the goods to the contract.

19.—(1) Where there is a contract for the sale of specific goods or where goods are subsequently appropriated to the contract, the seller may, by the terms of the contract or appropriation, reserve the right of disposal of the goods until certain conditions are fulfilled. In such case, notwithstanding the delivery of the goods to the buyer, or to a carrier or other bailee or custodier for the purpose of transmission to the buyer, the property in the goods does not pass to the buyer until the conditions imposed by the seller are fulfilled.

(2) Where goods are shipped, and by the bill of lading the goods are deliverable to the order of the seller or his agent, the seller is prima facie demmed to reserve the right of disposal.

(3) Where the seller of goods draws on the buyer for the price, and transmits the bill of exchange and bill of lading to the buyer together to secure acceptance or payment of the bill of exchange, the buyer is bound to return the bill of lading if he does not honour the bill of exchange, and if he wrongfully retains the bill of lading the property in the goods does not pass to him.

20. Unless otherwise agreed, the goods remain at the seller's risk until the property therein is transferred to the buyer, but when the property therein is transferred to the buyer, the goods are at the buyer's risk whether delivery has been made or not.

Provided that where delivery has been delayed through the fault of either buyer or seller the goods are at the risk of the party in fault as regards any loss which might not have occurred but for such fault.

Provided also that nothing in this section shall affect the duties or liabilities of either seller or buyer as a bailee or custodier of the goods of the other party.

Transfer of Title

21.—(1) Subject to the provisions of this Act, where goods are sold by a person who is not the owner thereof, and who does not sell them under the authority or with the consent of the owner, the buyer acquires no better title to the goods than the seller had, unless the owner of the goods is by his conduct precluded from denying the seller's authority to sell.

(2) Provided also that nothing in this Act shall affect:

(a) The provisions of the Factors Acts, or any enactment enabling the apparent owner of goods to dispose of them as if he were the true owner thereof;

(b) The validity of any contract of sale under any special common law or statutory power of sale or under the order of a court of competent jurisdiction.

22.—(1) Where goods are sold in market overt, according to the usage of the market, the buyer acquires a good title to the goods, provided he buys them in good faith and without notice of any defect or want of title on the part of the seller.

(2) Nothing in this section shall affect the law relating to the sale of horses.

(3) The provisions of this section do not apply to Scotland.

23. When the seller of goods has a voidable title thereto, but his title has not been avoided at the time of the sale, the buyer acquires a good title to the goods, provided he buys them in good faith and without notice of the seller's defect of title.

24.—(1) Where goods have been stolen and the offender is prosecuted to conviction, the property in the goods so stolen revests in the person who was the owner of the goods, or his personal representative, notwithstanding any intermediate dealing with them, whether by sale in market overt or otherwise.

(2) Notwithstanding any enactment to the contrary, where goods have been obtained by fraud or other wrongful means not amounting to larcency, the property in such goods shall not revest in the person who was the owner of the goods, or his personal representative, by reason only of the conviction of the offender.

(3) The provisions of this section do not apply to Scotland.

25.—(1) Where a person having sold goods continues or is in possession of the goods, or of the documents of title to the goods, the delivery or transfer by that person, or by a mercantile agent acting for him, of the goods or documents of title under any sale, pledge, or other disposition thereof, to any person receiving the same in good faith and without notice of the previous sale, shall have the same effect as if the person making the delivery or transfer were expressly authorized by the owner of the goods to make the same.

(2) Where a person having bought or agreed to buy goods obtains, with the consent of the seller, possession of the goods or the documents of title to the goods, the delivery or transfer by that person, or by a mercantile agent acting for him, of the goods or documents of title, under any sale, pledge, or other disposition thereof, to any person receiving the same in good faith and without notice of any lien or other right of the original seller in respect of the goods, shall have the same effect as if the person making the delivery or transfer were a mercantile agent in possession of the goods or documents of title with the consent of the owner.

(3) In this section the term 'mercantile agent' has the same meaning as in the Factors Acts.

26.—(1) A writ of *fieri facias* or other writ of execution against goods shall bind the property in the goods of the execution debtor as from the time when the writ is delivered to the sheriff to be executed; and, for the better manifestation of such time, it shall be the duty of the sheriff, without fee, upon the receipt of any such writ to endorse upon the back thereof the hour, day, month, and year when he received the same.

Provided that no such writ shall prejudice the title to such goods acquired by any person in good faith and for valuable consideration, unless such person had at the time when he acquired his title notice that such writ or any other writ by virtue of which the goods of the execution debtor might be seized or attached had been delivered to and remained unexecuted in the hands of the sheriff.

(2) In this section the term 'sheriff' includes any officer charged with the enforcement of a writ of execution.

(3) The provisions of this section do not apply to Scotland.

PART III
PERFORMANCE OF THE CONTRACT

27. It is the duty of the seller to deliver the goods, and of the buyer to accept and pay for them, in accordance with the terms of the contract of sale.

28. Unless otherwise agreed, delivery of the goods and payment of the price are concurrent conditions, that is to say, the seller must be ready and willing to give possession of the goods to the buyer in exchange for the price and the buyer must be ready and willing to pay the price in exchange for possession of the goods.

29.—(1) Whether it is for the buyer to take possession of the goods or for the seller to send them to the buyer is a question depending in each case on the contract, express or implied, between the parties. Apart from any such contract, express or implied, the place of delivery is the seller's place of business, if he have one, and if not, his residence: Provided that, if the contract be for the sale of specific goods, which to the knowledge of the parties when the contract is made are in some other place, then that place is the place of delivery.

(2) Where under the contract of sale the seller is bound to send the goods to the buyer, but no time for sending them is fixed, the seller is bound to send them within a reasonable time.

(3) Where the goods at the time of sale are in the possession of a third person, there is no delivery by seller to buyer unless and until such third person acknowledges to the buyer that he holds the goods on his behalf; provided that nothing in this section shall affect the operation of the issue or transfer of any document of title to goods.

(4) Demand or tender of delivery may be treated as ineffectual unless made at a reasonable hour. What is a reasonable hour is a question of fact.

(5) Unless otherwise agreed, the expenses of and incidental to putting the goods into a deliverable state must be borne by the seller.

30.—(1) Where the seller delivers to the buyer a quantity of goods less than he contracted to sell, the buyer may reject them, but if the buyer accepts the goods so delivered he must pay for them at the contract rate.

(2) Where the seller delivers to the buyer a quantity of goods larger than he contracted to sell, the buyer may accept the goods included in the contract and reject the rest, or he may reject the whole. If the buyer accepts the whole of the goods so delivered he must pay for them at the contract rate.

(3) Where the seller delivers to the buyer the goods he contracted to sell mixed with goods of a different description not included in the contract, the buyer may accept the goods which are in accordance with the contract and reject the rest, or he may reject the whole.

(4) The provisions of this section are subject to any usage of trade, special agreement, or course of dealing between the parties.

31.—(1) Unless otherwise agreed, the buyer of goods is not bound to accept delivery thereof by instalments.

(2) Where there is a contract for the sale of goods to be delivered by stated instalments, which are to be separately paid for, and the seller makes defective deliveries in respect of one or more instalments, or the buyer neglects or refuses to take delivery of or pay for one or more instalments, it is a question in each case depending on the terms of the contract and the circumstances of the case, whether the breach of contract is a repudiation of the whole contract or whether it is a severable breach giving rise to a claim for compensation but not to a right to treat the whole contract as repudiated.

32.—(1) Where, in pursuance of a contract of sale, the seller is authorised or required to send the goods to the buyer, delivery of the goods to a carrier, whether named by the buyer or not, for the purpose of transmission to the buyer is prima facie deemed to be a delivery of the goods to the buyer.

(2) Unless otherwise authorised by the buyer, the seller must make such contract with the carrier on behalf of the buyer as may be reasonable having regard to the nature of the goods and the other circumstances of the case. If the seller omit so to do, and the goods are lost or damaged in course of transit, the buyer may decline to treat the delivery to the carrier as a delivery to himself, or may hold the seller responsible in damages.

(3) Unless otherwise agreed, where goods are sent by the seller to the buyer by a route involving sea transit, under circumstances in which it is usual to insure, the seller must give such notice to the buyer as may enable him to insure them during their sea transit, and, if the seller fails to do so, the goods shall be deemed to be at his risk during such sea transit.

33. Where the seller of goods agrees to deliver them at his own risk at a place other than that where they are when sold, the buyer must, nevertheless, unless otherwise agreed, take any risk of deterioration in the goods necessarily incident to the course of transit.

34.—(1) Where goods are delivered to the buyer, which he has not previously examined, he is not deemed to have accepted them unless and until he has had a reasonable opportunity of examining them for the purpose of ascertaining whether they are in conformity with the contract.

(2) Unless otherwise agreed, when the seller tenders delivery of goods to the buyer, he is bound on request, to afford the buyer a reasonable opportunity of examining the goods for the purpose of ascertaining whether they are in conformity with the contract.

35. The buyer is deemed to have accepted the goods when he intimates to the seller that he has accepted them, or when the goods have been delivered to him, and he does any act in relation to them which is inconsistent with the ownership of the seller, or when after the lapse of a reasonable time, he retains the goods without intimating to the seller that he has rejected them.

36. Unless otherwise agreed, where goods are delivered to the buyer, and he refuses to accept them having the right so to do, he is not bound to return them to the seller but it is sufficient if he intimates to the seller that he refuses to accept them.

37. When the seller is ready and willing to deliver the goods, and requests the buyer to take delivery, and the buyer does not within a reasonable time after such request take delivery of the goods, he is liable to the seller for any loss occasioned by his neglect or refusal to take delivery, and also for a reasonable charge for the care and custody of the goods: Provided that nothing in this section shall affect the rights of the seller where the neglect or refusal of the buyer to take delivery amounts to a repudiation of the contract.

PART IV

RIGHTS OF UNPAID SELLER AGAINST THE GOODS

38.—(1) The seller of goods is deemed to be an 'unpaid seller' within the meaning of this Act—

(a) When the whole of the price has not been paid or tendered;

(b) When a bill of exchange or other negotiable instrument has been received as conditional payment, and the condition on which it was received has not been fulfilled by reason of the dishonour of the instrument or otherwise.

(2) In this Part of this Act the term 'seller' includes any person who is in the position of a seller, as, for instance, an agent of the seller to whom the bill of lading has been indorsed, or a consignor or agent who has himself paid, or is directly responsible for, the price.

39.—(1) Subject to the provisions of this Act, and of any statute in that behalf, notwithstanding that the property in the goods may have passed to the buyer, the unpaid seller of goods, as such, has by implication of law:

(a) A lien on the goods or right to retain them for the price while he is in possession of them;

(b) In case of the insolvency of the buyer, a right of stopping the goods *in transitu* after he has parted with the possession of them;

(c) A right of re-sale as limited by this Act.

(2) Where the property in goods has not passed to the buyer, the unpaid

seller has, in addition to his other remedies, a right of withholding delivery similar to and co-extensive with his rights of lien and stoppage *in transitu* where the property has passed to the buyer.

40. In Scotland a seller of goods may attach the same while in his own hands or possession by arrestment or poinding; and such arrestment or poinding shall have the same operation and effect in a competition or otherwise as an arrestment or poinding by a third party.

Unpaid Seller's Lien

41.—(1) Subject to the provisions of this Act, the unpaid seller of goods who is in possession of them is entitled to retain possession of them until payment or tender of the price in the following cases, namely:

    (a) Where the goods have been sold without any stipulation as to credit;

    (b) Where the goods have been sold on credit, but the term of credit has expired;

    (c) Where the buyer becomes insolvent.

(2) The seller may exercise his right of lien notwithstanding that he is in possession of the goods as agent or bailee or custodier for the buyer.

42. Where an unpaid seller has made part delivery of the goods, he may exercise his right of lien or retention on the remainder, unless such part delivery has been made under such circumstances as to show an agreement to waive the lien or right of retention.

43.—(1) The unpaid seller of goods loses his lien or right of retention thereon:

    (a) When he delivers the goods to a carrier or other bailee or custodier for the purpose of transmission to the buyer without reserving the right of disposal of the goods;

    (b) When the buyer or his agent lawfully obtains possession of the goods;

    (c) By waiver thereof.

(2) The unpaid seller of goods, having a lien or right of retention thereon, does not lose his lien or right of retention by reason only that he has obtained judgment or decree for the price of the goods.

Stoppage 'in Transitu'

44. Subject to the provisions of this Act, when the buyer of goods becomes insolvent, the unpaid seller who has parted with the possession of the goods has the right of stopping them *in transitu*, that is to say, he may resume possession of the goods as long as they are in course of transit, and may retain them until payment or tender of the price.

45.—(1) Goods are deemed to be in course of transit from the time when they are delivered to a carrier by land or water, or other bailee or custodier for the purpose of transmission to the buyer, until the buyer, or his agent in that behalf, takes delivery of them from such carrier or other bailee or custodier.

(2) If the buyer or his agent in that behalf obtains delivery of the goods before their arrival at the appointed destination, the transit is at an end.

(3) If, after the arrival of the goods at the appointed destination, the

carrier or other bailee or custodier acknowledges to the buyer, or his agent, that he holds the goods on his behalf and continues in possession of them as bailee or custodier for the buyer, or his agent, the transit is at an end, and it is immaterial that a further destination for the goods may have been indicated by the buyer.

(4) If the goods are rejected by the buyer, and the carrier or other bailee or custodier continues in possession of them, the transit is not deemed to be at an end, even if the seller has refused to receive them back.

(5) When goods are delivered to a ship chartered by the buyer it is a question depending on the circumstances of the particular case, whether they are in the possession of the master as a carrier, or as agent to the buyer.

(6) Where the carrier or other bailee or custodier wrongfully refuses to deliver the goods to the buyer, or his agent in that behalf, the transit is deemed to be at an end.

(7) Where part delivery of the goods has been made to the buyer, or his agent in that behalf, the remainder of the goods may be stopped *in transitu*, unless such part delivery has been made under such circumstances as to show an agreement to give up possession of the whole of the goods.

46.—(1) The unpaid seller may exercise his right of stoppage *in transitu* either by taking actual possession of the goods, or by giving notice of his claim to the carrier or other bailee or custodier in whose possession the goods are. Such notice may be given either to the person in actual possession of the goods or to his principal. In the latter case the notice, to be effectual, must be given at such time and under such circumstances that the principal, by the exercise of reasonable diligence, may communicate it to his servant or agent in time to prevent a delivery to the buyer.

(2) When notice stoppage *in transitu* is given by the seller to the carrier, or other bailee or custodier in possession of the goods, he must re-deliver the goods to, or according to the directions of, the seller. The expenses of such re-delivery must be borne by the seller.

Re-sale by Buyer or Seller

47. Subject to the provisions of this Act, the unpaid seller's right of lien or retention or stoppage *in transitu* is not affected by any sale, or other disposition of the goods which the buyer may have made, unless the seller has assented thereto.

Provided that where a document of title to goods has been lawfully transferred to any person as buyer or owner of the goods, and that person transfers the document to a person who takes the document in good faith and for valuable consideration, then, if such last-mentioned transfer was by way of sale the unpaid seller's right of lien or retention or stoopage *in transitu* is defeated, and if such last-mentioned transfer was made by way of pledge or other disposition for value, the unpaid seller's right of lien or retention or stoppage *in transitu* can only be exercised subject to the rights of the transferee.

48.—(1) Subject to the provisions of this section, a contract of sale is not rescinded by the mere exercise by an unpaid seller of his right of lien or retention or stoppage *in transitu*.

(2) Where an unpaid seller who has exercised his right of lien or retention or stoppage *in transitu* re-sells the goods, the buyer acquires a good title thereto as against the original buyer.

(3) Where the goods are of a perishable nature, or where the unpaid seller gives notice to the buyer of his intention to re-sell, and the buyer does not within a reasonable time pay or tender the price, the unpaid seller may re-sell the goods and recover from the original buyer damages for any loss occasioned by his breach of contract.

(4) Where the seller expressly reserves the right of re-sale in case the buyer should make default, and on the buyer making default, re-sells the goods, the original contract of sale is thereby rescinded, but without prejudice to any claim the seller may have for damages.

PART V
ACTIONS FOR BREACH OF THE CONTRACT
Remedies of the Seller

49.—(1) Where, under a contract of sale, the property in the goods has passed to the buyer, and the buyer wrongfully neglects or refuses to pay for the goods according to the terms of the contract, the seller may maintain an action against him for the price of the goods.

(2) Where, under a contract of sale, the price is payable on a day certain irrespective of delivery, and the buyer wrongfully neglects or refuses to pay such price, the seller may maintain an action for the price, although the property in the goods has not passed, and the goods have not been appropriated to the contract.

(3) Nothing in this section shall prejudice the right of the seller in Scotland to recover interest on the price from the date of tender of the goods, or from the date on which the price was payable, as the case may be.

50.—(1) Where the buyer wrongfully neglects or refuses to accept and pay for the goods, the seller may maintain an action against him for damages for non-acceptance.

(2) The measure of damages is the estimated loss directly and naturally resulting, in the ordinary course of events, from the buyer's breach of contract.

(3) Where there is an available market for the goods in question the measure of damages is prima facie to be ascertained by the difference between the contract price and the market or current price at the time or times when the goods ought to have been accepted or, if no time was fixed for acceptance, then at the time of the refusal to accept.

Remedies of the Buyer

51.—(1) Where the seller wrongfully neglects or refuses to deliver the goods to the buyer, the buyer may maintain an action against the seller for damages for non-delivery.

(2) The measure of damages is the estimated loss directly and naturally

resulting, in the ordinary course of events, from the seller's breach of contract.

(3) Where there is an available market for the goods in question the measure of damages is prima facie to be ascertained by the difference between the contract price and the market or current price of the goods at the time or times when they ought to have been delivered, or, if no time was fixed, then at the time of the refusal to deliver.

52. In any action for breach of contract to deliver specific or ascertained goods the Court may, if it thinks fit, on the application of the Plaintiff, by its judgment or decree direct that the contract shall be performed specifically, without giving the Defendant the option of retaining the goods on payment of damages. The judgment or decree may be unconditional, or upon such terms and conditions as to damages, payment of the price, and otherwise, as to the Court may seem just, and the application by the Plaintiff may be made at any time before judgment or decree.

The provisions of this section shall be deemed to be supplementary to, and not in derogation of, the right of specific implement in Scotland.

53.—(1) Where there is a breach of warranty by the seller, or where the buyer elects, or is compelled, to treat any breach of a condition on the part of the seller as a breach of warranty, the buyer is not by reason only of such breach of warranty entitled to reject the goods; but he may

(a) set up against the seller the breach of warranty in diminution or extinction of the price; or

(b) maintain an action against the seller for damages for the breach of warranty.

(2) The measure of damages for breach of warranty is the estimated loss directly and naturally resulting, in the ordinary course of events, from the breach of warranty.

(3) In the case of breach of warranty of quality such loss is prima facie the difference between the value of the goods at the time of delivery to the buyer and the value they would have had if they had answered to the warranty.

(4) The fact that the buyer has set up the breach of warranty in diminution or extinction of the price does not prevent him from maintaining an action for the same breach of warranty if he has suffered further damage.

(5) Nothing in this section shall prejudice or affect the buyer's right of rejection in Scotland as declared by this Act.

54. Nothing in this Act shall affect the right of the buyer or the seller to recover interest or special damages in any case where by law interest or special damages may be recoverable, or to recover money paid where the consideration for the payment of it has failed.

PART VI
SUPPLEMENTARY

* 55. Where any right, duty, or liability would arise under a contract of sale by implication of law, it may be negatived or varied by express agreement

*See SG(IT)A, Section 5, page 269, and UCTA, Schedule 3 page 300.

or by the course of dealing between the parties, or by usage, if the usage be such as to bind both parties to the contract.

56. Where, by this Act, any reference is made to a reasonable time the question what is a reasonable time is a question of fact.

57. Where any right, duty, or liability is declared by this Act, it may, unless otherwise by this Act provided, be enforced by action.

58. In the case of a sale by auction:

(1) Where goods are put up for sale by auction in lots, each lot is prima facie deemed to be the subject of a separate contract of sale:

(2) A sale by auction is complete when the auctioneer announces its completion by the fall of the hammer, or in other customary manner. Until such announcement is made any bidder may retract his bid:

(3) Where a sale by auction is not notified to the subject to a right to bid on behalf of the seller, it shall not be lawful for the seller to bid himself or to employ any person to bid at such sale, or for the auctioneer knowingly to take any bid from the seller or any such person: Any sale contravening this rule may be treated as fraudulent by the buyer:

(4) A sale by auction may be notified to be subject to a reserve or upset price, and a right to bid may also be reserved expressly by or on behalf of the seller.

Where a right to bid is expressly reserved, but not otherwise, the seller, or any one person on his behalf, may bid at the auction.

59. In Scotland where a buyer has elected to accept goods which he might have rejected, and to treat a breach of contract as only giving rise to a claim for damages, he may, in an action by the seller for the price, be required, in the discretion of the Court before which the action depends, to consign or pay into court the price of the goods, or part thereof, or to give other reasonable security fur the due payment thereof.

60. The enactments mentioned in the schedule to this Act are hereby repealed as from the commencement of this Act to the extent in that schedule mentioned.

Provided that such repeal shall not affect anything done or suffered, or any right, title, or interest acquired or accrued before the commencement of this Act, or any legal proceeding or remedy in respect of any such thing, right, title or interest.

61.—(1) The rules in bankruptcy relating to contracts of sale shall continue to apply thereto, notwithstanding anything in this Act contained.

(2) The rules of the common law, including the law merchant, save in so far as they are inconsistent with the express provisions of this Act, and in particular the rules relating to the law of principal and agent and the effect of fraud, misrepresentation, duress or coercion, mistake, or other invalidating cause, shall continue to apply to contracts for the sale of goods.

(3) Nothing in this Act or in any repeal effected thereby shall affect the enactments relating to bills of sale, or any enactment relating to the sale of goods which is not expressly repealed by this Act.

(4) The provisions of this Act relating to contracts of sale do not apply to

any transaction in the form of a contract of sale which is intended to operate by way of mortgage, pledge, charge, or other security.

(5) Nothing in this Act shall prejudice or affect the landlord's right of hypothec or sequestration for rent in Scotland.

* 62.—(1) In this Act, unless the context or subject matter otherwise requires:

'Action' includes counter-claim and set off, and in Scotland condescendence and claim and compensation:

'Bailee' in Scotland includes custodier:

'Buyer' means a person who buys or agrees to buy goods:

'Contract of sale' includes an agreement to sell as well as a sale:

'Defendant' includes in Scotland defender, respondent, and claimant in a multiplepoinding:

'Delivery' means voluntary transfer of possession from one person to another:

'Document of title to goods' has the same meaning as it has in Factors Acts:

'Factors Acts' mean the Factors Act, 1889, the Factors (Scotland) Act, 1890, and any enactment amending or substituted for the same:

'Fault' means wrongful act or default:

'Future goods' means goods to be manufactured or acquired by the seller after the making of the contract of sale:

'Goods' include all chattels personal other than things in action and money, and in Scotland all corporeal moveables except money. The term includes emblements, industrial growing crops, and things attached to or forming part of the land which are agreed to be severed before sale or under the contract of sale:

'Lien' in Scotland includes right of retention:

'Plaintiff' includes pursuer, complainer, claimant in a multiplepoinding and defendant or defender counter-claiming:

'Property' means the general property in goods, and not merely a special property:

'Quality of goods' includes their state or condition.

'Sale' includes a bargain and sale as well as a sale and delivery:

'Seller' means a person who sells or agrees to sell goods:

'Specific goods' means goods identified and agreed upon at the time a contract of sale is made:

'Warranty' as regards England and Ireland means an agreement with reference to goods which are the subject of a contract of sale, but collateral to the main purpose of such contract, the breach of which gives rise to a claim for damages, but not to a right to reject the goods and treat the contract as repudiated.

As regards Scotland a breach of warranty shall be deemed to be a failure to perform a material part of the contract.

(2) A thing is deemed to be done 'in good faith' within the meaning of this Act when it is in fact done honestly, whether it be done negligently or not.

(3) A person is deemed to be insolvent within the meaning of this Act who either has ceased to pay his debts in the ordinary course of business, or

*See SG(IT)A, Section 15, page 275, and Section 7, page 270.

cannot pay his debts as they become due, whether he has committed an act of bankruptcy or not, and whether he has become a notour bankrupt or not.

(4) Goods are in a 'deliverable state' within the meaning of this Act when they are in such a state that the buyer would under the contract be bound to take delivery of them.

63. This Act shall come into operation on the first day of January one thousand eight hundred and ninety-four.

64. This Act may be cited as the Sale of Goods Act, 1893.

Appendix 4

The Supply of Goods (Implied Terms) Act, 1973 (as amended)

Sections 4-7 and 12-15 of this Act have been amended or repealed by The Unfair Contract Terms Act, 1977. *Cross-references to the amending or repealing sections of the latter Act, which is reproduced in full in Appendix 5, are given here in the relevant place.*

ARRANGEMENT OF SECTIONS

Sale of goods

Hire-purchase agreements

Trading stamps

Miscellaneous

Supply of Goods (Implied Terms) Act 1973

1973 CHAPTER 13

An Act to amend the law with respect to the terms to be implied in contracts of sale of goods and hire-purchase agreements and on the exchange of goods for trading stamps, and with respect to the terms of conditional sale agreements; and for connected purposes.

[18th April 1973]

BE IT ENACTED by the Queen's most Excellent Majesty, by and with the advice and consent of the Lords Spiritual and Temporal, and Commons, in this present Parliament assembled, and by the authority of the same, as follows:—

Sale of Goods

1. For section 12 of the principal Act (implied conditions as to title, and implied warranties as to quiet possession and freedom from encumbrances) there shall be substituted the following section:—

Implied undertakings as to title, etc.

" Implied undertakings as to title, etc.

12.—(1) In every contract of sale, other than one to which subsection (2) of this section applies, there is—

> (*a*) an implied condition on the part of the seller that in the case of a sale, he has a right to sell the goods, and in the case of an agreement to sell, he will have a right to sell the goods at the time when the property is to pass; and

> (*b*) an implied warranty that the goods are free, and will remain free until the time when the property is to pass, from any charge or encumbrance not disclosed or known to

the buyer before the contract is made and that the buyer will enjoy quiet possession of the goods except so far as it may be disturbed by the owner or other person entitled to the benefit of any charge or encumbrance so disclosed or known.

(2) In a contract of sale, in the case of which there appears from the contract or is to be inferred from the circumstances of the contract an intention that the seller should transfer only such title as he or a third person may have, there is—

> (a) an implied warranty that all charges or encumbrances known to the seller and not known to the buyer have been disclosed to the buyer before the contract is made ; and

> (b) an implied warranty that neither—
>> (i) the seller ; nor
>> (ii) in a case where the parties to the contract intend that the seller should transfer only such title as a third person may have, that person ; nor
>> (iii) anyone claiming through or under the seller or that third person otherwise than under a charge or encumbrance disclosed or known to the buyer before the contract is made ;
>
> will disturb the buyer's quiet possession of the goods."

Sale by description.

2. Section 13 of the principal Act (sale by description) shall be renumbered as subsection (1) of that section, and at the end there shall be inserted the following subsection : —

> " (2) A sale of goods shall not be prevented from being a sale by description by reason only that, being exposed for sale or hire, they are selected by the buyer."

Implied undertakings as to quality or fitness.

3. For section 14 of the principal Act (implied undertakings as to quality or fitness) there shall be substituted the following section : —

" Implied undertakings as to quality or fitness.

14.—(1) Except as provided by this section, and section 15 of this Act and subject to the provisions of any other enactment, there is no implied condition or warranty as to the quality or fitness for any particular purpose of goods supplied under a contract or sale.

(2) Where the seller sells goods in the course of a business, there is an implied condition that the goods supplied under the contract are of merchantable quality, except that there is no such condition—

  (a) as regards defects specifically drawn to the buyer's attention before the contract is made ; or

  (b) if the buyer examines the goods before the contract is made, as regards defects which that examination ought to reveal.

(3) Where the seller sells goods in the course of a business and the buyer, expressly or by implication, makes known to the seller any particular purpose for which the goods are being bought, there is an implied condition that the goods supplied under the contract are reasonably fit for that purpose, whether or not that is a purpose for which such goods are commonly supplied, except where the circumstances show that the buyer does not rely, or that it is unreasonable for him to rely, on the seller's skill or judgment.

(4) An implied condition or warranty as to quality or fitness for a particular purpose may be annexed to a contract of sale by usage.

(5) The foregoing provisions of this section apply to a sale by a person who in the course of a business is acting as agent for another as they apply to a sale by a principal in the course of a business, except where that other is not selling in the course of a business and either the buyer knows that fact or reasonable steps are taken to bring it to the notice of the buyer before the contract is made.

(6) In the application of subsection (3) above to an agreement for the sale of goods under which the purchase price or part of it is payable by instalments any reference to the seller shall include a reference to the person by whom any antecedent negotiations are conducted ; and section 58(3) and (5) of the Hire- 1965 c. 66. Purchase Act 1965, section 54(3) and (5) of the Hire- 1965 c. 67. Purchase (Scotland) Act 1965 and section 65(3) and (5) of the Hire-Purchase Act (Northern Ireland) 1966 1966 c. 42, (meaning of antecedent negotiations and related (N.I.). expressions) shall apply in relation to this subsection as they apply in relation to each of those Acts, but as if a reference to any such agreement were included in the references in subsection (3) of each of those sections to the agreements there mentioned."

Exclusion of implied terms and conditions.

*4. For section 55 of the principal Act (exclusion of implied terms and conditions) there shall be substituted the following section:—

"Exclusion of implied terms and conditions.

55.—(1) Where any right, duty or liability would arise under a contract of sale of goods by implication of law, it may be negatived or varied by express agreement, or by the course of dealing between the parties, or by usage if the usage is such as to bind both parties to the contract, but the foregoing provision shall have effect subject to the following provisions of this section.

(2) An express condition or warranty does not negative a condition or warranty implied by this Act unless inconsistent therewith.

(3) In the case of a contract of sale of goods, any term of that or any other contract exempting from all or any of the provisions of section 12 of this Act shall be void.

(4) In the case of a contract of sale of goods, any term of that or any other contract exempting from all or any of the provisions of section 13, 14 or 15 of this Act shall be void in the case of a consumer sale and shall, in any other case, not be enforceable to the extent that it is shown that it would not be fair or reasonable to allow reliance on the term.

(5) In determining for the purposes of subsection (4) above whether or not reliance on any such term would be fair or reasonable regard shall be had to all the circumstances of the case and in particular to the following matters—

(a) the strength of the bargaining positions of the seller and buyer relative to each other, taking into account, among other things, the availability of suitable alternative products and sources of supply;

(b) whether the buyer received an inducement to agree to the term or in accepting it had an opportunity of buying the goods or suitable alternatives without it from any source of supply;

(c) whether the buyer knew or ought reasonably to have known of the existence and extent of the term (having regard, among other things, to any custom of the trade and any previous course of dealing between the parties);

(d) where the term exempts from all or any of the provisions of section 13, 14 or 15 of

*Sub-sections 3-11 repealed by UCTA.

this Act if some condition is not complied with, whether it was reasonable at the time of the contract to expect that compliance with that condition would be practicable ;

(e) whether the goods were manufactured, processed, or adapted to the special order of the buyer.

(6) Subsection (5) above shall not prevent the court from holding, in accordance with any rule of law, that a term which purports to exclude or restrict any of the provisions of section 13, 14 or 15 of this Act is not a term of the contract.

(7) In this section " consumer sale " means a sale of goods (other than a sale by auction or by competitive tender) by a seller in the course of a business where the goods—

(a) are of a type ordinarily bought for private use or consumption ; and

(b) are sold to a person who does not buy or hold himself out as buying them in the course of a business.

(8) The onus of proving that a sale falls to be treated for the purposes of this section as not being a consumer sale shall lie on the party so contending.

(9) Any reference in this section to a term exempting from all or any of the provisions of any section of this Act is a reference to a term which purports to exclude or restrict, or has the effect of excluding or restricting, the operation of all or any of the provisions of that section, or the exercise of a right conferred by any provision of that section, or any liability of the seller for breach of a condition or warranty implied by any provision of that section.

(10) It is hereby declared that any reference in this section to a term of a contract includes a reference to a term which although not contained in a contract is incorporated in the contract by another term of the contract.

(11) This section is subject to section 61(6) of this Act."

* 5.—(1) After section 55 of the principal Act there shall be inserted the following section :—   Conflict of laws.

"Conflict of laws.   55A. Where the proper law of a contract for the sale of goods would, apart from a term that it should be the law of some other country or a term

---

*Section 5(1) repealed by UCTA.

to the like effect, be the law of any part of the United Kingdom, or where any such contract contains a term which purports to substitute, or has the effect of substituting, provisions of the law of some other country for all or any of the provisions of sections 12 to 15 and 55 of this Act, those sections shall, notwithstanding that term but subject to section 61(6) of this Act, apply to the contract."

1967 c. 45.

(2) In section 1(4) of the Uniform Laws on International Sales Act 1967 (which provides that no provision of the law of any part of the United Kingdom shall be regarded as a mandatory provision for the purposes of the Uniform Law on the International Sale of Goods so as to override the choice of the parties) for the words from " no provision " to the end of the subsection there shall be substituted the words " no provision of the law of any part of the United Kingdom, except sections 12 to 15, 55 and 55A of the Sale of Goods Act 1893, shall be regarded as a mandatory provision within the meaning of that Article."

56 & 57 Vict. c. 71.

International sales.

*6. In section 61 of the principal Act (savings) there shall be inserted after subsection (5) thereof the following subsection—

" (6) Nothing in section 55 or 55A of this Act shall prevent the parties to a contract for the international sale of goods from negativing or varying any right, duty or liability which would otherwise arise by implication of law under sections 12 to 15 of this Act."

Interpretation.

*7.—(1) In section 62(1) of the principal Act (definitions) at the appropriate points in alphabetical order there shall be inserted the following definitions:

" business " includes a profession and the activities of any government department (including a department of the Government of Northern Ireland), local authority or statutory undertaker ;

" contract for the international sale of goods " means a contract of sale of goods made by parties whose places of business (or, if they have none, habitual residences) are in the territories of different States (the Channel Islands and the Isle of Man being treated for this purpose as different States from the United Kingdom) and in the case of which one of the following conditions is satisfied, that is to say—

(a) the contract involves the sale of goods which are at the time of the conclusion of the contract in the course of carriage or will be carried from the

---

*Section 6 and part of Section 7 from "contract for the international..." to beginning of Section 7(2) repealed by UCTA.

territory of one State to the territory of another ; or

    (*b*) the acts constituting the offer and acceptance have been effected in the territories of different States ; or

    (*c*) delivery of the goods is to be made in the territory of a State other than that within whose territory the acts constituting the offer and the acceptance have been effected."

(2) After section 62(1) of the principal Act there shall be inserted the following subsection : —

    " (1A) Goods of any kind are of merchantable quality within the meaning of this Act if they are as fit for the purpose or purposes for which goods of that kind are commonly bought as it is reasonable to expect having regard to any description applied to them, the price (if relevant) and all the other relevant circumstances ; and any reference in this Act to unmerchantable goods shall be construed accordingly."

Hire-purchase agreements

8.—(1) In every hire-purchase agreement, other than one to which subsection (2) below applies, there is— *[Implied terms as to title.]*

    (*a*) an implied condition on the part of the owner that he will have a right to sell the goods at the time when the property is to pass ; and

    (*b*) an implied warranty that the goods are free, and will remain free until the time when the property is to pass, from any charge or encumbrance not disclosed or known to the hirer before the agreement is made and that the hirer will enjoy quiet possession of the goods except so far as it may be disturbed by any person entitled to the benefit of any charge or encumbrance so disclosed or known.

(2) In a hire-purchase agreement, in the case of which there appears from the agreement or is to be inferred from the circumstances of the agreement an intention that the owner should transfer only such title as he or a third person may have, there is—

    (*a*) an implied warranty that all charges or encumbrances known to the owner and not known to the hirer have been disclosed to the hirer before the agreement is made ; and

    (*b*) an implied warranty that neither—

        (i) the owner ; nor

(ii) in a case where the parties to the agreement intend that any title which may be transferred shall be only such title as a third person may have, that person ; nor

(iii) anyone claiming through or under the owner or that third person otherwise than under a charge or encumbrance disclosed or known to the hirer before the agreement is made ;

will disturb the hirer's quiet possession of the goods.

Letting by description.

9.—(1) Where under a hire purchase agreement goods are let by description, there is an implied condition that the goods will correspond with the description ; and if under the agreement the goods are let by reference to a sample as well as a description, it is not sufficient that the bulk of the goods corresponds with the sample if the goods do not also correspond with the description.

(2) Goods shall not be prevented from being let by description by reason only that, being exposed for sale or hire, they are selected by the hirer.

Implied undertakings as to quality or fitness.

10.—(1) Except as provided by this section and section 11 below and subject to the provisions of any other enactment, including any enactment of the Parliament of Northern Ireland, there is no implied condition or warranty as to the quality or fitness for any particular purpose of goods let under a hire-purchase agreement.

(2) Where the owner lets goods under a hire purchase agreement in the course of a business, there is an implied condition that the goods are of merchantable quality, except that there is no such condition—

(*a*) as regards defects specifically drawn to the hirer's attention before the agreement is made ; or

(*b*) if the hirer examines the goods before the agreement is made, as regards defects which that examination ought to reveal.

(3) Where the owner lets goods under a hire purchase agreement in the course of a business and the hirer, expressly or by implication, makes known to the owner or the person by whom any antecedent negotiations are conducted, any particular purpose for which the goods are being hired, there is an implied condition that the goods supplied under the agreement are reasonably fit for that purpose, whether or not that is a purpose for which such goods are commonly supplied, except where the

circumstances show that the hirer does not rely, or that it is unreasonable for him to rely, on the skill or judgment of the owner or that person.

(4) An implied condition or warranty as to quality or fitness for a particular purpose may be annexed to a hire-purchase agreement by usage.

(5) The foregoing provisions of this section apply to a hire-purchase agreement made by a person who in the course of a business is acting as agent for the owner as they apply to an agreement made by the owner in the course of a business, except where the owner is not letting in the course of a business and either the hirer knows that fact or reasonable steps are taken to bring it to the notice of the hirer before the agreement is made.

(6) Section 58(3) and (5) of the Hire-Purchase Act 1965, section 54(3) and (5) of the Hire-Purchase (Scotland) Act 1965 and section 65(3) and (5) of the Hire-Purchase Act (Northern Ireland) 1966 (meaning of antecedent negotiations and related expressions) shall apply in relation to subsection (3) above as they apply in relation to each of those Acts. 1965 c. 66. 1965 c. 67. 1966 c. 42 (N.I.).

11. Where under a hire-purchase agreement goods are let Samples. by reference to a sample, there is an implied condition—

    (*a*) that the bulk will correspond with the sample in quality ; and

    (*b*) that the hirer will have a reasonable opportunity of comparing the bulk with the sample ; and

    (*c*) that the goods will be free from any defect, rendering them unmerchantable, which would not be apparent on reasonable examination of the sample.

* **12.**—(1) An express condition or warranty does not negative Exclusion of a condition or warranty implied by this Act unless inconsistent implied therewith. terms and conditions.

(2) A term of a hire purchase agreement or any other agreement exempting from all or any of the provisions of section 8 above shall be void.

(3) A term of a hire purchase agreement or any other agreement exempting from all or any of the provisions of section 9, 10 or 11 above shall be void in the case of a consumer agreement and shall, in any other case, not be enforceable to the extent that it is shown that it would not be fair or reasonable to allow reliance on the term.

(4) In determining for the purpose of subsection (3) above whether or not reliance on any such term would be fair or

*Sub-sections 12(2)-12(9) repealed by UCTA.

reasonable regard shall be had to all the circumstances of the case and in particular to the following matters—

    (a) the strength of the bargaining positions of the owner and hirer relative to each other, taking into account, among other things, the availability of suitable alternative products and sources of supply ;

    (b) whether the hirer received an inducement to agree to the term or in accepting it had an opportunity of acquiring the goods or suitable alternatives without it from any source of supply ;

    (c) whether the hirer knew or ought reasonably to have known of the existence and extent of the term (having regard, among other things, to any custom of the trade and any previous course of dealing between the parties) ;

    (d) where the term exempts from all or any of the provisions of section 9, 10 or 11 above if some condition is not complied with, whether it was reasonable at the time of the agreement to expect that compliance with that condition would be practicable ;

    (e) whether the goods were manufactured, processed or adapted to the special order of the hirer.

(5) Subsection (4) above shall not prevent the court from holding, in accordance with any rule of law, that a term which purports to exclude or restrict any of the provisions of section 9, 10 or 11 above is not a term of the hire-purchase agreement.

(6) In this section " consumer agreement " means a hire-purchase agreement where the owner makes the agreement in the course of a business and the goods to which the agreement relates—

    (a) are of a type ordinarily supplied for private use or consumption ; and

    (b) are hired to a person who does not hire or hold himself out as hiring them in the course of a business.

(7) The onus of proving that a hire-purchase agreement falls to be treated for the purposes of this section as not being a consumer agreement shall lie on the party so contending.

(8) Any reference in this section to a term exempting from all or any of the provisions of any section of this Act is a reference to a term which purports to exclude or restrict, or has the effect of excluding or restricting, the operation of all or any of the provisions of that section, or the exercise of a right conferred by any provision of that section, or any liability of the owner for breach of a condition or warranty implied by any provision of that section.

(9) It is hereby declared that any reference in this section to a term of an agreement includes a reference to a term which although not contained in an agreement is incorporated in the agreement by another term of the agreement.

*13. Where the proper law of a hire purchase agreement would, Conflict of apart from a term that it should be the law of some other laws. country or a term to the like effect, be the law of any part of the United Kingdom, or where any such agreement contains a term which purports to substitute, or has the effect of substituting, provisions of the law of some other country for all or any of the provisions of sections 8 to 12 above, those sections shall, notwithstanding that term, apply to the agreement.

*14.—(1) Section 11(1)(c) of the principal Act (whereby in Special certain circumstances a breach of a condition in a contract of provisions as sale is treated only as a breach of warranty) shall not apply to to conditional conditional sale agreements which are agreements for consumer sale sales. agreements.

(2) In England and Wales and Northern Ireland a breach of a condition (whether express or implied) to be fulfilled by the seller under any such agreement shall be treated as a breach of warranty, and not as grounds for rejecting the goods and treating the agreement as repudiated, if (but only if) it would have fallen to be so treated had the condition been contained or implied in a corresponding hire-purchase agreement as a condition to be fulfilled by the owner.

*15.—(1) In sections 8 to 14 above and this section— Supple-
" conditional sale agreement ", " hire-purchase agreement ", mentary.
" hirer " and " owner " have the same meanings respectively as in the Hire-Purchase Act 1965 or, as the case 1965 c. 66.
may be, the Hire-Purchase (Scotland) Act 1965 ; 1965 c. 67.
" business " includes a profession and the activities of any
government department (including a department of the
Government of Northern Ireland), local authority or
statutory undertaker ;
" consumer sale " has the same meaning as in section 55 of
the principal Act, as amended by section 4 above ; and
" condition " and " warranty ", in relation to Scotland, mean
stipulation, and any stipulation referred to in sections
8(1)(a) 9, 10 and 11 above shall be deemed to be
material to the agreement.

(2) In the application of subsection (1) above to Northern Ireland—
(a) " hirer " has the same meaning as in section 65(1) of
the Hire Purchase Act (Northern Ireland) 1966 ; and 1966 c. 42
(N.I.).

---

*Section 13 repealed by UCTA and Sections 14 and 15 amended by UCTA, Schedule 3, page 300.

1965 c. 66.
1966 c. 42
(N.I.).

(*b*) subject to paragraph (*a*) above, for the reference to the Hire-Purchase Act 1965 there shall be substituted a reference to the Hire-Purchase Act (Northern Ireland) 1966.

(3) Goods of any kind are of merchantable quality within the meaning of section 10(2) above if they are as fit for the purpose or purposes for which goods of that kind are commonly bought as it is reasonable to expect having regard to any description applied to them, the price (if relevant) and all the other relevant circumstances; and in section 11 above " unmerchantable " shall be construed accordingly.

(4) In section 14(2) above " corresponding hire-purchase agreement " means, in relation to a conditional sale agreement, a hire-purchase agreement relating to the same goods as the conditional sale agreement and made between the same parties and at the same time and in the same circumstances and, as nearly as may be, in the same terms as the conditional sale agreement.

(5) Nothing in sections 8 to 13 above shall prejudice the operation of any other enactment including any enactment of the Parliament of Northern Ireland or any rule of law whereby any condition or warranty, other than one relating to quality or fitness, is to be implied in any hire-purchase agreement.

Trading Stamps

Terms to be implied on redemption of trading stamps for goods.

1964 c. 71.

16.—(1) For section 4 of the Trading Stamps Act 1964 (warranties to be implied on redemption of trading stamps for goods) there shall be substituted the following section:—

" Warranties to be implied on redemption of trading stamps for goods.

4.—(1) In every redemption of trading stamps for goods, notwithstanding any terms to the contrary on which the redemption is made, there is—

(*a*) an implied warranty on the part of the promoter of the trading stamp scheme that he has a right to give the goods in exchange;

(*b*) an implied warranty that the goods are free from any charge or encumbrance not disclosed or known to the person obtaining the goods before, or at the time of, redemption and that that person will enjoy quiet possession of the goods except so far as it may be disturbed by the owner or other person entitled to the benefit of any charge or encumbrance so disclosed or known;

(c) an implied warranty that the goods are of merchantable quality, except that there is no such warranty—

  (i) as regards defects specifically drawn to the attention of the person obtaining the goods before or at the time of redemption; or

  (ii) if that person examines the goods before or at the time of redemption, as regards defects which that examination ought to reveal.

(2) Goods of any kind are of merchantable quality within the meaning of this section if they are as fit for the purpose or purposes for which goods of that kind are commonly bought as it is reasonable to expect having regard to any description applied to them and all the other relevant circumstances.

(3) In the application of this section to Scotland for any reference to a warranty there shall be substituted a reference to a stipulation."

(2) The section so substituted, without subsection (3) thereof, shall be substituted for section 4 of the Trading Stamps Act 1965 c. 6 (Northern Ireland) 1965 (warranties to be implied on redemption (N.I.). of trading stamps for goods).

Miscellaneous

17.—(1) It is hereby declared that this Act extends to Northern Ireland.

Northern Ireland.

(2) For the purposes of section 6 of the Government of Ireland 1920 c. 67. Act 1920 this Act shall, so far as it relates to matters within the powers of the Parliament of Northern Ireland, be deemed to be an Act passed before the appointed day within the meaning of that section.

18.—(1) This Act may be cited as the Supply of Goods Short title, (Implied Terms) Act 1973. citation, interpretation, (2) In this Act " the principal Act " means the Sale of Goods commence- Act 1893. ment, repeal and saving. (3) This Act shall come into operation at the expiration of a 56 & 57 Vict. period of one month beginning with the date on which it is c. 71. passed.

1965 c. 66.
1965 c. 67.
1966 c. 42
(N.I.).

(4) Sections 17 to 20 and 29(3)(c) of each of the following Acts, that is to say, the Hire-Purchase Act 1965, the Hire-Purchase (Scotland) Act 1965 and the Hire Purchase Act (Northern Ireland) 1966 (provisions as to conditions, warranties and stipulations in hire-purchase agreements) shall cease to have effect.

(5) This Act does not apply to contracts of sale or hire-purchase agreements made before its commencement.

Appendix 5

The Unfair Contract Terms Act, 1977

ARRANGEMENT OF SECTIONS

PART I

AMENDMENT OF LAW FOR ENGLAND AND WALES AND NORTHERN IRELAND

Introductory

Section
1. Scope of Part I.

Avoidance of liability for negligence, breach of contract, etc.
2. Negligence liability.
3. Liability arising in contract.
4. Unreasonable indemnity clauses.

Liability arising from sale or supply of goods
5. " Guarantee " of consumer goods.
6. Sale and hire-purchase.
7. Miscellaneous contracts under which goods pass.

Other provisions about contracts
8. Misrepresentation.
9. Effect of breach.
10. Evasion by means of secondary contract.

Explanatory provisions
11. The " reasonableness " test.
12. " Dealing as consumer ".
13. Varieties of exemption clause.
14. Interpretation of Part I.

PART II

AMENDMENT OF LAW FOR SCOTLAND

PART III

PROVISIONS APPLYING TO WHOLE OF UNITED KINGDOM

Miscellaneous

General

Unfair Contract Terms Act 1977

1977 CHAPTER 50

An Act to impose further limits on the extent to which under the law of England and Wales and Northern Ireland civil liability for breach of contract, or for negligence or other breach of duty, can be avoided by means of contract terms and otherwise, and under the law of Scotland civil liability can be avoided by means of contract terms.   [26th October 1977]

BE IT ENACTED by the Queen's most Excellent Majesty, by and with the advice and consent of the Lords Spiritual and Temporal, and Commons, in this present Parliament assembled, and by the authority of the same, as follows:—

PART I

AMENDMENT OF LAW FOR ENGLAND AND WALES AND NORTHERN IRELAND

Introductory

1.—(1) For the purposes of this Part of this Act, "negligence" means the breach—

Scope of Part I.

    (*a*) of any obligation, arising from the express or implied terms of a contract, to take reasonable care or exercise reasonable skill in the performance of the contract;

    (*b*) of any common law duty to take reasonable care or exercise reasonable skill (but not any stricter duty);

(c) of the common duty of care imposed by the Occupiers' Liability Act 1957 or the Occupiers' Liability Act (Northern Ireland) 1957.

(2) This Part of this Act is subject to Part III; and in relation to contracts, the operation of sections 2 to 4 and 7 is subject to the exceptions made by Schedule 1.

(3) In the case of both contract and tort, sections 2 to 7 apply (except where the contrary is stated in section 6(4)) only to business liability, that is liability for breach of obligations or duties arising—

(a) from things done or to be done by a person in the course of a business (whether his own business or another's); or

(b) from the occupation of premises used for business purposes of the occupier;

and references to liability are to be read accordingly.

(4) In relation to any breach of duty or obligation, it is immaterial for any purpose of this Part of this Act whether the breach was inadvertent or intentional, or whether liability for it arises directly or vicariously.

Avoidance of liability for negligence, breach of contract, etc.

Negligence liability.

2.—(1) A person cannot by reference to any contract term or to a notice given to persons generally or to particular persons exclude or restrict his liability for death or personal injury resulting from negligence.

(2) In the case of other loss or damage, a person cannot so exclude or restrict his liability for negligence except in so far as the term or notice satisfies the requirement of reasonableness.

(3) Where a contract term or notice purports to exclude or restrict liability for negligence a person's agreement to or awareness of it is not of itself to be taken as indicating his voluntary acceptance of any risk.

Liability arising in contract.

3.—(1) This section applies as between contracting parties where one of them deals as consumer or on the other's written standard terms of business.

(2) As against that party, the other cannot by reference to any contract term—

(a) when himself in breach of contract, exclude or restrict any liability of his in respect of the breach; or

(b) claim to be entitled—

(i) to render a contractual performance substantially different from that which was reasonably expected of him, or

(ii) in respect of the whole or any part of his contractual obligation, to render no performance at all,

except in so far as (in any of the cases mentioned above in this subsection) the contract term satisfies the requirement of reasonableness.

4.—(1) A person dealing as consumer cannot by reference to any contract term be made to indemnify another person (whether a party to the contract or not) in respect of liability that may be incurred by the other for negligence or breach of contract, except in so far as the contract term satisfies the requirement of reasonableness. *Unreasonable indemnity clauses.*

(2) This section applies whether the liability in question—

(*a*) is directly that of the person to be indemnified or is incurred by him vicariously ;

(*b*) is to the person dealing as consumer or to someone else.

Liability arising from sale or supply of goods

5.—(1) In the case of goods of a type ordinarily supplied for private use or consumption, where loss or damage— *" Guarantee " of consumer goods.*

(*a*) arises from the goods proving defective while in consumer use ; and

(*b*) results from the negligence of a person concerned in the manufacture or distribution of the goods,

liability for the loss or damage cannot be excluded or restricted by reference to any contract term or notice contained in or operating by reference to a guarantee of the goods.

(2) For these purposes—

(*a*) goods are to be regarded as " in consumer use " when a person is using them, or has them in his possession for use, otherwise than exclusively for the purposes of a business ; and

(*b*) anything in writing is a guarantee if it contains or purports to contain some promise or assurance (however worded or presented) that defects will be made good by complete or partial replacement, or by repair, monetary compensation or otherwise.

(3) This section does not apply as between the parties to a contract under or in pursuance of which possession or ownership of the goods passed.

6.—(1) Liability for breach of the obligations arising from— *Sale and hire-purchase.*

(*a*) section 12 of the Sale of Goods Act 1893 (seller's implied undertakings as to title, etc.) ; *56 & 57 Vict. c. 71.*

    (*b*) section 8 of the Supply of Goods (Implied Terms) Act 1973 (the corresponding thing in relation to hire-purchase),

cannot be excluded or restricted by reference to any contract term.

(2) As against a person dealing as consumer, liability for breach of the obligations arising from—

    (*a*) section 13, 14 or 15 of the 1893 Act (seller's implied undertakings as to conformity of goods with description or sample, or as to their quality or fitness for a particular purpose) ;

    (*b*) section 9, 10 or 11 of the 1973 Act (the corresponding things in relation to hire-purchase),

cannot be excluded or restricted by reference to any contract term.

(3) As against a person dealing otherwise than as consumer, the liability specified in subsection (2) above can be excluded or restricted by reference to a contract term, but only in so far as the term satisfies the requirement of reasonableness.

(4) The liabilities referred to in this section are not only the business liabilities defined by section 1(3), but include those arising under any contract of sale of goods or hire-purchase agreement.

Miscellaneous contracts under which goods pass.

7.—(1) Where the possession or ownership of goods passes under or in pursuance of a contract not governed by the law of sale of goods or hire-purchase, subsections (2) to (4) below apply as regards the effect (if any) to be given to contract terms excluding or restricting liability for breach of obligation arising by implication of law from the nature of the contract.

(2) As against a person dealing as consumer, liability in respect of the goods' correspondence with description or sample, or their quality or fitness for any particular purpose, cannot be excluded or restricted by reference to any such term.

(3) As against a person dealing otherwise than as consumer, that liability can be excluded or restricted by reference to such a term, but only in so far as the term satisfies the requirement of reasonableness.

(4) Liability in respect of—

    (*a*) the right to transfer ownership of the goods, or give possession ; or

    (*b*) the assurance of quiet possession to a person taking goods in pursuance of the contract,

cannot be excluded or restricted by reference to any such term PART I
except in so far as the term satisfies the requirement of
reasonableness.

(5) This section does not apply in the case of goods passing 1964 c. 71.
on a redemption of trading stamps within the Trading Stamps 1965 c. 6.
Act 1964 or the Trading Stamps Act (Northern Ireland) 1965. (N.I.).

Other provisions about contracts

8.—(1) In the Misrepresentation Act 1967, the following is Misrepre-
substituted for section 3— sentation.

"Avoidance 3. If a contract contains a term which would 1967 c. 7.
of provision exclude or restrict—
excluding
liability for
misrepre-
sentation.   (*a*) any liability to which a party to a contract
        may be subject by reason of any misrepre-
        sentation made by him before the contract
        was made ; or

    (*b*) any remedy available to another party to the
        contract by reason of such a misrepresenta-
        tion,

that term shall be of no effect except in so far as it
satisfies the requirement of reasonableness as stated
in section 11(1) of the Unfair Contract Terms Act
1977 ; and it is for those claiming that the term
satisfies that requirement to show that it does.".

(2) The same section is substituted for section 3 of the Mis- 1967 c. 14
representation Act (Northern Ireland) 1967. (N.I.).

9.—(1) Where for reliance upon it a contract term has to Effect of
satisfy the requirement of reasonableness, it may be found to breach.
do so and be given effect accordingly notwithstanding that the
contract has been terminated either by breach or by a party
electing to treat it as repudiated.

(2) Where on a breach the contract is nevertheless affirmed
by a party entitled to treat it as repudiated, this does not of itself
exclude the requirement of reasonableness in relation to any
contract term.

10. A person is not bound by any contract term prejudicing Evasion by
or taking away rights of his which arise under, or in connection means of
with the performance of, another contract, so far as those rights secondary
extend to the enforcement of another's liability which this Part contract.
of this Act prevents that other from excluding or restricting.

PART I

The " reasonableness " test.
1967 c. 7.
1967 c. 14. (N.I.).

Explanatory provisions

11.—(1) In relation to a contract term, the requirement of reasonableness for the purposes of this Part of this Act, section 3 of the Misrepresentation Act 1967 and section 3 of the Misrepresentation Act (Northern Ireland) 1967 is that the term shall have been a fair and reasonable one to be included having regard to the circumstances which were, or ought reasonably to have been, known to or in the contemplation of the parties when the contract was made.

(2) In determining for the purposes of section 6 or 7 above whether a contract term satisfies the requirement of reasonableness, regard shall be had in particular to the matters specified in Schedule 2 to this Act ; but this subsection does not prevent the court or arbitrator from holding, in accordance with any rule of law, that a term which purports to exclude or restrict any relevant liability is not a term of the contract.

(3) In relation to a notice (not being a notice having contractual effect), the requirement of reasonableness under this Act is that it should be fair and reasonable to allow reliance on it, having regard to all the circumstances obtaining when the liability arose or (but for the notice) would have arisen.

(4) Where by reference to a contract term or notice a person seeks to restrict liability to a specified sum of money, and the question arises (under this or any other Act) whether the term or notice satisfies the requirement of reasonableness, regard shall be had in particular (but without prejudice to subsection (2) above in the case of contract terms) to—

(a) the resources which he could expect to be available to him for the purpose of meeting the liability should it arise ; and

(b) how far it was open to him to cover himself by insurance.

(5) It is for those claiming that a contract term or notice satisfies the requirement of reasonableness to show that it does.

" Dealing as consumer ".

12.—(1) A party to a contract " deals as consumer " in relation to another party if—

(a) he neither makes the contract in the course of a business nor holds himself out as doing so ; and

(b) the other party does make the contract in the course of a business ; and

(c) in the case of a contract governed by the law of sale of
goods or hire-purchase, or by section 7 of this Act,
the goods passing under or in pursuance of the contract
are of a type ordinarily supplied for private use or
consumption.

(2) But on a sale by auction or by competitive tender the
buyer is not in any circumstances to be regarded as dealing as
consumer.

(3) Subject to this, it is for those claiming that a party does
not deal as consumer to show that he does not.

13.—(1) To the extent that this Part of this Act prevents the Varieties of
exclusion or restriction of any liability it also prevents— exemption
clause.

(a) making the liability or its enforcement subject to
restrictive or onerous conditions ;

(b) excluding or restricting any right or remedy in respect
of the liability, or subjecting a person to any prejudice
in consequence of his pursuing any such right or
remedy ;

(c) excluding or restricting rules of evidence or procedure ;
and (to that extent) sections 2 and 5 to 7 also prevent excluding
or restricting liability by reference to terms and notices which
exclude or restrict the relevant obligation or duty.

(2) But an agreement in writing to submit present or future
differences to arbitration is not to be treated under this Part of
this Act as excluding or restricting any liability.

14. In this Part of this Act— Interpretation
" business " includes a profession and the activities of any of Part I.
government department or local or public authority ;

" goods " has the same meaning as in the Sale of Goods 56 & 57 Vict.
Act 1893 ; c. 71.

" hire-purchase agreement " has the same meaning as in the
Consumer Credit Act 1974 ; 1974 c. 39.

" negligence " has the meaning given by section 1(1) ;

" notice " includes an announcement, whether or not in
writing, and any other communication or pretended
communication ; and

" personal injury " includes any disease and any impairment of physical or mental condition.

PART II

AMENDMENT OF LAW FOR SCOTLAND

Scope of
Part II.

15.—(1) This Part of this Act applies only to contracts, is subject to Part III of this Act and does not affect the validity of any discharge or indemnity given by a person in consideration of the receipt by him of compensation in settlement of any claim which he has.

(2) Subject to subsection (3) below, sections 16 to 18 of this Act apply to any contract only to the extent that the contract—

(a) relates to the transfer of the ownership or possession of goods from one person to another (with or without work having been done on them);

(b) constitutes a contract of service or apprenticeship;

(c) relates to services of whatever kind, including (without prejudice to the foregoing generality) carriage, deposit and pledge, care and custody, mandate, agency, loan and services relating to the use of land;

(d) relates to the liability of an occupier of land to persons entering upon or using that land;

(e) relates to a grant of any right or permission to enter upon or use land not amounting to an estate or interest in the land.

(3) Notwithstanding anything in subsection (2) above, sections 16 to 18—

(a) do not apply to any contract to the extent that the contract—

(i) is a contract of insurance (including a contract to pay an annuity on human life);

(ii) relates to the formation, constitution or dissolution of any body corporate or unincorporated association or partnership;

(b) apply to—

a contract of marine salvage or towage;

a charter party of a ship or hovercraft;

a contract for the carriage of goods by ship or hovercraft; or,

a contract to which subsection (4) below relates,

only to the extent that—

(i) both parties deal or hold themselves out as dealing in the course of a business (and then only in so far as the contract purports to exclude or restrict liability for breach of duty in respect of death or personal injury); or

(ii) the contract is a consumer contract (and then only in favour of the consumer).

(4) This subsection relates to a contract in pursuance of which goods are carried by ship or hovercraft and which either—

    (a) specifies ship or hovercraft as the means of carriage over part of the journey to be covered ; or

    (b) makes no provision as to the means of carriage and does not exclude ship or hovercraft as that means,

in so far as the contract operates for and in relation to the carriage of the goods by that means.

16.—(1) Where a term of a contract purports to exclude or Liability for restrict liability for breach of duty arising in the course of any breach of business or from the occupation of any premises used for business duty. purposes of the occupier, that term—

    (a) shall be void in any case where such exclusion or restriction is in respect of death or personal injury ;

    (b) shall, in any other case, have no effect if it was not fair and reasonable to incorporate the term in the contract.

(2) Subsection (1)(a) above does not affect the validity of any discharge and indemnity given by a person, on or in connection with an award to him of compensation for pneumoconiosis attributable to employment in the coal industry, in respect of any further claim arising from his contracting that disease.

(3) Where under subsection (1) above a term of a contract is void or has no effect, the fact that a person agreed to, or was aware of, the term shall not of itself be sufficient evidence that he knowingly and voluntarily assumed any risk.

17.—(1) Any term of a contract which is a consumer contract Control of or a standard form contract shall have no effect for the purpose unreasonable of enabling a party to the contract— exemptions in consumer or

    (a) who is in breach of a contractual obligation, to exclude standard form or restrict any liability of his to the consumer or custo- contracts. mer in respect of the breach ;

    (b) in respect of a contractual obligation, to render no performance, or to render a performance substantially different from that which the consumer or customer reasonably expected from the contract ;

if it was not fair and reasonable to incorporate the term in the contract.

(2) In this section " customer " means a party to a standard form contract who deals on the basis of written standard terms of business of the other party to the contract who himself deals in the course of a business.

PART II
Unreasonable
indemnity
clauses in
consumer
contracts.

18.—(1) Any term of a contract which is a consumer contract shall have no effect for the purpose of making the consumer indemnify another person (whether a party to the contract or not) in respect of liability which that other person may incur as a result of breach of duty or breach of contract, if it was not fair and reasonable to incorporate the term in the contract.

(2) In this section " liability " means liability arising in the course of any business or from the occupation of any premises used for business purposes of the occupier.

" Guarantee "
of consumer
goods.

19.—(1) This section applies to a guarantee—

(*a*) in relation to goods which are of a type ordinarily supplied for private use or consumption ; and

(*b*) which is not a guarantee given by one party to the other party to a contract under or in pursuance of which the ownership or possession of the goods to which the guarantee relates is transferred.

(2) A term of a guarantee to which this section applies shall be void in so far as it purports to exclude or restrict liability for loss or damage (including death or personal injury)—

(*a*) arising from the goods proving defective while—

(i) in use otherwise than exclusively for the purposes of a business ; or

(ii) in the possession of a person for such use ; and

(*b*) resulting from the breach of duty of a person concerned in the manufacture or distribution of the goods.

(3) For the purposes of this section, any document is a guarantee if it contains or purports to contain some promise or assurance (however worded or presented) that defects will be made good by complete or partial replacement, or by repair, monetary compensation or otherwise.

Obligations
implied by
law in sale
and hire-
purchase
contracts.
56 & 57
Vict. c. 71.
1973 c. 13.

20.—(1) Any term of a contract which purports to exclude or restrict liability for breach of the obligations arising from—

(*a*) section 12 of the Sale of Goods Act 1893 (seller's implied undertakings as to title etc.) ;

(*b*) section 8 of the Supply of Goods (Implied Terms) Act 1973 (implied terms as to title in hire-purchase agreements),

shall be void.

(2) Any term of a contract which purports to exclude or PART II
restrict liability for breach of the obligations arising from—

    (a) section 13, 14 or 15 of the said Act of 1893 (seller's implied undertakings as to conformity of goods with description or sample, or as to their quality or fitness for a particular purpose) ;

    (b) section 9, 10 or 11 of the said Act of 1973 (the corresponding provisions in relation to hire-purchase),

shall—

        (i) in the case of a consumer contract, be void against the consumer ;

        (ii) in any other case, have no effect if it was not fair and reasonable to incorporate the term in the contract.

21.—(1) Any term of a contract to which this section applies Obligations
purporting to exclude or restrict liability for breach of an implied by
obligation— law in other
contracts for
    (a) such as is referred to in subsection (3)(a) below— the supply of
goods.
        (i) in the case of a consumer contract, shall be void against the consumer, and

        (ii) in any other case, shall have no effect if it was not fair and reasonable to incorporate the term in the contract ;

    (b) such as is referred to in subsection (3)(b) below, shall have no effect if it was not fair and reasonable to incorporate the term in the contract.

(2) This section applies to any contract to the extent that it relates to any such matter as is referred to in section 15(2)(a) of this Act, but does not apply to—

    (a) a contract of sale of goods or a hire-purchase agreement ; or

    (b) a charterparty of a ship or hovercraft unless it is a consumer contract (and then only in favour of the consumer).

(3) An obligation referred to in this subsection is an obligation incurred under a contract in the course of a business and arising by implication of law from the nature of the contract which relates—

    (a) to the correspondence of goods with description or sample, or to the quality or fitness of goods for any particular purpose ; or

    (b) to any right to transfer ownership or possession of goods, or to the enjoyment of quiet possession of goods.

(4) Nothing in this section applies to the supply of goods on a redemption of trading stamps within the Trading Stamps Act 1964 c. 71.
1964.

PART II
Consequence
of breach.

22. For the avoidance of doubt, where any provision of this Part of this Act requires that the incorporation of a term in a contract must be fair and reasonable for that term to have effect—

(a) if that requirement is satisfied, the term may be given effect to notwithstanding that the contract has been terminated in consequence of breach of that contract;

(b) for the term to be given effect to, that requirement must be satisfied even where a party who is entitled to rescind the contract elects not to rescind it.

Evasion by
means of
secondary
contract.

23. Any term of any contract shall be void which purports to exclude or restrict, or has the effect of excluding or restricting—

(a) the exercise, by a party to any other contract, of any right or remedy which arises in respect of that other contract in consequence of breach of duty, or of obligation, liability for which could not by virtue of the provisions of this Part of this Act be excluded or restricted by a term of that other contract;

(b) the application of the provisions of this Part of this Act in respect of that or any other contract.

The
" reasonable-
ness " test.

24.—(1) In determining for the purposes of this Part of this Act whether it was fair and reasonable to incorporate a term in a contract, regard shall be had only to the circumstances which were, or ought reasonably to have been, known to or in the contemplation of the parties to the contract at the time the contract was made.

(2) In determining for the purposes of section 20 or 21 of this Act whether it was fair and reasonable to incorporate a term in a contract, regard shall be had in particular to the matters specified in Schedule 2 to this Act; but this subsection shall not prevent a court or arbiter from holding, in accordance with any rule of law, that a term which purports to exclude or restrict any relevant liability is not a term of the contract.

(3) Where a term in a contract purports to restrict liability to a specified sum of money, and the question arises for the purposes of this Part of this Act whether it was fair and reasonable to incorporate the term in the contract, then, without prejudice to subsection (2) above, regard shall be had in particular to—

(a) the resources which the party seeking to rely on that term could expect to be available to him for the purpose of meeting the liability should it arise;

(*b*) how far it was open to that party to cover himself by insurance.

(4) The onus of proving that it was fair and reasonable to incorporate a term in a contract shall lie on the party so contending.

25.—(1) In this Part of this Act—
"breach of duty" means the breach—

> (*a*) of any obligation, arising from the express or implied terms of a contract, to take reasonable care or exercise reasonable skill in the performance of the contract ;
>
> (*b*) of any common law duty to take reasonable care or exercise reasonable skill ;
>
> (*c*) of the duty of reasonable care imposed by section 2(1) of the Occupiers' Liability (Scotland) Act 1960 ;

"business" includes a profession and the activities of any government department or local or public authority ;

"consumer" has the meaning assigned to that expression in the definition in this section of "consumer contract" ;

"consumer contract" means a contract (not being a contract of sale by auction or competitive tender) in which—

> (*a*) one party to the contract deals, and the other party to the contract ("the consumer") does not deal or hold himself out as dealing, in the course of a business, and
>
> (*b*) in the case of a contract such as is mentioned in section 15(2)(*a*) of this Act, the goods are of a type ordinarily supplied for private use or consumption ;

and for the purposes of this Part of this Act the onus of proving that a contract is not to be regarded as a consumer contract shall lie on the party so contending ;

"goods" has the same meaning as in the Sale of Goods Act 1893 ;

"hire-purchase agreement" has the same meaning as in section 189(1) of the Consumer Credit Act 1974 ;

"personal injury" includes any disease and any impairment of physical or mental condition.

(2) In relation to any breach of duty or obligation, it is immaterial for any purpose of this Part of this Act whether the act or omission giving rise to that breach was inadvertent or

PART II   intentional, or whether liability for it arises directly or vicariously.

(3) In this Part of this Act, any reference to excluding or restricting any liability includes—

(a) making the liability or its enforcement subject to any restrictive or onerous conditions ;

(b) excluding or restricting any right or remedy in respect of the liability, or subjecting a person to any prejudice in consequence of his pursuing any such right or remedy ;

(c) excluding or restricting any rule of evidence or procedure ;

(d) excluding or restricting any liability by reference to a notice having contractual effect,

but does not include an agreement to submit any question to arbitration.

(4) In subsection (3)(d) above " notice " includes an announcement, whether or not in writing, and any other communication or pretended communication.

(5) In sections 15 and 16 and 19 to 21 of this Act, any reference to excluding or restricting liability for breach of an obligation or duty shall include a reference to excluding or restricting the obligation or duty itself.

PART III

PROVISIONS APPLYING TO WHOLE OF UNITED KINGDOM

Miscellaneous

International
supply
contracts.

26.—(1) The limits imposed by this Act on the extent to which a person may exclude or restrict liability by reference to a contract term do not apply to liability arising under such a contract as is described in subsection (3) below.

(2) The terms of such a contract are not subject to any requirement of reasonableness under section 3 or 4: and nothing in Part II of this Act shall require the incorporation of the terms of such a contract to be fair and reasonable for them to have effect.

(3) Subject to subsection (4), that description of contract is one whose characteristics are the following—

(a) either it is a contract of sale of goods or it is one under or in pursuance of which the possession or ownership of goods passes ; and (*b*) it is made by parties whose places of business (or, if they have none, habitual residences) are in the territories of different States (the Channel Islands and the Isle of Man being treated for this purpose as different States from the United Kingdom).

(4) A contract falls within subsection (3) above only if either—

(*a*) the goods in question are, at the time of the conclusion of the contract, in the course of carriage, or will be carried, from the territory of one State to the territory of another ; or

(*b*) the acts constituting the offer and acceptance have been done in the territories of different States ; or

(*c*) the contract provides for the goods to be delivered to the territory of a State other than that within whose territory those acts were done.

27.—(1) Where the proper law of a contract is the law of any part of the United Kingdom only by choice of the parties (and apart from that choice would be the law of some country outside the United Kingdom) sections 2 to 7 and 16 to 21 of this Act do not operate as part of the proper law. Choice of law clauses.

(2) This Act has effect notwithstanding any contract term which applies or purports to apply the law of some country outside the United Kingdom, where (either or both)—

(*a*) the term appears to the court, or arbitrator or arbiter to have been imposed wholly or mainly for the purpose of enabling the party imposing it to evade the operation of this Act ; or

(*b*) in the making of the contract one of the parties dealt as consumer, and he was then habitually resident in the United Kingdom, and the essential steps necessary for the making of the contract were taken there, whether by him or by others on his behalf.

(3) In the application of subsection (2) above to Scotland, for paragraph (*b*) there shall be substituted—

" (*b*) the contract is a consumer contract as defined in Part II of this Act, and the consumer at the date when the contract was made was habitually resident in the United Kingdom, and the essential steps necessary for the making of the contract were taken there, whether by him or by others on his behalf.".

28.—(1) This section applies to a contract for carriage by sea of a passenger or of a passenger and his luggage where the provisions of the Athens Convention (with or without modification) do not have, in relation to the contract, the force of law in the United Kingdom. Temporary provision for sea carriage of passengers.

PART III   (2) In a case where—

    (a) the contract is not made in the United Kingdom, and

    (b) neither the place of departure nor the place of destination under it is in the United Kingdom,

a person is not precluded by this Act from excluding or restricting liability for loss or damage, being loss or damage for which the provisions of the Convention would, if they had the force of law in relation to the contract, impose liability on him.

(3) In any other case, a person is not precluded by this Act from excluding or restricting liability for that loss or damage—

    (a) in so far as the exclusion or restriction would have been effective in that case had the provisions of the Convention had the force of law in relation to the contract; or

    (b) in such circumstances and to such extent as may be prescribed, by reference to a prescribed term of the contract.

(4) For the purposes of subsection (3)(a), the values which shall be taken to be the official values in the United Kingdom of the amounts (expressed in gold francs) by reference to which liability under the provisions of the Convention is limited shall be such amounts in sterling as the Secretary of State may from time to time by order made by statutory instrument specify.

(5) In this section,—

    (a) the references to excluding or restricting liability include doing any of those things in relation to the liability which are mentioned in section 13 or section 25(3) and (5); and

    (b) " the Athens Convention " means the Athens Convention relating to the Carriage of Passengers and their Luggage by Sea, 1974; and

    (c) " prescribed " means prescribed by the Secretary of State by regulations made by statutory instrument;

and a statutory instrument containing the regulations shall be subject to annulment in pursuance of a resolution of either House of Parliament.

Saving for other relevant legislation.
    29.—(1) Nothing in this Act removes or restricts the effect of, or prevents reliance upon, any contractual provision which—

    (a) is authorised or required by the express terms or necessary implication of an enactment; or

(*b*) being made with a view to compliance with an international agreement to which the United Kingdom is a
party, does not operate more restrictively than is contemplated by the agreement.

(2) A contract term is to be taken—

(*a*) for the purposes of Part I of this Act, as satisfying the
requirement of reasonableness ; and

(*b*) for those of Part II, to have been fair and reasonable to
incorporate,

if it is incorporated or approved by, or incorporated pursuant to
a decision or ruling of, a competent authority acting in the
exercise of any statutory jurisdiction or function and is not a
term in a contract to which the competent authority is itself
a party.

(3) In this section—

" competent authority " means any court, arbitrator or
arbiter, government department or public authority ;

" enactment " means any legislation (including subordinate
legislation) of the United Kingdom or Northern Ireland
and any instrument having effect by virtue of such
legislation ; and

" statutory " means conferred by an enactment.

30.—(1) In section 3 of the Consumer Protection Act 1961 Obligations
(provisions against marketing goods which do not comply with under
safety requirements), after subsection (1) there is inserted— Consumer
Protection
" (1A) Any term of an agreement which purports to ex- Acts.
clude or restrict, or has the effect of excluding or restricting, 1961 c. 40.
any obligation imposed by or by virtue of that section, or
any liability for breach of such an obligation, shall be void.".

(2) The same amendment is made in section 3 of the Consumer 1965 c. 14
Protection Act (Northern Ireland) 1965. (N.I.).

General

31.—(1) This Act comes into force on 1st February 1978. Commencement;
(2) Nothing in this Act applies to contracts made before the amendments;
date on which it comes into force ; but subject to this, it applies repeals.
to liability for any loss or damage which is suffered on or after
that date.

(3) The enactments specified in Schedule 3 to this Act are
amended as there shown.

(4) The enactments specified in Schedule 4 to this Act are
repealed to the extent specified in column 3 of that Schedule.

PART III
Citation and
extent.

32.—(1) This Act may be cited as the Unfair Contract Terms Act 1977.

(2) Part I of this Act extends to England and Wales and to Northern Ireland ; but it does not extend to Scotland.

(3) Part II of this Act extends to Scotland only.

(4) This Part of this Act extends to the whole of the United Kingdom.

SCHEDULES

SCHEDULE 1

Section 1(2).

Scope of sections 2 to 4 and 7

1. Sections 2 to 4 of this Act do not extend to—

(a) any contract of insurance (including a contract to pay an annuity on human life) ;

(b) any contract so far as it relates to the creation or transfer of an interest in land, or to the termination of such an interest, whether by extinction, merger, surrender, forfeiture or otherwise ;

(c) any contract so far as it relates to the creation or transfer of a right or interest in any patent, trade mark, copyright, registered design, technical or commercial information or other intellectual property, or relates to the termination of any such right or interest ;

(d) any contract so far as it relates—

(i) to the formation or dissolution of a company (which means any body corporate or unincorporated association and includes a partnership), or

(ii) to its constitution or the rights or obligations of its corporators or members ;

(e) any contract so far as it relates to the creation or transfer of securities or of any right or interest in securities.

2. Section 2(1) extends to—

(a) any contract of marine salvage or towage ;

(b) any charterparty of a ship or hovercraft ; and

(c) any contract for the carriage of goods by ship or hovercraft ;

but subject to this sections 2 to 4 and 7 do not extend to any such contract except in favour of a person dealing as consumer.

3. Where goods are carried by ship or hovercraft in pursuance of a contract which either—

(a) specifies that as the means of carriage over part of the journey to be covered, or

(b) makes no provision as to the means of carriage and does not exclude that means,

then sections 2(2), 3 and 4 do not, except in favour of a person dealing as consumer, extend to the contract as it operates for and in relation to the carriage of the goods by that means.

4. Section 2(1) and (2) do not extend to a contract of employment, except in favour of the employee.

5. Section 2(1) does not affect the validity of any discharge and indemnity given by a person, on or in connection with an award to him of compensation for pneumoconiosis attributable to employment in the coal industry, in respect of any further claim arising from his contracting that disease.

Sections 11(2)
and 24(2).

SCHEDULE 2

" Guidelines " for Application of Reasonableness Test

The matters to which regard is to be had in particular for the purposes of sections 6(3), 7(3) and (4), 20 and 21 are any of the following which appear to be relevant—

(a) the strength of the bargaining positions of the parties relative to each other, taking into account (among other things) alternative means by which the customer's requirements could have been met ;

(b) whether the customer received an inducement to agree to the term, or in accepting it had an opportunity of entering into a similar contract with other persons, but without having to accept a similar term ;

(c) whether the customer knew or ought reasonably to have known of the existence and extent of the term (having regard, among other things, to any custom of the trade and any previous course of dealing between the parties) ;

(d) where the term excludes or restricts any relevant liability if some condition is not complied with, whether it was reasonable at the time of the contract to expect that compliance with that condition would be practicable ;

(e) whether the goods were manufactured, processed or adapted to the special order of the customer.

Section 31(3).

SCHEDULE 3

Amendment of Enactments

56 & 57 Vict.
c. 71.

In the Sale of Goods Act 1893—

(a) in section 55(1), for the words " the following provisions of this section " substitute " the provisions of the Unfair Contract Terms Act 1977 " ;

(b) in section 62(1), in the definition of " business ", for " local authority or statutory undertaker " substitute " or local or public authority ".

1973 c. 13.
1974 c. 39.

In the Supply of Goods (Implied Terms) Act 1973 (as originally enacted and as substituted by the Consumer Credit Act 1974)—

(a) in section 14(1) for the words from " conditional sale " to the end substitute " a conditional sale agreement where the buyer deals as consumer within Part I of the Unfair Contract Terms Act 1977 or, in Scotland, the agreement is a consumer contract within Part II of that Act " ;

(b) in section 15(1), in the definition of " business ", for " local authority or statutory undertaker " substitute " or local or public authority ".

SCHEDULE 4

REPEALS

Chapter	Short title	Extent of repeal
56 & 57 Vict. c. 71.	Sale of Goods Act 1893.	In section 55, subsections (3) to (11). Section 55A. Section 61(6). In section 62(1) the definition of " contract for the international sale of goods ".
1962 c. 46.	Transport Act 1962.	Section 43(7).
1967 c. 45.	Uniform Laws on International Sales Act 1967.	In section 1(4), the words " 55 and 55A ".
1972 c. 33.	Carriage by Railway Act 1972.	In section 1(1), the words from " and shall have " onwards.
1973 c. 13.	Supply of Goods (Implied Terms) Act 1973.	Section 5(1). Section 6. In section 7(1), the words from " contract for the international sale of goods " onwards. In section 12, subsections (2) to (9). Section 13. In section 15(1), the definition of " consumer sale ".

The repeals in sections 12 and 15 of the Supply of Goods (Implied Terms) Act 1973 shall have effect in relation to those sections as originally enacted and as substituted by the Consumer Credit Act 1974 c. 39. 1974.

Extracts from *The Health and Safety at Work etc. Act, 1974*

General duties

2.—(1) It shall be the duty of every employer to ensure, so far as is reasonably practicable, the health, safety and welfare at work of all his employees.

(2) Without prejudice to the generality of an employer's duty under the preceding subsection, the matters to which that duty extends include in particular—

(a) the provision and maintenance of plant and systems of work that are, so far as is reasonably practicable, safe and without risks to health ;

(b) arrangements for ensuring, so far as is reasonably practicable, safety and absence of risks to health in connection with the use, handling, storage and transport of articles and substances ;

(c) the provision of such information, instruction, training and supervision as is necessary to ensure, so far as is reasonably practicable, the health and safety at work of his employees ;

(d) so far as is reasonably practicable as regards any place of work under the employer's control, the maintenance of it in a condition that is safe and without risks to health and the provision and maintenance of means of access to and egress from it that are safe and without such risks ;

(e) the provision and maintenance of a working environment for his employees that is, so far as is reasonably practicable, safe, without risks to health, and adequate as regards facilities and arrangements for their welfare at work.

(3) Except in such cases as may be prescribed, it shall be the duty of every employer to prepare and as often as may be appropriate revise a written statement of his general policy with respect to the health and safety at work of his employees and the organisation and arrangements for the time being in force for carrying out that policy, and to bring the statement and any revision of it to the notice of all of his employees.

(4) Regulations made by the Secretary of State may provide for the appointment in prescribed cases by recognised trade unions (within the meaning of the regulations) of safety representatives from amongst the employees, and those representatives shall represent the employees in consultations with the employers under subsection (6) below and shall have such other functions as may be prescribed.

(5) Regulations made by the Secretary of State may provide for the election in prescribed cases by employees of safety representatives from amongst the employees, and those representatives shall represent the employees in consultations with the employers under subsection (6) below and may have such other functions as may be prescribed.

(6) It shall be the duty of every employer to consult any such representatives with a view to the making and maintenance of arrangements which will enable him and his employees to co-operate effectively in promoting and developing measures to ensure the health and safety at work of the employees, and in checking the effectiveness of such measures.

(7) In such cases as may be prescribed it shall be the duty of every employer, if requested to do so by the safety representatives mentioned in subsections (4) and (5) above, to establish, in accordance with regulations made by the Secretary of State, a safety committee having the function of keeping under review the measures taken to ensure the health and safety at work of his employees and such other functions as may be prescribed.

3.—(1) It shall be the duty of every employer to conduct his undertaking in such a way as to ensure, so far as is reasonably practicable, that persons not in his employment who may be affected thereby are not thereby exposed to risks to their health or safety.

(2) It shall be the duty of every self-employed person to conduct his undertaking in such a way as to ensure, so far as is reasonably practicable, that he and other persons (not being his employees) who may be affected thereby are not thereby exposed to risks to their health or safety.

(3) In such cases as may be prescribed, it shall be the duty of every employer and every self-employed person, in the prescribed circumstances and in the prescribed manner, to give to persons (not being his employees) who may be affected by the way in which he conducts his undertaking the prescribed information about such aspects of the way in which he conducts his undertaking as might affect their health or safety.

6.—(1) It shall be the duty of any person who designs, manufactures, imports or supplies any article for use at work—

(a) to ensure, so far as is reasonably practicable, that the article is so designed and constructed as to be safe and without risks to health when properly used ;

(b) to carry out or arrange for the carrying out of such testing and examination as may be necessary for the performance of the duty imposed on him by the preceding paragraph ;

(c) to take such steps as are necessary to secure that there will be available in connection with the use of the article at work adequate information about the use for which it is designed and has been tested, and about any conditions necessary to ensure that, when put to that use, it will be safe and without risks to health.

(2) It shall be the duty of any person who undertakes the design or manufacture of any article for use at work to carry out or arrange for the carrying out of any necessary research with a view to the discovery and, so far as is reasonably practicable, the elimination or minimisation of any risks to health or safety to which the design or article may give rise.

(3) It shall be the duty of any person who erects or installs any article for use at work in any premises where that article is to be used by persons at work to ensure, so far as is reasonably practicable, that nothing about the way in which it is erected or installed makes it unsafe or a risk to health when properly used.

(4) It shall be the duty of any person who manufactures, imports or supplies any substance for use at work—

(*a*) to ensure, so far as is reasonably practicable, that the substance is safe and without risks to health when properly used ;

(*b*) to carry out or arrange for the carrying out of such testing and examination as may be necessary for the performance of the duty imposed on him by the preceding paragraph ;

(*c*) to take such steps as are necessary to secure that there will be available in connection with the use of the substance at work adequate information about the results of any relevant tests which have been carried out on or in connection with the substance and about any conditions necessary to ensure that it will be safe and without risks to health when properly used.

(5) It shall be the duty of any person who undertakes the manufacture of any substance for use at work to carry out or arrange for the carrying out of any necessary research with a view to the discovery and, so far as is reasonably practicable, the elimination or minimisation of any risks to health or safety to which the substance may give rise.

(6) Nothing in the preceding provisions of this section shall be taken to require a person to repeat any testing, examination or research which has been carried out otherwise than by him or at his instance, in so far as it is reasonable for him to rely on the results thereof for the purposes of those provisions.

(7) Any duty imposed on any person by any of the preceding provisions of this section shall extend only to things done in the course of a trade, business or other undertaking carried on by him (whether for profit or not) and to matters within his control.

(8) Where a person designs, manufactures, imports or supplies an article for or to another on the basis of a written undertaking by that other to take specified steps sufficient to ensure, so far as is reasonably practicable, that the article will be safe and without risks to health when properly used, the undertaking shall have the effect of relieving the first-mentioned person from the duty imposed by subsection (1)(*a*) above to such extent as is reasonable having regard to the terms of the undertaking.

(9) Where a person (" the ostensible supplier ") supplies any article for use at work or substance for use at work to another (" the customer ") under a hire-purchase agreement, conditional sale agreement or credit-sale agreement, and the ostensible supplier—

(a) carries on the business of financing the acquisition of goods by others by means of such agreements ; and

(b) in the course of that business acquired his interest in the article or substance supplied to the customer as a means of financing its acquisition by the customer from a third person (" the effective supplier "),

the effective supplier and not the ostensible supplier shall be treated for the purposes of this section as supplying the article or substance to the customer, and any duty imposed by the preceding provisions of this section on suppliers shall accordingly fall on the effective supplier and not on the ostensible supplier.

(10) For the purposes of this section an article or substance is not to be regarded as properly used where it is used without regard to any relevant information or advice relating to its use which has been made available by a person by whom it was designed, manufactured, imported or supplied.

7. It shall be the duty of every employee while at work—

(a) to take reasonable care for the health and safety of himself and of other persons who may be affected by his acts or omissions at work ; and

(b) as regards any duty or requirement imposed on his employer or any other person by or under any of the relevant statutory provisions, to co-operate with him so far as is necessary to enable that duty or requirement to be performed or complied with.

8. No person shall intentionally or recklessly interfere with or misuse anything provided in the interests of health, safety or welfare in pursuance of any of the relevant statutory provisions.

9. No employer shall levy or permit to be levied on any employee of his any charge in respect of anything done or provided in pursuance of any specific requirement of the relevant statutory provisions.

Health and safety regulations and approved codes of practice

15.—(1) Subject to the provisions of section 50, the Secretary of State shall have power to make regulations under this section (in this part referred to as " health and safety regulations ") for any of the general purposes of this Part except as regards matters relating exclusively to agricultural operations.

(2) Without prejudice to the generality of the preceding subsection, health and safety regulations may for any of the general purposes of this Part make provision for any of the purposes mentioned in Schedule 3.

(3) Health and safety regulations—

(a) may repeal or modify any of the existing statutory provisions ;

(b) may exclude or modify in relation to any specified class of case any of the provisions of sections 2 to 9 or any of the existing statutory provisions ;

(c) may make a specified authority or class of authorities responsible, to such extent as may be specified, for the enforcement of any of the relevant statutory provisions.

(4) Health and safety regulations—

(a) may impose requirements by reference to the approval of the Commission or any other specified body or person ;

(b) may provide for references in the regulations to any specified document to operate as references to that document as revised or re-issued from time to time.

(5) Health and safety regulations—

(a) may provide (either unconditionally or subject to conditions, and with or without limit of time) for exemptions from any requirement or prohibition imposed by or under any of the relevant statutory provisions ;

(b) may enable exemptions from any requirement or prohibition imposed by or under any of the relevant statutory provisions to be granted (either unconditionally or subject to conditions, and with or without limit of time) by any specified person or by any person authorised in that behalf by a specified authority.

(6) Health and safety regulations—

    (*a*) may specify the persons or classes of persons who, in the event of a contravention of a requirement or prohibition imposed by or under the regulations, are to be guilty of an offence, whether in addition to or to the exclusion of other persons or classes of persons ;

    (*b*) may provide for any specified defence to be available in proceedings for any offence under the relevant statutory provisions either generally or in specified circumstances ;

    (*c*) may exclude proceedings on indictment in relation to offences consisting of a contravention of a requirement or prohibition imposed by or under any of the existing statutory provisions, sections 2 to 9 or health and safety regulations ;

    (*d*) may restrict the punishments which can be imposed in respect of any such offence as is mentioned in paragraph (*c*) above.

(7) Without prejudice to section 35, health and safety regulations may make provision for enabling offences under any of the relevant statutory provisions to be treated as having been committed at any specified place for the purpose of bringing any such offence within the field of responsibility of any enforcing authority or conferring jurisdiction on any court to entertain proceedings for any such offence.

(8) Health and safety regulations may take the form of regulations applying to particular circumstances only or to a particular case only (for example, regulations applying to particular premises only).

(9) If an Order in Council is made under section 84(3) providing that this section shall apply to or in relation to persons, premises or work outside Great Britain then, notwithstanding the Order, health and safety regulations shall not apply to or in relation to aircraft in flight, vessels, hovercraft or offshore installations outside Great Britain or persons at work outside Great Britain in connection with submarine cables or submarine pipelines except in so far as the regulations expressly so provide.

(10) In this section " specified " means specified in health and safety regulations.

16.—(1) For the purpose of providing practical guidance with respect to the requirements of any provision of sections 2 to 7 or of health and safety regulations or of any of the existing statutory provisions, the Commission may, subject to the following subsection and except as regards matters relating exclusively to agricultural operations—

(a) approve and issue such codes of practice (whether prepared by it or not) as in its opinion are suitable for that purpose ;

(b) approve such codes of practice issued or proposed to be issued otherwise than by the Commission as in its opinion are suitable for that purpose.

(2) The Commission shall not approve a code of practice under subsection (1) above without the consent of the Secretary of State, and shall, before seeking his consent, consult—

(a) any government department or other body that appears to the Commission to be appropriate (and, in particular, in the case of a code relating to electro-magnetic radiations, the National Radiological Protection Board) ; and

(b) such government departments and other bodies, if any, as in relation to any matter dealt with in the code, the Commission is required to consult under this section by virtue of directions given to it by the Secretary of State.

(3) Where a code of practice is approved by the Commission under subsection (1) above, the Commission shall issue a notice in writing—

(a) identifying the code in question and stating the date on which its approval by the Commission is to take effect ; and

(b) specifying for which of the provisions mentioned in subsection (1) above the code is approved.

(4) The Commission may—

(a) from time to time revise the whole or any part of any code of practice prepared by it in pursuance of this section ;

(b) approve any revision or proposed revision of the whole or any part of any code of practice for the time being approved under this section ;

and the provisions of subsections (2) and (3) above shall, with the necessary modifications, apply in relation to the approval of any revision under this subsection as they apply in relation to the approval of a code of practice under subsection (1) above.

(5) The Commission may at any time with the consent of the Secretary of State withdraw its approval from any code of practice approved under this section, but before seeking his consent shall consult the same government departments and other bodies as it would be required to consult under subsection (2) above if it were proposing to approve the code.

(6) Where under the preceding subsection the Commission withdraws its approval from a code of practice approved under this section, the Commission shall issue a notice in writing identifying the code in question and stating the date on which its approval of it is to cease to have effect.

(7) References in this Part to an approved code of practice are references to that code as it has effect for the time being by virtue of any revision of the whole or any part of it approved under this section.

(8) The power of the Commission under subsection (1)(*b*) above to approve a code of practice issued or proposed to be issued otherwise than by the Commission shall include power to approve a part of such a code of practice ; and accordingly in this Part " code of practice " may be read as including a part of such a code of practice.

21. If an inspector is of the opinion that a person—

  (*a*) is contravening one or more of the relevant statutory provisions ; or

  (*b*) has contravened one or more of those provisions in circumstances that make it likely that the contravention will continue or be repeated,

he may serve on him a notice (in this Part referred to as " an improvement notice ") stating that he is of that opinion, specifying the provision or provisions as to which he is of that opinion, giving particulars of the reasons why he is of that opinion, and requiring that person to remedy the contravention or, as the case may be, the matters occasioning it within such period (ending not earlier than the period within which an appeal against the notice can be brought under section 24) as may be specified in the notice.

22.—(1) This section applies to any activities which are being or are about to be carried on by or under the control of any person, being activities to or in relation to which any of the relevant statutory provisions apply or will, if the activities are so carried on, apply.

(2) If as regards any activities to which this section applies an inspector is of the opinion that, as carried on or about to be carried on by or under the control of the person in question, the activities involve or, as the case may be, will involve a risk of serious personal injury, the inspector may serve on that person a notice (in this Part referred to as " a prohibition notice ").

(3) A prohibition notice shall—

(*a*) state that the inspector is of the said opinion ;

(*b*) specify the matters which in his opinion give or, as the case may be, will give rise to the said risk ;

(*c*) where in his opinion any of those matters involves or, as the case may be, will involve a contravention of any of the relevant statutory provisions, state that he is of that opinion, specify the provision or provisions as to which he is of that opinion, and give particulars of the reasons why he is of that opinion ; and

(*d*) direct that the activities to which the notice relates shall not be carried on by or under the control of the person on whom the notice is served unless the matters specified in the notice in pursuance of paragraph (*b*) above and any associated contraventions of provisions so specified in pursuance of paragraph (*c*) above have been remedied.

(4) A direction given in pursuance of subsection (3)(*d*) above shall take immediate effect if the inspector is of the opinion, and states it, that the risk of serious personal injury is or, as the case may be, will be imminent, and shall have effect at the end of a period specified in the notice in any other case.

25.—(1) Where, in the case of any article or substance found by him in any premises which he has power to enter, an inspector has reasonable cause to believe that, in the circumstances in which he finds it, the article or substance is a cause of imminent danger of serious personal injury, he may seize it and cause it to be rendered harmless (whether by destruction or otherwise).

(2) Before there is rendered harmless under this section—

(*a*) any article that forms part of a batch of similar articles ; or

(*b*) any substance,

the inspector shall, if it is practicable for him to do so, take a sample thereof and give to a responsible person at the premises where the article or substance was found by him a portion of the sample marked in a manner sufficient to identify it.

(3) As soon as may be after any article or substance has been seized and rendered harmless under this section, the inspector shall prepare and sign a written report giving particulars of the circumstances in which the article or substance was seized and so dealt with by him, and shall—

(*a*) give a signed copy of the report to a responsible person at the premises where the article or substance was found by him ; and

(*b*) unless that person is the owner of the article or substance, also serve a signed copy of the report on the owner ;

and if, where paragraph (*b*) above applies, the inspector cannot after reasonable enquiry ascertain the name or address of the owner, the copy may be served on him by giving it to the person to whom a copy was given under the preceding paragraph.

36.—(1) Where the commission by any person of an offence under any of the relevant statutory provisions is due to the act or default of some other person, that other person shall be guilty of the offence, and a person may be charged with and convicted of the offence by virtue of this subsection whether or not proceedings are taken against the first-mentioned person.

(2) Where there would be or have been the commission of an offence under section 33 by the Crown but for the circumstance that that section does not bind the Crown, and that fact is due to the act or default of a person other than the Crown, that person shall be guilty of the offence which, but for that circumstance, the Crown would be committing or would have committed, and may be charged with and convicted of that offence accordingly.

(3) The preceding provisions of this section are subject to any provision made by virtue of section 15(6).

37.—(1) Where an offence under any of the relevant statutory provisions committed by a body corporate is proved to have been committed with the consent or connivance of, or to have been attributable to any neglect on the part of, any director, manager, secretary or other similar officer of the body corporate or a person who was purporting to act in any such capacity, he as well as the body corporate shall be guilty of that offence and shall be liable to be proceeded against and punished accordingly.

(2) Where the affairs of a body corporate are managed by its members, the preceding subsection shall apply in relation to the acts and defaults of a member in connection with his functions of management as if he were a director of the body corporate.

40. In any proceedings for an offence under any of the relevant statutory provisions consisting of a failure to comply with a duty or requirement to do something so far as is practicable or so far as is reasonably practicable, or to use the best practicable means to do something, it shall be for the accused to prove (as the case may be) that it was not practicable or not reasonably practicable to do more than was in fact done to satisfy the duty or requirement, or that there was no better practicable means than was in fact used to satisfy the duty or requirement.

47.—(1) Nothing in this Part shall be construed—

(*a*) as conferring a right of action in any civil proceedings in respect of any failure to comply with any duty imposed by sections 2 to 7 or any contravention of section 8 ; or

(*b*) as affecting the extent (if any) to which breach of a duty imposed by any of the existing statutory provisions is actionable ; or

(*c*) as affecting the operation of section 12 of the Nuclear Installations Act 1965 (right to compensation by virtue of certain provisions of that Act).

(2) Breach of a duty imposed by health and safety regulations or agricultural health and safety regulations shall, so far as it causes damage, be actionable except in so far as the regulations provide otherwise.

(3) No provision made by virtue of section 15(6)(*b*) shall afford a defence in any civil proceedings, whether brought by

virtue of subsection (2) above or not; but as regards any duty imposed as mentioned in subsection (2) above health and safety regulations or, as the case may be, agricultural health and safety regulations may provide for any defence specified in the regulations to be available in any action for breach of that duty.

(4) Subsections (1)(*a*) and (2) above are without prejudice to any right of action which exists apart from the provisions of this Act, and subsection (3) above is without prejudice to any defence which may be available apart from the provisions of the regulations there mentioned.

(5) Any term of an agreement which purports to exclude or restrict the operation of subsection (2) above, or any liability arising by virtue of that subsection shall be void, except in so far as health and safety regulations or, as the case may be, agricultural health and safety regulations provide otherwise.

(6) In this section " damage " includes the death of, or injury to, any person (including any disease and any impairment of a person's physical or mental condition).

SCHEDULE 3

Subject-Matter of Health and Safety Regulations

1.—(1) Regulating or prohibiting—
   (*a*) the manufacture, supply or use of any plant ;
   (*b*) the manufacture, supply, keeping or use of any substance ;
   (*c*) the carrying on of any process or the carrying out of any operation.

(2) Imposing requirements with respect to the design, construction, guarding, siting, installation, commissioning, examination, repair, maintenance, alteration, adjustment, dismantling, testing or inspection of any plant.

(3) Imposing requirements with respect to the marking of any plant or of any articles used or designed for use as components in any plant, and in that connection regulating or restricting the use of specified markings.

(4) Imposing requirements with respect to the testing, labelling or examination of any substance.

(5) Imposing requirements with respect to the carrying out of research in connection with any activity mentioned in sub-paragraphs (1) to (4) above.

2.—(1) Prohibiting the importation into the United Kingdom or the landing or unloading there of articles or substances of any specified description, whether absolutely or unless conditions imposed by or under the regulations are complied with.

(2) Specifying, in a case where an act or omission in relation to such an importation, landing or unloading as is mentioned in the preceding sub-paragraph constitutes an offence under a provision of this Act and of the Customs and Excise Act 1952, the Act under which the offence is to be punished.

3.—(1) Prohibiting or regulating the transport of articles or substances of any specified description.

(2) Imposing requirements with respect to the manner and means of transporting articles or substances of any specified description, including requirements with respect to the construction, testing and marking of containers and means of transport and the packaging and labelling of articles or substances in connection with their transport.

4.—(1) Prohibiting the carrying on of any specified activity or the doing of any specified thing except under the authority and in accordance with the terms and conditions of a licence, or except with the consent or approval of a specified authority.

(2) Providing for the grant, renewal, variation, transfer and revocation of licences (including the variation and revocation of conditions attached to licences).

5. Requiring any person, premises or thing to be registered in any specified circumstances or as a condition of the carrying on of any specified activity or the doing of any specified thing.

6.—(1) Requiring, in specified circumstances, the appointment (whether in a specified capacity or not) of persons (or persons with specified qualifications or experience, or both) to perform specified functions, and imposing duties or conferring powers on persons appointed (whether in pursuance of the regulations or not) to perform specified functions.

(2) Restricting the performance of specified functions to persons possessing specified qualifications or experience.

7. Regulating or prohibiting the employment in specified circumstances of all persons or any class of persons.

8.—(1) Requiring the making of arrangements for securing the health of persons at work or other persons, including arrangements for medical examinations and health surveys.

(2) Requiring the making of arrangements for monitoring the atmospheric or other conditions in which persons work.

9. Imposing requirements with respect to any matter affecting the conditions in which persons work, including in particular such matters as the structural condition and stability of premises, the means of access to and egress from premises, cleanliness, temperature, lighting, ventilation, overcrowding, noise, vibrations, ionising and other radiations, dust and fumes.

10. Securing the provision of specified welfare facilities for persons at work, including in particular such things as an adequate water supply, sanitary conveniences, washing and bathing facilities, ambulance and first-aid arrangements, cloakroom accommodation, sitting facilities and refreshment facilities.

11. Imposing requirements with respect to the provision and use in specified circumstances of protective clothing or equipment, including clothing affording protection against the weather.

12. Requiring in specified circumstances the taking of specified precautions in connection with the risk of fire.

13.—(1) Prohibiting or imposing requirements in connection with the emission into the atmosphere of any specified gas, smoke or dust or any other specified substance whatsoever.

(2) Prohibiting or imposing requirements in connection with the emission of noise, vibrations or any ionising or other radiations.

(3) Imposing requirements with respect to the monitoring of any such emission as is mentioned in the preceding sub-paragraphs.

14. Imposing requirements with respect to the instruction, training and supervision of persons at work.

15.—(1) Requiring, in specified circumstances, specified matters to be notified in a specified manner to specified persons.

(2) Empowering inspectors in specified circumstances to require persons to submit written particulars of measures proposed to be taken to achieve compliance with any of the relevant statutory provisions.

16. Imposing requirements with respect to the keeping and preservation of records and other documents, including plans and maps.

17. Imposing requirements with respect to the management of animals.

18. The following purposes as regards premises of any specified description where persons work, namely—

(*a*) requiring precautions to be taken against dangers to which the premises or persons therein are or may be exposed by reason of conditions (including natural conditions) existing in the vicinity ;

(*b*) securing that persons in the premises leave them in specified circumstances.

19. Conferring, in specified circumstances involving a risk of fire or explosion, power to search a person or any article which a person has with him for the purpose of ascertaining whether he has in his possession any article of a specified kind likely in those circumstances to cause a fire or explosion, and power to seize and dispose of any article of that kind found on such a search.

20. Restricting, prohibiting or requiring the doing of any specified thing where any accident or other occurrence of a specified kind has occurred.

21. As regards cases of any specified class, being a class such that the variety in the circumstances of particular cases within it calls for the making of special provision for particular cases, any of the following purposes, namely—

(*a*) conferring on employers or other persons power to make rules or give directions with respect to matters affecting health or safety ;

(*b*) requiring employers or other persons to make rules with respect to any such matters ;

(*c*) empowering specified persons to require employers or other persons either to make rules with respect to any such matters or to modify any such rules previously made by virtue of this paragraph ; and

(*d*) making admissible in evidence without further proof, in such circumstances and subject to such conditions as may be specified, documents which purport to be copies of rules or rules of any specified class made under this paragraph.

22. Conferring on any local or public authority power to make byelaws with respect to any specified matter, specifying the authority or person by whom any byelaws made in the exercise of that power need to be confirmed, and generally providing for the procedure to be followed in connection with the making of any such byelaws.

Interpretation

23.—(1) In this Schedule "specified" means specified in health and safety regulations.

(2) It is hereby declared that the mention in this Schedule of a purpose that falls within any more general purpose mentioned therein is without prejudice to the generality of the more general purpose.

Summary of the Pearson Committee Report

The Royal Commission on Civil Liability and Compensation for Personal Injury, under the Chairmanship of Lord Pearson, published its massive report in March 1978. Only a small section is directed to the particular issue of product liability. Its concern was not merely in altering the law, but examining all the means by which our society compensates the victims of accidents, whether through the law courts, insurance or state benefits.

The Chapter (22) on 'Products' owes much to the Report of the Law Commissions, and reaches many of the same conclusions for the same reasons.

The Committee came to the view that the present law was unsatisfactory. It considered four ways in which the situation might be altered:

1   Altering the rules of contract.
2   Reversing the burden of proof in tort (delict) actions.
3   Introducing a 'no-fault' system.
4   Strict liability.

The first two were rejected for much the same reasons as those given by the Law Commissions.

A 'no-fault' system, i.e. a system of automatic compensation for people injured by products, was rejected on the basis that such a scheme would be very difficult to finance especially since there is no existing system of compulsory product liability insurance on which to impose a levy.

The Committee therefore opted for a system of strict liability:

1   The Strasbourg Convention and the EEC Directive indicate a strong trend towards strict liability for products.
2   Purchasers of products already enjoy strict liability against their supplier: it seems right to extend these benefits.
3   Since producers claim credit for successful products they should accept responsibility for their defective products.
4   It might act as an encouragement or inducement to the highest possible safety standards.
5   The producer is the person best able to arrange insurance cover.

Defect

The Committee adopted the definition used in the Strasbourg Convention: 'a product has a defect when it does not provide the safety which a person is entitled to expect, having regard to all the circumstances, including the presentation of the product'. The consumer must use the product carefully and in accordance with instructions.

Producers and distributors

Although principle would point to placing strict liability on the final producer alone, this system would often work unfairly against both the final producer — who might be a fairly small link in the chain — and against an injured person who might find himself deprived of a remedy. The net should be spread wider to include component manufacturers. However, the component manufacturer should not be liable if the part was made to faulty technical specifications supplied to him, or if the part was unsuitable for incorporation in the final product.

A distributor who supplies a defective product should be strictly liable unless he disclosed the name of either the manufacturer or his own supplier. This rule should apply without exception — even covering the retailers of primary products.

'Own branding' of goods indicates a greater acceptance of responsibility for the quality of those goods. Where an injury is caused by a defective 'own brand' product, both retailer and producer should be strictly liable.

It was argued that, where goods are made to a specification, the maker should not be liable if it is defective because of the specification. The Committee rejected this view: again the producer is in a better position to insure: if he feels that the specification is defective he can either refuse to do the work or obtain an indemnity. There might also well be the defence of contributory negligence where the specifier himself is injured.

The Committee felt that it was essential for the remedy to be available whether the goods were manufactured here or abroad. They accordingly recommended that importers of defective goods should be strictly liable.

Defences

It should be a defence to show:
1   That the product was not defective.
2   That the injury was not caused by the defect.
3   That the defendant was *not* in fact the producer (importer, etc).
4   That the producer did not put the product into circulation, e.g. it was stolen.
5   That the product was not defective at the time he put it into circulation (but, for example, it became so because of negligent servicing).
6   That it was not put into circulation in the course of a business (you can still sell the remainder of your home crop of apples).
7   That the injured person was wholly – or partly – responsible for his own injuries (contributory negligence).

It should not be a defence:
a   That the producer had withdrawn, or attempted to withdraw, the product from the market. However, in the particular case of aircraft where there are continual alterations in the instructions given to the operator, the maker might obtain an indemnity where he could show

that the operator had wilfully or negligently ignored instructions.

b   That the defect was one of 'design development' and not manufacture. That would create an enormous gap in the cover.

c   That the product had been officially scrutinised by a Safety Board, etc. The fact that a product has official approval does not diminish responsibility for it.

d   There should be no power to contract out of liability.

Restrictions on liability

The Committee rejected restrictions both on the amount of any individual claim or on the total amount for any one product. In the former case it would not be possible to fix an amount appropriate for all products, in the latter case, since the victims of a defective product may only emerge slowly, there would be an unacceptable conflict of interests — to compensate quickly and to ensure that all were compensated.

There should be a time limit of 10 years from the putting into circulation of the product, beyond which strict liability would cease, and a person injured by a defective product should start proceedings within 3 years of the date when the claimant became aware of 'the damage, the defect and the producer'.

Possible exclusions

It was argued that certain classes of product should not be subject to strict liability.

1   *Drugs*   Despite the particular problems, especially relating to development, and the practical impossibility of testing adequately to eliminate all risks, the Committee were not prepared to make them a special case. It is, after all, concern about drugs that is one of the chief forces behind the call for stricter liability.

2   *Human blood and organs*   The Report recommends that these *should* be regarded as products, and the

'authorities responsible for distributing them' should be regarded as the producer.

3   *Products incorporated into immovables*   For materials incorporated into a building. Liability should remain with the makers even after incorporation. Any exclusion would give rise to indefensible anomalies.

Liability for Defective Products — summary of the report by the Law Commission and the Scottish Law Commission

In making their report, published in June 1977, the two Commissions were well aware that it would shortly be overshadowed by the (then) forthcoming Pearson Committee Report (Royal Commission on Civil Liability and Compensation for Personal Injury). However, they state quite emphatically that the overlap did not impede their work.

The scope of the Report is, at the same time, both narrower and wider than that of the Pearson Committee: narrower in that it is concerned only with liability for defective products, wider in that it is not restricted to compensation for personal injuries but also considers compensation for other forms of loss (property damage, etc.)

The Law Commissions published a consultative document in which they sought representations from interested bodies (manufacturers, importers, distributors . . . insurers . . . consumers . . . and, of course, lawyers) on four major questions:

1   Whether the existing law was satisfactory,
2   Whether change should come through an extension of the law of contract, or
3   By altering the general requirement in the law of tort (delict) that an injured person must (usually) show a failure to take reasonable care, or
4   Whether some form of strict liability should be introduced in respect of defective products.

The response to this consultative document indicated widespread dissatisfaction with the existing law: most felt that change should *not* be effected through the law of contract. There was some support for the view that it should be on the producer of a defective product to show that he had taken reasonable care for the safety of the consumer. Finally 'a weighty body of opinion' (from which most of the manufacturers and producers consulted were conspicuously absent) favoured the imposition of some form of strict liability.

1 Criticisms of the present law

The situation, at present, is concisely stated in paragraph 20 of the Report: 'Where a person suffers personal injury, damage to property or certain other losses as the result of a product being defective he may recover compensation in the form of damages by proving a breach of contract, or the commission of a tort (delict) or, in certain circumstances, the breach of statutory duty.'

Criticism of the existing law can be made in the following respects:

1　Unless an injured party can prove *fault*, he has no remedy in the absence of a contractual relationship (which imposes strict liability).
2　In the absence of (provable) fault by the manufacturer, contractual remedies lie against the final seller who is seldom regarded as being responsible for the quality and safety of the product.
3　Thus there may be a chain of claims — multiplying litigation.
4　Even if a product can be shown to be defective, the present law requires a party to show that the defect existed at the time the product left the producer.
5　Even though the doctrine of *res ipsa loquitur* (the facts speak for themselves) may assist a party in showing fault, he is still at a disadvantage in relation to access to the relevant evidence and scientific expertise.

2 Possible ways of meeting these criticisms

1　The law of contract might be extended to permit the

ultimate purchaser to sue the producer direct (thus leap-frogging the chain) and/or to create 'third-party rights', giving the ultimate consumer remedies against the final supplier in cases where there was no contractual relation between them. The former is an artificial device which still restricts the remedy to the final purchaser who is not necessarily the ultimate consumer. The latter provides a remedy for all consumers — but against the wrong person: the right of redress should be directed against the person who created the risk and is in the best position to exercise control over the quality and safety of the product.

Note: the American law of product liability went through a stage or providing remedies through bending the rules of contract before progressing to remedies in tort (delict).

2   Easing the burdens on the plaintiff in a tort action. Although a plaintiff's task would be made easier by requiring the producer to establish that he had taken reasonable care, the Law Commissions were of the opinion that such a step does not go far enough. A plaintiff would still be handicapped by his lack of technical knowledge. Trials would still be a battle of experts and many injured parties would continue to be without a remedy.

3   Introduction of strict liability for injuries resulting from defective products. The Commissions concluded that such a step is justified — and that liability should lie on the producer:

a   The loss should be on the creator of the risk — who can spread the cost via his prices.

b   Liability should be on those best able to exercise control over quality and safety — and that means, almost invariably, the producer.

c   The producer is in the best position to insure against the risks: first party insurance against personal injury is expensive — and rare.

d   The public put their reliance in the producer and not the supplier.

e   Of all methods, it gives rise to the least complicated procedural and evidentiary problems.

f   By enabling parties to sue direct, litigation would be kept to the minimum.

g   It is desirable to keep the list of potentially liable parties
to the minimum necessary to ensure that an adequate
remedy is available' — the more people who are potentially liable, the higher the insurance bill as each obtains
adequate cover. Therefore, wherever practicable, strict
liability should *not* extend beyond the producer to
intermediaries (see Section 6 of the Health and Safety
at Work Act).

There is one further 'policy consideration' — in providing
adequate redress for those injured by defective products, the
laws should not commercially damage British industry. The
Report concluded, however, that the risk of putting reputable
producers out of business is both slight and justifiable.

3   The Proposals

Defective products

A product can be considered to be defective in two senses —
'unsafe' or 'unmerchantable'. The latter is concerned with
quality and performance and can reasonably be left to the
law of contract. So the essence of the definition of 'defective'
should be a 'lack of safety'. Clearly certain products have in
them a patently 'dangerous element', e.g. razor blades. It is not
sought to make the manufacturers of such items strictly
liable merely because it is, by design, potentially dangerous.
The Report therefore recommends that 'a product should be
regarded as defective if it does not comply with the standard
of reasonable safety that a person is entitled to expect of it
— but the standard of safety should be determined objectively
having regard to all the circumstances in which the product
has been put into circulation, and the use or uses to which it
would be reasonable for the product to be put in those circumstances'. Knives may unjam toast stuck in a toaster — but
it is not a reason for making the manufacturer liable to the
electrocuted user that he failed to insulate the handle!

The defectiveness of a product can be judged either at the
time when it is put into circulation, or at the time of the
accident. Accepting that time and innovation rapidly overtake
events it would not be right that products should become
defective merely because the standards applicable to them

have improved. The essential time is the date when the product was put into circulation.

Although strict liability is particularly appropriate to the case of mass produced goods – the Law Commissions did not want to restrict it to those producers. After all, 'where articles are individually made, the public expectation is, if anything, higher than in relation to mass-produced goods'.

It was not part of the Law Commissions' brief to consider liability for defective buildings (immovables), but the two Commissions disagreed on the question whether liability for defective materials used in the construction of a building should continue after their incorporation into the building. The Scottish Law Commission suggested that it should cease, liability being assessed under the general principles applying to buildings. The English and Welsh Commission saw no reason why strict liability should not continue.

Who should be liable?

Since it was felt that, as a matter of policy, strict liability should be imposed on the person best able to control quality, the Law Commissions agreed that in general it should not be extended to middlemen. They would, of course, remain potentially liable under the ordinary rules of contract. But there are three situations where such an extension would be justified.

1   *Own-brand products*   It is fair to say that by holding the goods out as his own the retailer assumes responsibility not only for their quality but also for their safety: he has, after all, a large degree of control in their manufacture. The producer would, of course, remain strictly liable.

2   *Anonymous goods*   The Report follows the lead of the Strasbourg Convention and recommends that a supplier should be strictly liable for goods that carry no indication of their producer *unless* he discloses either the identity of the manufacturer, or that of his own supplier. Thus a claim would not fail for want of an identifiable defendant.

3   *Imported goods*   Again a claim should not fail because

the producer is unidentifiable or protected by being outside the jurisdiction. The Report accordingly recommends that an importer of a defective product 'should answer for the quality of those goods' to any person who might be injured by them. 'He creates the risk by importing the product into the jurisdiction for commercial purposes.'

Should liability be strict for all products?

Certain products, because of their special natures, called for special consideration by the Law Commissions, and brought about the main areas of disagreement between the two Commissions.

1   *Nuclear occurrences*   The law already lays down strict liability on the licensee of a nuclear site in respect of 'nuclear occurrences'. The Commissions did not want to alter these arrangements.

2   *Pharmaceuticals*   Despite strong representations that some things were a 'special case', the Report clearly recommends that they should not be so treated. Even though a certain degree of danger and the possibility of harmful side effects are inherent risks, the Report proposes that drugs should nevertheless satisfy the standard of reasonable safety — due regard being had to any instructions and warnings supplied. However the Scots were swayed by the arguments that insurance cover might well be prohibitive — if obtainable at all — and suggested that the State should consider accepting a degree of responsibility — especially since it administers the system of NHS prescriptions. Such matters being outside the orbit of their brief, further discussion was left to the Royal Commission.

3   *Components*   The (English) Law Commission felt that liability for defects in components should rest with the component manufacturer — principally because it is he who has control over quality and has the better opportunity to check safety. However, manufacturers of components cannot be held responsible if they are used in a way for which they were never designed — so

'provided that the component is properly made to whatever specifications are required and is reasonably safe for reasonable use at the time of supply . . . the component maker would not be liable'.

The Scottish Law Commission, on the other hand, were of the opinion that liability should rest on the final manufacturer. Components are often made to the specifications of an ultimate manufacturer. If they are not, then the component maker will often be unable to say what the ultimate destination will be, and so may not be able to obtain adequate insurance cover.

4   *Natural products*   The English Law Commission were unable to draw any sensible line between natural and industrial producers: even so-called fresh foods have generally been the subject of a process — either by spraying or fertilising. It concluded that it should not 'recommend the exclusion of any natural products, even those few which can be said to have been subjected to no process whatsoever . . .'.

The Scottish Law Commission disagreed: the risks involved in agricultural or fishery production 'may usually be laid at the door of nature or of a polluter rather than of the producer'. Again the producer is often not the party best able to meet the risks — as likely as not he will be a farmer working on his own. They accordingly recommend that 'consideration should be given to the exclusion of producers of primary agricultural and fishery products from the regime of strict liability'.

Defences

The Report concluded that there should not be a special defence that the product was as safe as the state of art would allow. 'We think that the injured person should be compensated by the producer however careful he had been.'

However, where a consumer 'assumes a risk' by ignoring whatever instructions or warnings were given — he should not be allowed to claim. Similarly the producer should be allowed to raise the defence of 'contributory negligence' — if the injured party has failed to take reasonable care for his own safety then his damages are reduced proportionately to his degree of fault for his injuries.

Attempts to contract out of liability for negligence would of course be governed by *The Unfair Contract Terms Act, 1977*, Section 2. These provisions should be extended to strict liability.

Calculation of Damages

Compensation resulting from strict liability should be assessed on the same basis as under a claim in the existing law of tort (delict).

The Commissions decided against recommending any financial limits — either on individual claims or 'globally' (by setting a total liability in respect of a product).

Strict liability should be restricted to claims for death or personal injury. The Commissions believed that first party insurance in relation to property ought generally to be encouraged, and recommended against extending strict liability to property-loss claims. These would, of course, still be possible through the existing law of contract and tort (delict).

Appendix 9

The Congenital Disabilities (Civil Liability) Act, 1976

Congenital Disabilities (Civil Liability) Act 1976

1976 CHAPTER 28

An Act to make provision as to civil liability in the case of children born disabled in consequence of some person's fault; and to extend the Nuclear Installations Act 1965, so that children so born in consequence of a breach of duty under that Act may claim compensation.

[22nd July 1976]

BE IT ENACTED by the Queen's most Excellent Majesty, by and with the advice and consent of the Lords Spiritual and Temporal, and Commons, in this present Parliament assembled, and by the authority of the same, as follows:—

1.—(1) If a child is born disabled as the result of such an occurrence before its birth as is mentioned in subsection (2) below, and a person (other than the child's own mother) is under this section answerable to the child in respect of the occurrence, the child's disabilities are to be regarded as damage resulting from the wrongful act of that person and actionable accordingly at the suit of the child. *Civil liability to child born disabled.*

(2) An occurrence to which this section applies is one which—

    (*a*) affected either parent of the child in his or her ability to have a normal, healthy child ; or

    (*b*) affected the mother during her pregnancy, or affected her or the child in the course of its birth, so that the child is born with disabilities which would not otherwise have been present.

(3) Subject to the following subsections, a person (here referred to as " the defendant ") is answerable to the child if he was liable in tort to the parent or would, if sued in due time, have been so ; and it is no answer that there could not have been such liability because the parent suffered no actionable injury, if there was a breach of legal duty which, accompanied by injury, would have given rise to the liability.

(4) In the case of an occurrence preceding the time of conception, the defendant is not answerable to the child if at that time either or both of the parents knew the risk of their child being born disabled (that is to say, the particular risk created by the occurrence) ; but should it be the child's father who is the defendant, this subsection does not apply if he knew of the risk and the mother did not.

(5) The defendant is not answerable to the child, for anything he did or omitted to do when responsible in a professional capacity for treating or advising the parent, if he took reasonable care having due regard to then received professional opinion applicable to the particular class of case ; but this does not mean that he is answerable only because he departed from received opinion.

(6) Liability to the child under this section may be treated as having been excluded or limited by contract made with the parent affected, to the same extent and subject to the same restrictions as liability in the parent's own case ; and a contract term which could have been set up by the defendant in an action by the parent, so as to exclude or limit his liability to him or her, operates in the defendant's favour to the same, but no greater, extent in an action under this section by the child.

(7) If in the child's action under this section it is shown that the parent affected shared the responsibility for the child being born disabled, the damages are to be reduced to such extent as the court thinks just and equitable having regard to the extent of the parent's responsibility.

Liability of woman driving when pregnant. 2. A woman driving a motor vehicle when she knows (or ought reasonably to know) herself to be pregnant is to be regarded as being under the same duty to take care for the safety of her unborn child as the law imposes on her with respect to the safety of other people ; and if in consequence of her breach of that duty her child is born with disabilities which would not otherwise have been present, those disabilities are to be regarded as damage resulting from her wrongful act and actionable accordingly at the suit of the child.

3.—(1) Section 1 of this Act does not affect the operation of the Nuclear Installations Act 1965 as to liability for, and compensation in respect of, injury or damage caused by occurrences involving nuclear matter or the emission of ionising radiations. Disabled birth due to radiation.

1965 c. 57.

(2) For the avoidance of doubt anything which—

  (a) affects a man in his ability to have a normal, healthy child ; or

  (b) affects a woman in that ability, or so affects her when she is pregnant that her child is born with disabilities which would not otherwise have been present,

is an injury for the purposes of that Act.

(3) If a child is born disabled as the result of an injury to either of its parents caused in breach of a duty imposed by any of sections 7 to 11 of that Act (nuclear site licensees and others to secure that nuclear incidents do not cause injury to persons, etc.), the child's disabilities are to be regarded under the subsequent provisions of that Act (compensation and other matters) as injuries caused on the same occasion, and by the same breach of duty, as was the injury to the parent.

(4) As respects compensation to the child, section 13(6) of that Act (contributory fault of person injured by radiation) is to be applied as if the reference there to fault were to the fault of the parent.

(5) Compensation is not payable in the child's case if the injury to the parent preceded the time of the child's conception and at that time either or both of the parents knew the risk of their child being born disabled (that is to say, the particular risk created by the injury).

4.—(1) References in this Act to a child being born disabled or with disabilities are to its being born with any deformity, disease or abnormality, including predisposition (whether or not susceptible of immediate prognosis) to physical or mental defect in the future. Interpretation and other supplementary provisions.

(2) In this Act—

  (a) " born " means born alive (the moment of a child's birth being when it first has a life separate from its mother), and " birth " has a corresponding meaning ; and

  (b) " motor vehicle " means a mechanically propelled vehicle intended or adapted for use on roads.

(3) Liability to a child under section 1 or 2 of this Act is to be regarded—

  (a) as respects all its incidents and any matters arising or to arise out of it ; and (*b*) subject to any contrary context or intention, for the purpose of construing references in enactments and documents to personal or bodily injuries and cognate matters,

as liability for personal injuries sustained by the child immediately after its birth.

(4) No damages shall be recoverable under either of those sections in respect of any loss of expectation of life, nor shall any such loss be taken into account in the compensation payable in respect of a child under the Nuclear Installations Act 1965 as extended by section 3, unless (in either case) the child lives for at least 48 hours.

1965 c. 57.

(5) This Act applies in respect of births after (but not before) its passing, and in respect of any such birth it replaces any law in force before its passing, whereby a person could be liable to a child in respect of disabilities with which it might be born ; but in section 1(3) of this Act the expression " liable in tort " does not include any reference to liability by virtue of this Act, or to liability by virtue of any such law.

(6) References to the Nuclear Installations Act 1965 are to that Act as amended ; and for the purposes of section 28 of that Act (power by Order in Council to extend the Act to territories outside the United Kingdom) section 3 of this Act is to be treated as if it were a provision of that Act.

Crown application.

5. This Act binds the Crown.

Citation and extent.

6.—(1) This Act may be cited as the Congenital Disabilities (Civil Liability) Act 1976.

(2) This Act extends to Northern Ireland but not to Scotland.

Appendix 10

The Consumer Protection Act, 1961

Note: although The Consumer Safety Act, 1978, *has repealed* The Consumer Protection Act, 1961, *in its entirety, some relevant provisions of the former affecting the latter have not yet come into force.*

CHAPTER 40

An Act to make provision for the protection of consumers.

[19th July, 1961]

BE it enacted by the Queen's most Excellent Majesty, by and with the advice and consent of the Lords Spiritual and Temporal, and Commons, in this present Parliament assembled, and by the authority of the same, as follows:—

1.—(1) The Secretary of State may by regulations impose as respects any prescribed class of goods—

> (*a*) any such requirements, whether as to the composition or contents, design, construction, finish or packing of, or otherwise relating to, goods of that class or any component part thereof, as are in his opinion expedient to prevent or reduce risk of death or personal injury;

> (*b*) any such requirements for securing that goods of that class or any component part thereof are in the prescribed manner marked with or accompanied by any prescribed warning or instructions, or any prescribed form of warning or instructions, which in the opinion of the Secretary of State is or are expedient as aforesaid.

Safety requirements and instructions.

(2) Requirements may be imposed under this section either as respects all goods of a prescribed class or as respects any prescribed description of such goods, and either generally or in prescribed circumstances, and regulations under this section may make different provision for different cases.

(3) Regulations under this section may provide that the Schedule to this Act shall have effect in relation to goods of any class prescribed under this section, or to such goods and to goods of which such goods are a component part.

(4) A class or description of goods may be prescribed under this section notwithstanding that the goods are for use only as component parts of other goods (whether or not those other goods are goods of a prescribed class or description).

(5) It shall be the duty of the Secretary of State, before making any regulations under this section, to consult with such persons or bodies of persons as appear to him requisite.

(6) The power to make regulations conferred by this section shall be exerciseable by statutory instrument which shall be subject to annulment in pursuance of a resolution of either House of Parliament.

Prohibition on sale, etc. of goods not complying with regulations under s. 1.

2.—(1) Subject to the provisions of this section, no person shall sell, or have in his possession for the purpose of selling, any goods as respects which or a component part of which any requirements of regulations under the foregoing section are in force unless all requirements of the regulations relating to the goods or component part are complied with.

(2) Subject to the provisions of this section, no person shall sell, or have in his possession for the purpose of selling, a component part intended for, but not embodied in, any goods as respects which any requirements of regulations under the foregoing section are in force, being a component part such that if it were embodied in the goods any requirement of the regulations applicable to the goods would be contravened or not complied with.

(3) The foregoing provisions of this section shall not apply to a person—

(a) where he is selling, or as the case may be is in possession, otherwise than in the course of a business, or is acting as agent, or as the servant of the agent, of a person who was not acting in the course of a business in entrusting the goods to an agent ; or

(b) where he reasonably believes that the goods or component parts will not be used in Great Britain ; or

(c) in the case of a sale under a credit-sale agreement, if he has at no time had possession of the goods or component parts and only became the owner thereof at the time of entering into the agreement ; or

(d) where he is selling, or as the case may be is in possession for the purpose of selling, the goods or component parts as scrap, that is to say for the value of the materials of which the goods or parts are composed and not for use as finished articles ; or

(e) in the case of goods or component parts which have been damaged by, or in consequence of, fire or flooding, where he is selling, or as the case may be is in possession for the purpose of selling, the goods or component parts to a person who carries on a business of buying damaged goods and repairing or reconditioning them for resale, or to a person by whom the goods or parts were insured against damage.

(4) As respects any requirement relating to the manufacture of goods or a component part of goods, unless regulations under the foregoing section otherwise provide, subsections (1) and (2) of this section shall not apply in relation to goods or component parts manufactured before the imposition of the requirement, or if it is so provided by such regulations shall not apply in relation to such goods or component parts until a prescribed date.

(5) Regulations under the foregoing section may contain such other exemptions from the operation of subsections (1) and (2) of this section, applicable in such cases as may be prescribed, as appear to the Secretary of State necessary or expedient.

(6) If as respects goods of any class or description regulations under the foregoing section so provide, subsections (1) to (3) of this section (other than paragraphs (*d*) and (*e*) of subsection (3)) shall apply in relation to goods of that class or description as if references to selling or to a sale included references to letting under a hire-purchase agreement or on hire, and the reference to a sale under a credit-sale agreement were a reference to letting under a hire-purchase agreement:

Provided that subsections (1) and (2) of this section shall not apply—

(a) in a case of letting on hire, where the letting is incidental to the letting of premises ;

(b) in a case of possession for the purpose of letting on hire, where possession is for the purpose of a letting which is to be incidental to the letting of premises ;

(c) in any case of letting, where the letting was lawful at the time when it began.

3.—(1) Any obligation imposed by or by virtue of the foregoing section on any person not to sell, let or have possession of any goods or component part is a duty which is owed by him to any other person who may be affected by the contravention of or non-compliance with the requirement in question, and a breach of that duty is actionable (subject to the defences and other incidents applying to actions for breach of statutory duty). *Enforcement of s. 2.*

(2) Any person who contravenes the foregoing section shall be guilty of an offence and liable on summary conviction to a fine not exceeding one hundred pounds, or in the case of a second or subsequent offence to a fine not exceeding two hundred and fifty pounds or to imprisonment for a term not exceeding three months or to both:

Provided that a person shall not be convicted of an offence under this section by reason of a contravention of or failure to comply with any requirement imposed under section one of this Act in relation to the goods or component part in question if he proves that he had reasonable cause to believe that all such requirements were satisfied.

(3) Where an offence under this section committed by a body corporate is proved to have been committed with the consent or connivance of, or to be attributable to any neglect on the part of, any director, manager, secretary, or other similar officer of the body corporate, or any person purporting to act in any such capacity, he as well as the body corporate shall be deemed to be guilty of the offence.

In this subsection the expression " director ", in relation to any body corporate which is established by or under any enactment for the purpose of carrying on under national ownership any industry or part of an industry or undertaking and whose affairs are managed by its members, means a member of that body.

Expenses. **4.** There shall be defrayed out of moneys provided by Parliament any increase attributable to this Act in the sums payable out of moneys so provided by way of Rate-deficiency Grant or Exchequer Equalisation Grant under the enactments relating to local government in England and Wales or in Scotland.

Interpretation. **5.** In this Act the following expressions have the following meanings : —

" Act of 1932 " means the Hire Purchase and Small Debt (Scotland) Act, 1932, as amended by the Hire-Purchase Act, 1954 ;

" component part " includes an accessory ;

" credit-sale agreement " means an agreement for the sale of goods under which the whole or part of the purchase price is payable by instalments, except that, as respects Scotland, it does not include an agreement to sell under a contract to which the Act of 1932 applies ;

" hire-purchase agreement ", as respects England and Wales, has the same meaning as in the Hire-Purchase Act, 1938, and, as respects Scotland, means a contract to which the Act of 1932 applies ; and, as respects Scotland, references to letting under a hire-purchase agreement and to a hirer under such a letting shall include references to an agreement to sell under such a contract as aforesaid and to a purchaser under such an agreement respectively ;

" personal injury " includes disease or disability ;

" prescribed " means prescribed by regulations under section one of this Act.

6.—(1) Subject to the following provisions of this section, the Heating Appliances (Fireguards) Act, 1952, and the Oil Burners (Standards) Act, 1960, shall cease to have effect. *Repeals and transitional provisions.*

(2) In relation to goods of the following classes, that is to say gas fires, electric fires, oil heaters and component parts of oil heaters, this Act shall apply as if—

(a) any regulations made under the said Act of 1952 or the said Act of 1960 and in force at the commencement of this Act had been made under section one of this Act, and

(b) references in any such regulations to either of those Acts or any provision of those Acts were references to this Act or the corresponding provision thereof,

and any such regulations may be varied or revoked accordingly.

(3) Unless, and except in so far as, regulations under section one of this Act otherwise provide,—

(a) subsections (1) to (3) of section two of this Act shall apply in relation to goods of the said classes subject to the extensions specified in subsection (6) of that section, but without prejudice to the proviso to the said subsection (6) ;

(b) the Schedule to this Act shall have effect in relation to goods of those classes, but as if paragraph 7 provided that " local authority " should mean as respects England and Wales the council of a county borough, county district or metropolitan borough, or the Common Council of the City of London, and as respects Scotland a county or town council.

7.—(1) This Act may be cited as the Consumer Protection Act, 1961. *Short title, commencement and extent.*

(2) This Act shall come into operation on the expiration of the period of one month beginning with the day on which it is passed.

(3) This Act shall not extend to Northern Ireland.

SCHEDULE

PROVISIONS AS TO INSPECTION, TESTING AND ENFORCEMENT BY LOCAL AUTHORITIES

1.—(1) Subject to the provisions of this Schedule, an officer of a local authority authorised by them in writing in that behalf may, on producing if so required his authority, inspect any goods in relation to which this Schedule has effect for the purpose of determining—

    (*a*) whether the goods or any component part thereof are goods to which any prescribed requirements apply, and

    (*b*) if so, whether those requirements are complied with.

(2) Subject to the provisions of this Schedule. an officer of a local authority authorised by them in writing in that behalf may, on producing if so required his authority, inspect a component part intended for but not embodied in any goods in relation to which this Schedule has effect, for the purpose of determining—

    (*a*) whether it is one to which any prescribed requirements apply and if so whether those requirements are complied with, or

    (*b*) whether it is one which it is requisite to inspect in order to determine whether any prescribed requirements applying to goods comprising it would be compl'ed with when it was embodied in the goods, and if so whether those requirements would then be complied with.

2. A local authority may, subject to the provisions of this Schedule, purchase any goods for the purpose of carrying out a test to determine whether any prescribed requirements applicable to the goods or a component part thereof are complied with, or in the case of goods being a component part whether any prescribed requirements applicable to goods comprising it would be complied with when the part was embodied in the goods.

3. Regulations under section one of this Act may provide that in such cases as may be prescribed any test such as is referred to in the foregoing paragraph shall be carried out, at the expense of the local authority, by such person or body as may be authorised by or under the regulations to carry out the test, and may prescr be the manner in which any such test as is referred to in the foregoing paragraph is to be carried out.

4. An officer of a local authority shall not by virtue of paragraph 1 of this Schedule inspect any goods or component part, and a local authority shall not by virtue of paragraph 2 of this Schedule purchase any goods or component part, unless the goods or component part are kept in the area of the authority for the purpose of being sold or let in the course of a business.

5.—(1) Any person who wilfully obstructs any person in the exercise of his powers under paragraph 1 of this Schedule shall be guilty of an offence and liable on summary conviction to a fine not exceeding twenty pounds.

(2) Subsection (3) of section three of this Act shall apply in relation to an offence under this paragraph as it applies in relation to an offence under that section.

6. A local authority in England or Wales may institute proceedings for an offence under this Act committed in the area of the authority.

7. In this Schedule " local authority " as respects England and Wales means such of the following authorities, that is to say the councils of counties, county boroughs, county districts and metropolitan boroughs and the Common Council of the City of London as may be provided (either generally or for specified descriptions of areas) by regulations under section one of this Act relating to the goods in question, and as respects Scotland means a county or town council as may be so provided.

———— ∞ ————

Table of Statutes referred to in this Act

Short Title	Session and Chapter
Hire Purchase and Small Debt (Scotland) Act, 1932.	22 & 23 Geo. 5. c. 38.
Hire Purchase Act, 1938	1 & 2 Geo. 6. c. 53.
Heating Appliances (Fireguards) Act, 1952 ...	15 & 16 Geo. 6. & 1 Eliz. 2. c. 42.
Hire Purchase Act, 1954	2 & 3 Eliz. 2. c. 51.
Oil Burners (Standards) Act, 1960	8 & 9 Eliz. 2. c. 53.

Appendix 11

The Consumer Safety Act, 1978

ARRANGEMENT OF SECTIONS

Consumer Safety Act 1978

1978 CHAPTER 38

An Act to make further provision with respect to the safety of consumers and others. [20th July 1978]

B E IT ENACTED by the Queen's most Excellent Majesty, by and with the advice and consent of the Lords Spiritual and Temporal, and Commons, in this present Parliament assembled, and by the authority of the same, as follows:—

1.—(1) The Secretary of State may make regulations containing such provision authorised by subsections (2) and (3) of this section as the Secretary of State considers appropriate for the purpose of securing that goods are safe or that appropriate information is provided and inappropriate information is not provided in respect of goods ; and regulations in pursuance of this subsection are hereafter in this Act referred to as " safety regulations ".

Safety regulations in respect of goods.

(2) Safety regulations may contain provision—

(a) with respect to the composition or contents, design, construction, finish or packing of goods or with respect to other matters relating to goods ;

(b) for requiring goods to conform to a particular standard or to be approved or of a kind approved by a particular person and for requiring information to be given, and determining the manner in which it is to be given, for the purpose of indicating that the goods conform to that standard or are so approved or of such a kind ;

(c) with respect to standards for goods (which may be standards set out in the regulations or standards or parts of standards of which particulars have been published by any person in the United Kingdom or elsewhere) and with respect to the approval by the Secretary of State from time to time, for any purpose of the regulations, of standards or parts of standards of which particulars have been so published ;

(d) with respect to the giving, refusal, alteration and cancellation of approvals for goods or kinds of goods, with respect to the conditions and alteration of the conditions which may be attached to and the fees which may be charged for such approvals and with respect to appeals against refusals, alterations and cancellations of such approvals and against the conditions and alteration of conditions of such approvals ;

(e) with respect to the testing or inspection of goods, for determining the manner in which and person by whom any test or inspection required by the regulations is to be carried out and for determining the standards to be applied in carrying out such a test or inspection ;

(f) with respect to the ways of dealing with goods of which some or all do not satisfy a test prescribed by the regulations or a standard connected with a procedure so prescribed ;

(g) for requiring a warning or instructions or other information relating to goods to be marked on or to accompany the goods or to be given in some other manner in connection with the goods, and for securing that inappropriate information is not given in respect of goods either by means of misleading marks or otherwise ;

(h) for prohibiting persons from supplying, or from offering to supply, agreeing to supply, exposing for supply or possessing for supply, goods which the Secretary of State considers are not safe and goods in respect of which requirements of the regulations are not satisfied ;

(i) for prohibiting persons from supplying, or from offering to supply, agreeing to supply, exposing for supply or possessing for supply, goods which are designed to be used as component parts of other goods and which would if so used cause the other goods to contravene requirements of the regulations.

(3) Safety regulations may—

(a) make different provision for different circumstances or provision relating only to specified circumstances ;

(*b*) provide for exemptions from any provision of the
regulations ;

(*c*) contain such incidental and supplemental provisions as
the Secretary of State considers appropriate.

(4) Where the Secretary of State proposes to make safety
regulations it shall be his duty before he makes them to
consult such organisations as appear to him to be representative
of interests substantially affected by the proposal and such other
persons as he considers appropriate and, in the case of proposed
regulations relating to goods suitable for use at work, to consult
the Health and Safety Commission.

2.—(1) Where safety regulations prohibit a person from
supplying or offering or agreeing to supply goods or from
exposing or possessing goods for supply, then, subject to the
following provisions of this section, the person shall be guilty
of an offence if he contravenes the prohibition. *Offences against the safety regulations.*

(2) Where safety regulations require a person who makes or
processes goods in the course of carrying on a business—

(*a*) to carry out a particular test or use a particular procedure
in connection with the making or processing of the
goods with a view to ascertaining whether the goods
satisfy other requirements of the regulations ; or

(*b*) to deal or not to deal in a particular way with a quantity
of the goods of which the whole or part does not satisfy
the test or does not satisfy standards connected with
the procedure,

then, subject to the following provisions of this section, the person
shall be guilty of an offence if he does not comply with the
requirement.

(3) If a person contravenes a provision of safety regulations
which prohibits the provision, by means of a mark or otherwise, of information of a particular kind in connection with
goods, then, subject to the following provisions of this section,
he shall be guilty of an offence.

(4) A person who commits an offence in pursuance of the
preceding provisions of this section (hereafter in this section
referred to as " a relevant offence ") shall be liable on summary
conviction to imprisonment for a term not exceeding three
months and a fine of an amount not exceeding £1,000.

(5) Where the commission of a relevant offence by any person
is due to the act or default of some other person, the other person
shall be guilty of the offence and may be charged with and
convicted of it whether or not proceedings are taken against the
first-mentioned person.

(6) It shall be a defence to a charge of committing a relevant offence to prove that the accused took all reasonable steps and exercised all due diligence to avoid committing the offence ; but if in any case the defence provided by this subsection involves an allegation that the commission of the offence was due to the act or default of another person or due to reliance on information supplied by another person, the person charged shall not, without the leave of the court, be entitled to rely on the defence unless, within a period ending seven clear days before the hearing, he has served on the prosecutor a notice giving such information identifying or assisting in the identification of the other person as was then in his possession.

(7) Safety regulations may contain provision—

(a) for requiring persons on whom a duty is imposed by virtue of section 5 of this Act to have regard, in performing the duty so far as it relates to a provision of safety regulations, to matters specified in a direction issued by the Secretary of State with respect to that provision ;

(b) for securing that a person shall not be guilty of an offence by virtue of subsection (1) of this section unless it is proved that the goods in question do not conform to a particular standard ;

(c) for securing that proceedings for a relevant offence are not begun in England or Wales except by or with the consent of the Secretary of State or the Director of Public Prosecutions ;

(d) except in relation to Scotland, for enabling a magistrates' court to try an information in respect of a relevant offence if the information was laid within twelve months from the time when the offence was committed and, in relation to Scotland, for enabling summary proceedings for a relevant offence to be begun at any time within twelve months from the time when the offence was committed ;

and it is hereby declared that subsection (3) of the preceding section applies to safety regulations made by virtue of this subsection.

(8) Safety regulations shall not provide for a contravention of the regulations to be an offence.

Orders and notices to prohibit supply of goods or give warning of danger from goods.

3.—(1) The Secretary of State may—

(a) make orders (hereafter in this Act referred to as " prohibition orders ") prohibiting persons from supplying, or from offering to supply, agreeing to supply, exposing for supply or possessing for supply—

(i) any goods which the Secretary of State considers are not safe and which are described in the orders, and

(ii) any goods which are designed to be used as component parts of other goods and which would if so used cause the other goods to be goods described in the orders in pursuance of sub-paragraph (i) above;

(b) serve on any person a notice (hereafter in this Act referred to as a " prohibition notice ") prohibiting the person, except with the consent of the Secretary of State and in accordance with the conditions (if any) on which the consent is given, from supplying, or from offering to supply, agreeing to supply, exposing for supply or possessing for supply, any goods which the Secretary of State considers are not safe and which are described in the notice ;

(c) serve on any person a notice (hereafter in this Act referred to as a " notice to warn ") requiring the person to publish, in a form and manner and on occasions specified in the notice and at his own expense, a warning about any goods so specified which the Secretary considers are not safe and which the person supplies or has supplied.

(2) Part I of Schedule 1 to this Act shall have effect with respect to prohibition orders, Part II of that Schedule shall have effect with respect to prohibition notices and Part III of that Schedule shall have effect with respect to notices to warn ; and subsection (3) of section 1 of this Act shall apply to prohibition orders as it applies to safety regulations.

(3) A person who contravenes a prohibition order, a prohibition notice or a notice to warn shall be guilty of an offence and liable on summary conviction to imprisonment for a term not exceeding three months and a fine of an amount not exceeding £1,000 ; but it shall be a defence to a charge of committing an offence under this subsection to prove that the accused took all reasonable steps and exercised all due diligence to avoid committing the offence.

(4) If in any case the defence provided by the preceding subsection involves an allegation that the commission of the offence was due to the act or default of another person or to reliance on information supplied by another person, the person charged shall not, without the leave of the court, be entitled to rely on the defence unless, within a period ending seven clear days before the hearing, he has served on the prosecutor a notice giving such information identifying or assisting in the identification of the other person as was then in his possession.

(5) Where the commission by any person of an offence of contravening a prohibition order is due to the act or default of some other person the other person shall be guilty of the offence and may be charged with and convicted of the offence by virtue of this subsection whether or not proceedings are taken against the first-mentioned person.

Power to obtain information.

4.—(1) If the Secretary of State considers that, for the purpose of deciding whether to make, vary or revoke safety regulations or a prohibition order or to serve, vary or revoke a prohibition notice or to serve or revoke a notice to warn, he requires information which another person is likely to be able to furnish, the Secretary of State may serve on the other person a notice requiring the person—

    (a) to furnish to the Secretary of State, within a period specified in the notice, such information as is so specified ;

    (b) to produce such documents as are specified in the notice at a time and place so specified and to permit a person appointed by the Secretary of State for the purpose to take copies of the documents at that time and place ;

but a barrister, advocate or solicitor shall not be required by such a notice to furnish information contained in a privileged communication made by or to him in that capacity or to produce a document containing such a communication.

(2) A person who—

    (a) fails, without reasonable cause, to comply with a notice served on him in pursuance of the preceding subsection ; or

    (b) in purporting to comply with a requirement which by virtue of paragraph (a) of the preceding subsection is contained in a notice served on him in pursuance of that subsection, furnishes information which he knows is false in a material particular or recklessly furnishes information which is false in a material particular,

shall be guilty of an offence and, in the case of an offence under paragraph (a) of this subsection, liable on summary conviction to a fine not exceeding £1,000 and, in the case of an offence under paragraph (b) of this subsection, liable on conviction on indictment to a fine and on summary conviction to a fine of an amount not exceeding the statutory maximum.

(3) No information obtained by virtue of this section shall be disclosed except—

    (a) for the purpose of any criminal proceedings or any investigation with a view to such proceedings ; or (*b*) for the purpose of facilitating the performance by the Director General of Fair Trading of his functions under Part III of the Fair Trading Act 1973 or for the purpose of any proceedings under the said Part III ; or 1973 c. 41.

(*c*) for the purpose of enabling the Secretary of State to decide whether to make, vary or revoke safety regulations or a prohibition order or whether to serve, vary or revoke a prohibition notice or to serve or revoke a notice to warn ; or

(*d*) for the purpose of enabling the Secretary of State or a Northern Ireland Department to fulfil a Community obligation ; or

(*e*) in a prohibition notice, a notice to warn or a warning published as required by a notice to warn or in a warning about goods which is published by the Secretary of State ;

but the prohibition on disclosure imposed by this subsection does not apply to publicised information.

(4) A person who discloses information in contravention of the preceding subsection shall be guilty of an offence and liable, on conviction on indictment, to imprisonment for a term not exceeding two years and a fine and, on summary conviction, to a fine of an amount not exceeding the statutory maximum.

5.—(1) Subject to the following subsection, it shall be the duty of each weights and measures authority to enforce within its area the provisions of safety regulations and section 2 of this Act and the provisions of prohibition orders and prohibition notices and subsections (3) and (5) of section 3 of this Act so far as those subsections relate to such orders and notices. Enforcement.

(2) The Secretary of State may by regulations transfer the whole or part of the duty imposed on a weights and measures authority by the preceding subsection to another person who has agreed to the transfer ; and the regulations may, without prejudice to the generality of the preceding provisions of this subsection—

(*a*) make different provision for different circumstances ; and

(*b*) contain such incidental and supplemental provisions (including provision for the Secretary of State to defray expenses of a person on whom a duty is imposed by the regulations) as the Secretary of State considers appropriate.

(3) The provisions of Schedule 2 to this Act shall have effect for the purpose of facilitating—

(*a*) the enforcement by the Secretary of State of provisions mentioned in subsection (1) of this section ; and

(*b*) the performance of a duty imposed on a person by virtue of this section ;

but nothing in the preceding provisions of this subsection prejudices any powers which are exercisable by the Secretary of State apart from this subsection.

(4) If the Secretary of State directs a person on whom a duty is imposed by virtue of subsection (1) or (2) of this section to make a report to the Secretary of State, in such form and containing such particulars as are specified in the direction, on the exercise of the person's functions under this Act or, while the Consumer Protection Act 1961 remains in force, under this Act and that Act, it shall be the duty of the person to comply with the direction.

1961 c. 40.

(5) Nothing in the preceding provisions of this section or in regulations made by virtue of subsection (2) of this section authorises a weights and measures authority or a person specified in the regulations to institute proceedings in Scotland for an offence.

Civil
liability.

6.—(1) Any obligation imposed on a person by safety regulations or a prohibition order or a prohibition notice is a duty owed by him to any other person who may be affected by a failure to perform the obligation, and a breach of that duty is actionable (subject to the defences and other incidents applying to actions for breach of statutory duty).

(2) An agreement shall be void so far as it would, apart from this subsection, have the effect of excluding or restricting an obligation mentioned in the preceding subsection or liability for a breach of such an obligation.

(3) References in the preceding provisions of this section to an obligation imposed by safety regulations do not include such an obligation as to which the regulations state that those provisions do not apply to it.

(4) A contravention of any provision of safety regulations, a prohibition order or a prohibition notice and the commission of an offence under section 2 or 3 of this Act shall not affect the validity of any contract or rights arising under any contract except so far as the contract provides otherwise.

Supplemental.

7.—(1) The Secretary of State may make regulations with respect to the manner of giving information in pursuance of Schedule 1 or Schedule 2 to this Act.

(2) Any document required or authorised by virtue of this Act to be served on a person may be so served—

   (a) by delivering it to him or by leaving it at his proper address or by sending it by post to him at that address ; or

   (b) if the person is a body corporate, by serving it in accordance with the preceding paragraph on the secretary or clerk of that body ; or

   (c) if the person is a partnership, by serving it as aforesaid on a partner or on a person having control or management of the partnership business.

(3) For the purposes of the preceding subsection and section 26 of the Interpretation Act 1889 (which relates to the service of documents by post) in its application to the preceding subsection, the proper address of any person on whom a document is to be served by virtue of this Act shall be his last known address except that— 1889 c. 63.

   (a) in the case of service on a body corporate or its secretary or clerk it shall be the address of the registered or principal office of the body ;

   (b) in the case of service on a partnership or a partner or a person having the control or management of a partnership business it shall be the principal office of the partnership ;

and for the purposes of this subsection the principal office of a company registered outside the United Kingdom or a partnership carrying on business outside the United Kingdom is its principal office within the United Kingdom.

(4) Where an offence under any provision of this Act which has been committed by a body corporate is proved to have been committed with the consent or connivance of, or to be attributable to any neglect on the part of, a director, manager, secretary or other similar officer of the body corporate or any person who was purporting to act in any such capacity, he as well as the body corporate shall be guilty of that offence and shall be liable to be proceeded against and punished accordingly.

(5) Where the affairs of a body corporate are managed by its members the preceding subsection shall apply in relation to the acts and defaults of a member in connection with his functions of management as if he were a director of the body corporate

(6) Any power to make an order or regulations which is conferred on the Secretary of State by this Act shall be exercisable by statutory instrument and any statutory instrument made by virtue of this subsection, except an instrument containing safety regulations or containing only an order made by virtue

of section 12(2) of this Act, shall be subject to annulment in pursuance of a resolution of either House of Parliament.

(7) No safety regulations shall be made unless a draft of the regulations has been laid before and approved by a resolution of each House of Parliament.

1968 c. 29.

(8) In subsection (4) of section 2 of the Trade Descriptions Act 1968 (which provides that a description or mark applied to goods in pursuance of an enactment mentioned in that subsection shall be deemed not to be a trade description) after paragraph (*f*) there shall be inserted the words " (*g*) the Consumer Safety Act 1978 ", and in subsection (5)(*a*) of that section (which provides that where, under certain Acts including the Food and Drugs Act (Northern Ireland) 1958, the application of a description to goods is prohibited except in certain cases the description shall be deemed not to be a trade description when applied in those cases) after the figures " 1958 " there shall be inserted the words " or the Consumer Safety Act 1978 ".

Expenses etc and reports.

8.—(1) There shall be paid out of money provided by Parliament—

(*a*) any expenses incurred by a Minister of the Crown or government department in consequence of the provisions of this Act ; and

(*b*) any increase attributable to this Act in the sums payable out of money so provided under any other enactment ;

and any sums received by a Minister of the Crown or a government department by virtue of this Act shall be paid into the Consolidated Fund.

1961 c. 40.

(2) It shall be the duty of the Secretary of State to lay before each House of Parliament from time to time, and in any event not less than once in every five years, a report on the exercise of the functions under this Act and, while the Consumer Protection Act 1961 remains in force, of the functions under that Act, of the Secretary of State and of persons on whom duties are imposed by virtue of section 5 of this Act.

Interpretation.

9.—(1) Subject to the following subsection, for the purposes of this Act a person supplies goods only if, in the course of carrying on a business (whether or not a business of dealing in the goods in question) and either as principal or agent—

(*a*) he sells (otherwise than under a hire-purchase agreement), hires out or lends the goods to another person ; or

(*b*) he enters into a hire-purchase agreement, or a contract for work and materials, to furnish the goods to another person ; or (*c*) he exchanges the goods for any consideration (which may consist of trading stamps) other than money ; or

(*d*) he gives the goods to another person either as a prize or otherwise ;

and " supply " and related expressions shall be construed accordingly.

(2) In this Act any reference to supply does not include supply to a person with whom the goods in question were insured against damage and, except in relation to a notice to warn, does not include supply which is incidental to the letting or sale of land and, except in relation to a prohibition notice, does not include—

(*a*) supply to a person who carries on a business of buying such goods as those in question and repairing or re-conditioning them ; and

(*b*) supply by a sale of articles as scrap (that is to say for the value of materials included in the articles and not of the articles themselves) ;

and if a person supplies goods by hiring them out or lending them, then, for the purposes of this Act, he does not supply them by reason only of anything done in pursuance of the arrangements for the hiring out or loan.

(3) Where a person supplies goods to another person under a hire-purchase agreement, conditional sale agreement or credit-sale agreement or under an agreement for the hiring of goods (other than a hire-purchase agreement) and the first-mentioned person—

(*a*) carries on the business of financing the provision of goods for others by means of such agreements ; and

(*b*) in the course of that business acquired his interest in the goods supplied to the other person as a means of financing the provision of them for the other person by a further person,

the further person and not the first-mentioned person shall be treated for the purposes of this Act as supplying the goods to the other person.

(4) In this Act—

" conditional sale agreement ", " credit-sale agreement " and " hire-purchase agreement " have the meanings assigned to them by section 189(1) of the Consumer 1974 c. 39. Credit Act 1974, and for the purposes of this Act " goods " in the definitions of those expressions shall have the same meaning as in this Act ;

" contravention " includes failure to comply, and related expressions shall be construed accordingly ;

"goods" includes substances whether natural or manufactured and whether or not incorporated in or mixed with other goods and—

(a) in relation to a notice to warn, includes things comprised in land which by operation of law became land on becoming so comprised ; but

1955 c. 16
(4 & 5 Eliz. 2).
1970 c. 40.
1968 c. 67.

1971 c. 38.

(b) does not include food as defined in section 135(1) of the Food and Drugs Act 1955, feeding stuff and fertiliser as defined in section 66(1) of the Agriculture Act 1970, medicinal products within the meaning of the Medicines Act 1968 in respect of which there is in force a product licence within the meaning of that Act (except cosmetic and toilet products as defined by regulations made by the Secretary of State) and controlled drugs within the meaning of the Misuse of Drugs Act 1971, except drugs which are excepted from section 4(1)(b) of that Act (which makes it unlawful to supply a controlled drug) by regulations under section 7(1)(a) of that Act ;

"notice" means notice in writing ;

"personal injury" includes disease and any other impairment of a person's physical or mental condition ;

"prohibition order", "prohibition notice" and "notice to warn" have the meanings assigned to them by section 3(1) of this Act ;

"publicised information", in relation to a disclosure, means information which, before the disclosure occurred, was published in proceedings mentioned in paragraph (a) or (b) or in a warning mentioned in paragraph (e) of section 4(3) of this Act ;

"safe" means such as to prevent or adequately to reduce any risk of death and any risk of personal injury from the goods in question or from circumstances in which the goods might be used or kept, and for the purposes of section 1 of this Act the Secretary of State shall be entitled to consider that goods containing radioactive substances are safe or not safe by reference to the radiation from the goods and from other sources and to the consequences of the radiation for users of the goods and other persons ;

"safety regulations" has the meaning assigned to it by section 1(1) of this Act ; and

1977 c. 45.

"the statutory maximum" means the prescribed sum within the meaning of section 28 of the Criminal Law

Act 1977 as respects England and Wales and section 289B of the Criminal Procedure (Scotland) Act 1975 as respects Scotland (which is £1,000 or another sum fixed by order to take account of changes in the value of money) ; 1975 c. 21.

and references in this Act to the Secretary of State include any other Minister of the Crown in charge of a government department.

10.—(1). The enactments and instrument mentioned in the first and second columns of Schedule 3 to this Act are hereby repealed to the extent specified in the third column of that Schedule. Repeals and transitional provisions.

(2) If a draft of regulations under section 1 of the Consumer Protection Act 1961 is approved by a resolution of each House of Parliament, a statutory instrument containing the regulations shall not be subject to annulment in pursuance of subsection (6) of that section. 1961 c. 40.

(3) In section 3(2) of the said Act of 1961 (under which a person who sells or has certain other dealings in goods which do not comply with the requirements of regulations under that Act is punishable with a fine not exceeding £100 or, in the case of a second or subsequent conviction, with a fine not exceeding £250 and imprisonment for a term not exceeding three months) for the words from " one hundred pounds " to " two hundred and fifty pounds " there shall be substituted the words " one thousand pounds " ; and in paragraph 5 of the Schedule to that Act (under which a person who obstructs another person in the exercise of powers of inspection conferred on the other person by paragraph 1 of that Schedule is liable to a fine not exceeding £20) for the words " twenty pounds " there shall be substituted the words " two hundred pounds ".

(4) Section 5(1) of this Act shall apply to the provisions of sections 2 and 3(2), (2A) and (3) of the said Act of 1961 as it applies to the provisions of safety regulations.

(5) Subsections (2) to (4) of this section shall cease to have effect when the repeal of the said Act of 1961 by this Act comes into force.

(6) Subsection (4) of section 1 of this Act shall not apply to a proposal to make safety regulations if the Secretary of State is satisfied that the proposed regulations—

    (a) will relate only to goods in respect of which regulations under section 1 of the said Act of 1961 impose such requirements as are mentioned in section 1(1) of that Act ; and (*b*) will impose substantially similar requirements in respect of the goods ;

and it shall be the duty of the Secretary of State to include, in any safety regulations as respects which the said subsection (4) did not apply by virtue of this subsection, a statement that he was satisfied as aforesaid.

Application to Northern Ireland.

1965 c. 14 (N.I.).

11. This Act shall have effect, in its application to Northern Ireland, with the following modifications, namely,—

(*a*) safety regulations may revoke regulations in force under the Consumer Protection Act (Northern Ireland) 1965 ;

(*b*) in section 1(4) the words from " and in " onwards shall be omitted ;

(*c*) in paragraph (*c*) of subsection (7) of section 2 for the words " England or Wales " there shall be substituted the words " Northern Ireland " and at the end of that paragraph there shall be inserted the words " for Northern Ireland " ;

(*d*) in paragraph (*d*) of the said subsection (7) for the words " information " and " laid " there shall be substituted respectively the words " complaint " and " made " ;

(*e*) in section 5 for the references to a weights and measures authority there shall be substituted references to a district council ;

(*f*) section 8(1) shall be omitted ;

(*g*) in section 9(4)—

1955 c. 16 (4 & 5 Eliz. 2).

1958 c. 27 (N.I.).

(i) in the definition of " goods ", for the reference to section 135(1) of the Food and Drugs Act 1955 there shall be substituted a reference to section 70(1) of the Food and Drugs Act (Northern Ireland) 1958, and

(ii) in the definition of " statutory maximum ", for the reference to England and Wales there shall be substituted a reference to Northern Ireland,

1977 c. 45.

and for the purposes of the definition of " statutory maximum " as so amended the provisions of the Criminal Law Act 1977 which relate to the sum mentioned in that definition shall extend to Northern Ireland ;

1961 c. 40.

(*h*) in section 10(3) to (6) for the references to the Consumer Protection Act 1961 there shall be substituted references to the Consumer Protection Act (Northern Ireland) 1965 and in section 10(4) the word " (2A) " shall be omitted.

12.—(1) This Act may be cited as the Consumer Safety Act 1978.

(2) This Act shall come into force on such day as the Secretary of State may by order appoint ; and an order in pursuance of this subsection may appoint different days for different provisions of this Act or for different purposes of the same provision and may contain such transitional provisions as the Secretary of State considers appropriate.

Short title and commencement.

SCHEDULES

Section 3(2).

SCHEDULE 1

Prohibition Orders, Prohibition Notices And Notices To Warn

Part I

Prohibition Orders

1. If the Secretary of State proposes to make a prohibition order (hereafter in this Part of this Schedule referred to as "an order"), then, subject to paragraph 5 of this Schedule, it shall be his duty before he makes the order—

    (*a*) to publish, in such manner as he thinks fit and not less than 28 days before he makes the order, a notice stating—

        (i) that he proposes to make the order and, in such terms as he thinks fit, the proposed effect of the order, and

        (ii) that any person may make representations in writing to the Secretary of State about the proposed order before a date specified in the notice (which must be after the expiration of the period of 28 days beginning with the date of first publication of the notice); and

    (*b*) to consider any such representations made within that period.

2. The effect of an order must not be more restrictive, but may be less restrictive, than the proposed effect of it as stated in the notice aforesaid.

3. Without prejudice to the power to make a further order and subject to the following paragraph, an order shall cease to have effect at the expiration of a period specified in the order which must not be longer than twelve months beginning with the date on which the order comes into force.

4. An order may revoke a previous order or may vary it otherwise than by providing for it to be in force after the expiration of twelve months beginning with the date of the coming into force of the previous order.

5. Paragraphs 1 and 2 of this Schedule shall not apply to an order if the order contains a statement that in the opinion of the Secretary of State the risk of danger connected with the goods to which the order relates is such that the order must be made without delay.

Part II

Prohibition Notices

Preliminary

6. In this Part of this Schedule—

    "notice" means a prohibition notice;

    "notification" means a notification in writing; and

"the trader" in relation to a proposed notice or an actual notice means the person on whom the proposed notice is proposed to be served or on whom the actual notice has been served.

SCH. 1

7. A notice must specify the date on which it comes into force.

General procedure

8. If the Secretary of State proposes to serve a notice in respect of any goods, then, subject to paragraph 14 of this Schedule, it shall be his duty before he serves the notice to serve on the trader a notification—

(a) stating that the Secretary of State proposes to serve on him a notice in respect of the goods ; and

(b) specifying the goods in a manner sufficient to identify them and stating that, for the reasons set out in the notification, the Secretary of State considers that the goods are not safe ; and

(c) stating that the trader may make representations, in writing or both in writing and orally, for the purpose of satisfying the Secretary of State that the goods are safe but that if the trader intends to make such representations he must, before the expiration of the period of 14 days beginning with the day when the notification is served on him, inform the Secretary of State of his intention indicating whether the representations are to be in writing only or both in writing and oral.

9. Subject to paragraph 14 of this Schedule, the Secretary of State shall not serve a notice on the trader in respect of any goods before the expiration of the period of 14 days beginning with the day on which the Secretary of State served on him a notification in pursuance of the preceding paragraph relating to the goods ; and if within that period the trader informs the Secretary of State as mentioned in sub-paragraph (c) of the preceding paragraph, then—

(a) the Secretary of State shall not serve a notice on the trader in consequence of the notification before the expiration of the period of 28 days beginning with the day aforesaid ; and

(b) if during that period the trader makes to the Secretary of State such written representations as are mentioned in the said sub-paragraph (c) the Secretary of State shall not serve a notice on the trader in consequence of the notification before the Secretary of State has considered the report of a person appointed in pursuance of the following paragraph in consequence of the representations.

10. Where, in consequence of the service on the trader of a notification in pursuance of paragraph 8 of this Schedule, the trader informs the Secretary of State as mentioned in sub-paragraph (c) of that paragraph within the period so mentioned and makes to the Secretary of State within that period or the 14 days beginning with the end of that period such written representations as are so mentioned, it shall be the duty of the Secretary of State—

(a) to appoint a person to consider the written representations ; and

SCH. 1

(b) if the trader informed the Secretary of State in pursuance of the said sub-paragraph (c) that the representations would be both written and oral, to inform the trader of the place and time (which must not be before the expiration of the 14 days aforesaid and of 7 days beginning with the day when the information is given to the trader) at which the oral representations may be made to the person appointed ;

and the trader or his representative may at that place and time make to the person appointed oral representations for the purpose of satisfying the Secretary of State that the goods in question are safe and may call and examine witnesses in connection with the representations.

11. The person appointed in pursuance of the preceding paragraph to consider written representations with respect to any goods shall, after considering the representations, any oral representations made in pursuance of that paragraph with respect to the goods and any statements made by witnesses in connection with the oral representations, make a report (including recommendations) to the Secretary of State about the representations and the proposed notice.

12. If at any time after the Secretary of State has served a notification on the trader in pursuance of paragraph 8 of this Schedule the Secretary of State decides not to serve a notice on him in consequence of the notification, it shall be the duty of the Secretary of State to inform him of the decision ; and after the Secretary of State informs him of the decision the notification and anything done in consequence of it in pursuance of the preceding paragraphs of this Schedule shall be disregarded for the purposes of those paragraphs.

13. Where a notification is served on the trader in respect of any goods in pursuance of paragraph 8 of this Schedule, a notice served on him in consequence of the notification may relate to some only of those goods.

Special procedure

14. Paragraphs 8 to 13 of this Schedule shall not apply to a notice which contains a statement that the Secretary of State considers that the risk of danger connected with the goods to which the notice relates is such that the notice must come into force without delay ; and references to a notice in paragraphs 15 to 18 of this Schedule are to a notice containing such a statement.

15. A notice in respect of any goods must—
   (a) state that, for the reasons set out in the notice, the Secretary of State considers that the goods are not safe ; and
   (b) state that the trader may, at such time as the trader thinks fit, make representations in writing to the Secretary of State for the purpose of satisfying him that the goods are safe.

16. If representations in writing about a notice are made by the trader to the Secretary of State it shall be the duty of the Secretary of State to consider the representations and either to revoke the notice and to inform the trader that he has revoked it or—
   (a) to appoint a person to consider the representations ; and

(*b*) to serve on the trader a notification stating that he may make to the person appointed oral representations for the purpose mentioned in the preceding paragraph and specifying the place and time (which, except with the agreement of the trader, must not be before the expiration of 21 days beginning with the date of service of the notification) at which the oral representations may be made ;

and the trader or his representative may at that place and time make to the person appointed oral representations for the purpose aforesaid and may call and examine witnesses in connection with the representations.

17. The person appointed in pursuance of the preceding paragraph to consider written representations with respect to any goods shall, after considering the representations, any oral representations made in pursuance of that paragraph with respect to the goods and any statements made by witnesses in connection with the oral representations, make a report (including recommendations) to the Secretary of State about the representations and the notice in question.

18. Where the Secretary of State has appointed a person in pursuance of paragraph 16 of this Schedule to consider any representations relating to a notice then, without prejudice to the operation of paragraphs 19 and 20 of this Schedule, paragraphs 16 and 17 of this Schedule shall not apply to any subsequent representations in writing about the notice.

Other representations

19. If at any time the trader on whom a notice has been served makes representations in writing to the Secretary of State for the purpose of satisfying him that the goods to which the notice relates are safe and, by virtue of the preceding paragraph, paragraph 16 of this Schedule does not apply to the representations, it shall be the duty of the Secretary of State to consider the representations and to serve on the trader, before the expiration of one month beginning with the day when the Secretary of State receives the representations, a notification stating—

(*a*) that the Secretary of State will revoke the notice or vary it or declines to do so ; or

(*b*) that the Secretary of State has appointed a person to consider the representations and that the trader may make to the person appointed, at a place specified in the notification and a time so specified (which, except with the agreement of the trader, must not be before the expiration of the period of 21 days beginning with the date of service of the notification), oral representations for the purpose aforesaid ;

and the trader or his representative may at that place and time make to the person appointed oral representations for the purpose aforesaid and may call and examine witnesses in connection with the representations.

SCH. 1   20. The person appointed in pursuance of the preceding paragraph to consider written representations with respect to any goods shall, after considering the representations, any oral representations made in pursuance of that paragraph with respect to the goods and any statements made by witnesses in connection with the oral representations, make a report (including recommendations) to the Secretary of State about the representations and the notice in question.

Miscellaneous

21. The Secretary of State may revoke or vary a notice by serving on the trader a notification stating that the notice is revoked or, as the case may be, is varied as specified in the notification ; but the Secretary of State shall not have power to vary a notice so as to make the effect of the notice more restrictive for the trader.

22. It shall be the duty of the Secretary of State to consider any report made to him in pursuance of paragraph 17 or 20 of this Schedule and, after considering the report, to inform the trader of the Secretary of State's decision with respect to the notice in question.

23. Where the Secretary of State has appointed a time in pursuance of this Part of this Schedule for oral representations, he may appoint a later time or further times for the representations ; and where he does so references in this Part of this Schedule to the appointed time shall be construed as references to the later time or, as the case may be, as including the further times.

24. If a person discloses a secret manufacturing process or a trade secret contained in information obtained by him in consequence of the inclusion of the information in written or oral representations made in pursuance of this Part of this Schedule or in a statement made by a witness in connection with such oral representations, then, subject to the following paragraph, he shall be guilty of an offence and liable, on conviction on indictment, to imprisonment for a term not exceeding two years and a fine and, on summary conviction, to a fine of an amount not exceeding the statutory maximum ; and it is hereby declared that the reference above to written representations includes such written representations as are mentioned in paragraph 19 of this Schedule.

25. A person shall not be guilty of an offence under the preceding paragraph in consequence of his disclosure of a process or trade secret contained in information if—

    (a) the information was obtained by him as a person appointed by the Secretary of State in pursuance of this Part of this Schedule to consider the representations in question and the disclosure was made in his report to the Secretary of State about the representations or was made for the purpose of criminal proceedings or an investigation with a view to such proceedings ; or

    (b) the information was obtained by him otherwise than as a person so appointed and the disclosure was made as mentioned in paragraphs (a) to (e) of section 4(3) of this Act ; or

    (c) the disclosure was of publicised information.

PART III
NOTICES TO WARN

26. If the Secretary of State proposes to serve on a person a notice to warn in respect of any goods, it shall be the duty of the Secretary of State before he serves the notice to serve on the person a notification in writing—

(a) containing a draft of the notice and stating that the Secretary of State proposes to serve on the person such a notice in the form of the draft ; and

(b) stating that, for the reasons set out in the notification, the Secretary of State considers that the goods specified in the draft are not safe ; and

(c) stating that the person may make representations, in writing or both in writing and orally, for the purpose of satisfying the Secretary of State that the goods are safe but that if the person intends to make such representations he must, before the expiration of the period of 14 days beginning with the day when the notification is served on him, inform the Secretary of State of his intention indicating whether the representations are to be in writing only or both in writing and oral.

27. Paragraphs 9 to 13, 21 and 23 to 25 of this Schedule shall with the necessary modifications have effect in relation to a notice to warn as they have effect in relation to a prohibition notice but as if—

(a) the reference to paragraph 14 of this Schedule in the said paragraph 9 were omitted ;

(b) for the references to paragraph 8 of this Schedule in paragraphs 9, 10, 12 and 13 of this Schedule there were substituted references to the preceding paragraph ;

(c) in the said paragraph 13 for the words from " relate " onwards there were substituted the words " be less onerous than the draft of the notice contained in the notification " ;

(d) in the said paragraph 21 the words " or vary " and the words from " or, as " onwards were omitted ; and

(e) in paragraph 24 of this Schedule the words from " and it is " onwards were omitted and in that paragraph and paragraph 25 of this Schedule for the references to Part II of this Schedule there were substituted references to provisions of that Part as applied by this paragraph.

SCHEDULE 2
ENFORCEMENT
Preliminary

1. In this Schedule—

" enforcement authority " means the Secretary of State, any person on whom a duty is imposed by or under section 5 of this Act and any other person by whom that duty may be discharged in pursuance of arrangements made by virtue of any enactment ;

" officer ", in relation to an enforcement authority, means a person authorised in writing by the authority to assist the authority in performing such a duty as aforesaid or, where the authority is the Secretary of State, to assist him in enforcing relevant provisions ;

" premises " includes any place, any stall, and any ship, aircraft and other vehicle of any kind ; and

" relevant provisions " means provisions of safety regulations or a prohibition order or a prohibition notice.

Purchases

2. An enforcement authority shall have power to purchase goods, and to authorise any of its officers to purchase goods on behalf of the authority, for the purpose of ascertaining whether any relevant provisions are being complied with.

Powers to enter premises and to inspect and seize goods

3. An officer of an enforcement authority may, at all reasonable hours and on production, if required, of his credentials, exercise the following powers, that is to say—

(*a*) he may, for the purpose of ascertaining whether any relevant provisions have been contravened, inspect any goods and enter any premises other than premises used only as a dwelling ;

(*b*) he may, for the purpose of ascertaining whether an offence under section 2(2) of this Act has been committed, examine any procedure (including any arrangements for carrying out a test) connected with the production of goods ;

(*c*) if he has reasonable cause to suspect that relevant provisions have been contravened he may, for the purpose of ascertaining whether the provisions have been contravened, require any person carrying on a business or employed in connection with a business to produce any books or documents relating to the business and may take copies of, or of any entry in, any such book or document ;

(*d*) if he has reasonable cause to believe that relevant provisions have been contravened, he may seize and detain any goods for the purpose of ascertaining, by testing or otherwise, whether the provisions have been contravened ;

(*e*) he may seize and detain any goods (including documents) which he has reason to believe may be required as evidence in proceedings for an offence under section 2 of this Act or under section 3 of this Act so far as it relates to prohibition orders and prohibition notices ;

(*f*) he may, for the purpose of exercising his powers under sub-paragraph (*d*) or (*e*) above to seize goods, but only if and to the extent that it is reasonably necessary in order to secure that relevant provisions are complied with, require

any person having authority to do so to break open any
container and, if that person does not comply with the
requirement, he may do so himself.

4. An officer seizing any goods or documents in the exercise
of his powers under the preceding paragraph shall inform the person
from whom they are seized that the officer has seized them.

5. If a justice of the peace on sworn information in writing—

    (*a*) is satisfied that there is reasonable ground to believe either—

        (i) that any goods (including books and documents)
which an officer of an enforcement authority has power
under paragraph 3 of this Schedule to inspect are on any
premises and that their inspection is likely to disclose
evidence that relevant provisions have been contravened,
or

        (ii) that relevant provisions have been or are being or
are about to be contravened on any premises ; and

    (*b*) is also satisfied either—

        (i) that admission to the premises has been or is likely
to be refused and that notice of intention to apply for a
warrant under this paragraph has been given to the
occupier, or

        (ii) that an application for admission, or the giving of
such a notice, would defeat the object of the entry or
that the premises are unoccupied or that the occupier is
temporarily absent and it might defeat the object of the
entry to await his return,

the justice may by warrant under his hand, which shall continue in
force for a period of one month, authorise an officer of an enforcement authority to enter the premises, if need be by force.

In the application of this paragraph to Scotland " justice of the
peace " shall be construed as including a sheriff.

6. An officer entering any premises by virtue of this Schedule
may take with him such other persons and such equipment as
may appear to him necessary ; and on leaving any premises which he
has entered by virtue of a warrant under the preceding paragraph
he shall, if the premises are unoccupied or the occupier is temporarily absent, leave them as effectively secured against trespassers as
he found them.

7. If any person discloses to any person—

    (*a*) any information obtained by him in premises which he
has entered by virtue of this Schedule ; or

    (*b*) any information obtained by him in pursuance of this
Schedule ;

he shall, unless the disclosure was made for the purposes of proceedings for a breach of duty mentioned in section 6(1) of this Act and
does not disclose a secret manufacturing process or trade secret or

SCH. 2

was made as mentioned in paragraphs (*a*) to (*e*) of section 4(3) of this Act or in compliance with a direction under section 5(4) of this Act or was of publicised information, be guilty of an offence and liable, on conviction on indictment, to imprisonment for a term not exceeding two years and a fine and, on summary conviction, to a fine of an amount not exceeding the statutory maximum.

8. If any person who is not an officer of an enforcement authority purports to act as such under this Schedule he shall be guilty of an offence and liable on summary conviction to a fine not exceeding £1,000.

9. Nothing in this Schedule shall be taken to compel the production by a barrister, advocate or solicitor of a document containing a privileged communication made by or to him in that capacity or to authorise the taking of possession of any such document which is in his possession.

Obstruction

10. Any person who—

    (*a*) wilfully obstructs an officer of an enforcement authority acting in pursuance of this Schedule ; or

    (*b*) wilfully fails to comply with any requirement properly made to him by such an officer under this Schedule ; or

    (*c*) without reasonable cause fails to give such an officer so acting any other assistance or information which he may reasonably require of him for the purpose of the performance of his functions under this Schedule,

shall be guilty of an offence and liable on summary conviction to a fine not exceeding £200.

11. If any person, in giving any such information as is mentioned in the preceding paragraph, makes any statement which he knows is false in a material particular or recklessly makes a statement which is false in a material particular he shall be guilty of an offence and liable on conviction on indictment to a fine and on summary conviction to a fine of an amount not exceeding the statutory maximum.

12. Nothing in this Schedule shall be construed as requiring a person to answer any question or give any information if to do so might incriminate the person or the person's spouse.

Tests

13. Where any goods seized or purchased by an officer in pursuance of this Schedule are submitted to a test, then—

    (*a*) if the goods were seized, the officer shall inform the person mentioned in paragraph 4 of this Schedule of the result of the test ;

(*b*) if the goods were purchased and the test leads to the institution of proceedings for an offence under section 2 of this Act or under section 3 of this Act so far as it relates to prohibition orders and prohibition notices, the officer shall inform the person from whom the goods were purchased of the result of the test ;

and the officer shall, where as a result of the test such proceedings are instituted against any person, allow him to have the goods tested if it is reasonably practicable to do so.

14. The Secretary of State may by regulations provide that any test of goods seized or purchased by or on behalf of an enforcement authority in pursuance of this Schedule shall, in such cases as are specified in the regulations—

(*a*) be carried out at the expense of the authority in a manner so specified and by a person specified in or determined under the regulations ; or

(*b*) be carried out either as mentioned in sub-paragraph (*a*) above or by the authority in a manner specified in the regulations.

Compensation

15. Where, in the exercise of his powers under this Schedule, an officer of an enforcement authority seizes and detains any goods and their owner suffers loss by reason thereof or by reason that the goods, during the detention, are lost or damaged or deteriorate, then unless the owner is convicted of an offence under section 2 of this Act or under section 3 of this Act so far as it relates to prohibition orders and prohibition notices in relation to the goods, the authority shall be liable to compensate him for the loss so suffered.

16. Any disputed question as to the right to or the amount of any compensation payable under the preceding paragraph shall be determined by arbitration and, in Scotland, by a single arbiter appointed, failing agreement between the parties, by the sheriff.

SCHEDULE 3

REPEALS

Chapter or number	Short title	Extent of repeal
1961 c. 40.	The Consumer Protection Act 1961.	The whole Act.
1965 c. 14 (N.I.).	The Consumer Protection Act (Northern Ireland) 1965.	The whole Act.
1971 c. 15.	The Consumer Protection Act 1971.	The whole Act.
1972 c. 70.	The Local Government Act 1972.	In Schedule 29, paragraph 18(2).
1973 c. 65.	The Local Government (Scotland) Act 1973.	In Schedule 27, paragraphs 149 and 150.
1974 c. 39.	The Consumer Credit Act 1974.	In Schedule 4, paragraphs 20, 21, 46 and 47.
1977 c. 50.	The Unfair Contract Terms Act 1977.	Section 30.
S.I. 1977 No. 595 (N.I. 6).	The Consumer Protection and Advice (Northern Ireland) Order 1977.	Article 3.

Appendix 12

Consumer Safety Act Press Notice

The following is the text of a Press Notice issued on 28 September 1978 by the Department of Prices and Consumer Protection. This notice deals with the bringing into force of *The Consumer Safety Act, 1978*.

* * *

'Mr John Fraser, Minister of State for Prices and Consumer Protection, has today signed a Commencement Order which brings almost all the provisions of the Consumer Safety Act into force on 1 November this year.

This Act, introduced as a Private Member's Bill by Mr Neville Trotter MP and supported at all stages by the Government, gives the Secretary of State wider powers than those provided by *The Consumer Protection Act, 1961* (which it will eventually repeal) to take action on the safety of goods.

It will enable the Secretary of State to take urgent action if unsafe goods are found to be on sale. He will be able to serve on any trader a prohibition notice prohibiting him from continuing to supply specified goods which are considered to be unsafe. He will be able to make prohibition orders prohibiting the supply in the course of a business, i.e. by all traders, of any goods which he considers to be unsafe. He can also serve on any trader a 'notice to warn', requiring him to publish a warning about goods which he has been marketing and which are considered to be dangerous.

The Act gives to the Secretary of State powers similar to those under the 1961 Act to make regulations prescribing safety requirements as to composition, design and construction of goods, but the new powers are such that more extensive labelling requirements can be imposed, for example, that goods must bear such information as warning symbols, names of ingredients, first-aid instructions and name and address of manufacturer or supplier.

There will also be power, by means of Regulations, to require goods to be of a type approved by a specified body, to impose requirements as to the fitness for purposes of safety equipment; to prescribe quality control procedures relevant to the safety of goods and to provide in Regulations that compliance with an approved standard is deemed-to-satisfy a requirement of the Regulations for the purpose of criminal liability.

The Secretary of State will be empowered by the Act to serve on any person a notice requiring information to be provided for the purpose of enabling him to decide whether or not to make Regulations, serve prohibition orders or notices or warning notices in respect of goods of any kind.

Generally, enforcement of the new Act will be the duty of local weights and measures authorities. The Act gives wider enforcement powers and imposes higher maximum penalties for offences compared with those specified in the 1961 Act.

The Commencement Order brings into force all the provisions of the Act other than those which repeal *The Consumer Protection Act, 1961*, and *The Consumer Protection Act (Northern Ireland), 1965*, and legislation amending those Acts. But until those Acts are repealed the maximum fine for contravening regulations made under them will be increased and local weights and measures authorities will be under a duty to enforce the Acts.

Notes

1 *The Consumer Protection Acts, 1961 and 1971,* and the equivalent Northern Ireland legislation, will remain in operation until an order is made under the new Act repealing them. The regulations made under the existing legislation will remain in

force but will be replaced over a period by regulations made
under the new Act.

2   One of the provisions in the new Act now being brought
into operation, increases the maximum penalties of £100
(first offence) and £250 (subsequent offence) in Section 3(2)
of the 1961 Act to £1000 in either case. Another provision
makes the enforcement duty on weights and measures
authorities applicable to the Consumer Protection Act.

3   The Consumer Safety Act completed all its Parliamentary
stages on 14 July and received the Royal Assent on 20 July.

4   The Act includes a number of the provisions proposed in
the Green Paper on Consumer Safety (Cmnd 6398) issued by
the Government in February 1976.

5   The Act extends to the whole of the United Kingdom.

6   Goods excluded from its scope are food, feeding stuff,
fertiliser, medicinal products in respect of which there is in
force a product licence under *The Medicines Act, 1968*, and
controlled drugs within the meaning of *The Misuse of Drugs
Act, 1971*.

7   The powers provided by the Act are exercisable by any
Secretary of State and any other Minister of the Crown in
charge of a government department.

Existing and proposed regulations relating to the safety of consumer goods

Existing regulations

SI 1966 No. 1610	Stands for Carry-cots (Safety)
SI 1967 No. 839	Nightdresses (Safety)
SI 1969 No. 310	Electrical Appliances (Colour Code)
SI 1970 No. 811	Electrical Appliances (Colour Code): Amendment
SI 1971 No. 1961	Electric Blankets (Safety)
SI 1972 No. 1957	Cooking Utensils (Safety)
SI 1973 No. 2106	Heating Appliances (Fireguards)
SI 1974 No. 226	Pencils and Graphic Instruments (Safety)
SI 1974 No. 1367	Toys (Safety)
SI 1975 No. 1241	Glazed Ceramic Ware (Safety)
SI 1975 No. 1366	Electrical Equipment (Safety)
SI 1976 No. 2	Children's Clothing (Hood Cords)
SI 1976 No. 454	Vitreous Enamel-ware (Safety)
SI 1976 No. 1208	Electrical Equipment (Safety) (Amendment)
SI 1977 No. 167	Oil Heaters (Safety)
SI 1977 No. 1140	Aerosol Dispensers (EEC Requirements) (*see Note 1*)
SI 1978 No. 836	Babies Dummies (Safety)
Not yet published	Heating Appliances (Fireguards): Amendment
Not yet published	Perambulators and Pushchairs (Safety)
SI 1978 No. 209	Packaging and labelling of Dangerous Substances (*see Note 2*)
SI 1978 No. 1354	Cosmetic Products (*see Note 3*)

Notes

1   Made under Section 2 of *The European Communities Act, 1972*, and under *The Health and Safety at Work etc. Act, 1974.*
2   Made under Section 2 of *The European Communities Act, 1972.*
3   Made under the powers conferred by Section 2 of *The European Communities Act, 1972*, as well as those available under *The Consumer Protection Act, 1961.*

Regulations in course of preparation

Aerosol Dispensers (Safety) — these will be made under the new Act and will deal with aerosols which do not bear the '3' symbol and are not therefore within the scope of *The Aerosol Dispenser (EEC) Requirements Regulations, 1977.*

Costs — to be made under the 1978 Act.

Electrical Plugs, Sockets and Adaptors — to be made under the 1978 Act.

Materials and Articles Intended to Come into Contact with Food — to be made jointly by MAFF and DPCP under Section 2 of *The European Communities Act, 1972.*

Oil Lamps — to be made shortly under the *Consumer Protection Act.*

Paints, Varnishes, etc. (Packaging and Labelling) — to be made jointly by the Department of Employment and DPCP under the Health and Safety at Work Act and the Consumer Safety Act.

Radioactive Products — these will be made under the 1978 Act and will require radioactive consumer goods to be approved by a specified body before they can be marketed.

Strasbourg Convention

Preamble

The member states of the Council of Europe, signatory hereto,

Considering that the aim of the Council of Europe is to achieve a greater unity between its Members;

Considering the development of case law in the majority of member States extending liability of producers prompted by a desire to protect consumers taking into account the new production techniques and marketing and sales methods;

Desiring to ensure better protection of the public and, at the same time, to take producers' legitimate interests into account;

Considering that priority should be given to compensation for personal injury and death;

Aware of the importance of introducing special rules on the liability of producers at European level,

Have agreed as follows:

Article 1

1   Each Contracting State shall make its national law conform with the provisions of this Convention not later than the date of the entry into force of the Convention in respect of that State.

2   Each Contracting State shall communicate to the Secretary General of the Council of Europe, not later than the date of the entry into force of the Convention in respect of that State, any text adopted or a statement of the contents of the existing law which it relies on to implement the Convention.

Article 2

For the purpose of this Convention:

a   the term 'product' indicates all movables, natural or industrial, whether raw or manufactured, even though incorporated into another movable or into an immovable;

b   the term 'product' indicates the manufacturers of finished products or of component parts and the producers of natural products;

c   a product has a 'defect' when it does not provide the safety which a person is entitled to expect, having regard to all the circumstances including the presentation of the product;

d   a product has been 'put into circulation' when the producer has delivered it to another person.

Article 3

1   The producer shall be liable to pay compensation for death or personal injuries caused by a defect in his product.

2   Any person who has imported a product for putting it into circulation in the course of a business and any person who has presented a product as his product by causing his name, trademark or other distinguishing feature to appear on the product, shall be deemed to be producers for the purpose of this Convention and shall be liable as such.

3   When the product does not indicate the identity of the persons liable under paragraphs 1 and 2 of this Article, each supplier shall be deemed to be a producer for the purpose of this Convention and liable as such, unless he discloses, within a reasonable time, at the request of the claimant, the identity of the producer or of the person who supplied him with the product. The same shall apply, in the case of an imported product, if this product does not indicate the identity of the importer referred to in paragraph 2, even if the name of the producer is indicated.

4   In the case of damage caused by a defect in a product incorporated into another product, the producer of the incorporated product and the producer incorporating that product shall be liable.

5   Where several persons are liable under this Convention for the same damage, each shall be liable in full (*in solidum*).

Article 4

1   If the injured person or the person entitled to claim compensation has by his own fault contributed to the damage, the compensation may be reduced or disallowed having regard to all the circumstances.

2   The same shall apply if a person, for whom the injured person or the person entitled to claim compensation is responsible under national law, has contributed to the damage by his fault.

Article 5

1   A producer shall not be liable under this Convention if he proves:
a   that the product has not been put into circulation by him; or
b   that, having regard to the circumstances, it is probable that the defect which caused the damage did not exist at the time when the product was put into circulation by him or that this defect came into being afterwards; or
c   that the product was neither manufactured for sale, hire or any other form of distribution for the economic purposes of the producer nor manufactured or distributed in the course of his business.

2   The liability of a producer shall not be reduced when the damage is caused both by a defect in the product and by the act or omission of a third party.

Article 6

Proceedings for the recovery of the damages shall be subject to a limitation period of three years from the day the claimant became aware or should reasonably have been aware of the damage, the defect and the identity of the producer.

Article 7

The right to compensation under this Convention against a producer shall be extinguished if an action is not brought within ten years from the date on which the producer put into circulation the individual product which caused the damage.

Article 8

The liability of the producer under this Convention cannot be excluded or limited by any exemption or exoneration clause.

Article 9

This Convention shall not apply to:
a   the liability of producers *inter se* and their rights of recourse against third parties;
b   nuclear damage.

Article 10

Contracting States shall not adopt rules derogating from this Convention, even if these rules are more favourable to the victim.

Article 11

States may replace the liability of the producer, in a principal or subsidiary way, wholly or in part, in a general way, or for certain risks only, by the liability of a guarantee fund or other form of collective guarantee, provided that the victim shall receive protection at least equivalent to the protection he would have had under the liability scheme provided for this Convention.

Article 12

This Convention shall not affect any rights which a person suffering damage may have according to the ordinary rules of the law of contractual and extracontractual liability including any rules concerning the duties of a seller who sells goods in the course of his business.

Article 13

1   This Convention shall be open to signature by the member States of the Council of Europe. It shall be subject to ratification, acceptance or approval. Instruments of ratification, acceptance or approval shall be deposited with the Secretary General of the Council of Europe.

2   This Convention shall enter into force on the first day of the month following the expiration of a period of six months after the date of deposit of the third instrument of ratification, acceptance or approval.

3   In respect of a signatory State ratifying, accepting or approving subsequently, the Convention shall come into force on the first day of the month following the expiration of a period of six months after the date of the deposit of its instrument of ratification, acceptance or approval.

Article 14

1   After the entry into force of this Convention, the Committee of Ministers of the Council of Europe may invite any non-member State to accede thereto.

2   Such accession shall be effected by depositing with the Secretary General of the Council of Europe an instrument of accession which shall take effect on the first day of the month following the expiration of a period of six months after the date of its deposit.

Article 15

1   Any State may, at the time of signature or when depositing its instrument of ratification, acceptance, approval or accession, specify the territory or territories to which this Convention shall apply.

2   Any State may, when depositing its instrument of ratification, acceptance, approval or accession or at any later date, by declaration addressed to the Secretary General of the Council of Europe, extend this Convention to any other territory or territories specified in the declaration and for whose international relations it is responsible or on whose behalf it is authorised to give undertakings.

3   Any declaration made in pursuance of the preceding paragraph

may, in respect of any territory mentioned in such declaration, be withdrawn by means of a notification addressed to the Secretary General of the Council of Europe. Such withdrawal shall take effect on the first day of the month following the expiration of a period of six months after the date of receipt by the Secretary General of the Council of Europe of the declaration of withdrawal.

Article 16

1   Any State may, at the time of signature or when depositing its instrument of ratification, acceptance, approval or accession, or at any later date, by notification addressed to the Secretary General of the Council of Europe, declare that, in pursuance of an international agreement to which it is a Party it will not consider imports from one or more specified States also Parties to that agreement as imports for the purpose of paragraphs 2 and 3 of Article 3; in this case the person importing the product into any of these States from another State shall be deemed to be an importer for all the States Parties to this agreement.

2   Any declaration made in pursuance of the preceding paragraph may be withdrawn by means of a notification addressed to the Secretary General of the Council of Europe. Such withdrawal shall take effect the first day of the month following the expiration of a period of one month after the date of receipt by the Secretary General of the Council of Europe of the declaration of withdrawal.

Article 17

1   No reservation shall be made to the provisions of this Convention except those mentioned in the Annex to this Convention.

2   The Contracting State which has made one of the reservations mentioned in the Annex to this Convention may withdraw it by means of a declaration addressed to the Secretary General of the Council of Europe which shall become effective the first day of the month following the expiration of a period of one month after the date of its receipt by the Secretary General.

Article 18

1   Any Contracting State may, in so far as it is concerned, denounce

this Convention by means of a notification addressed to the Secretary General of the Council of Europe.

2   Such denunciation shall take effect on the first day of the month following the expiration of a period of six months after the date of receipt by the Secretary General of such notification.

Article 19

The Secretary General of the Council of Europe shall notify the member States of the Council and any State which has aceded to this Convention of:

a   any signature;
b   any deposit of an instrument of ratification, acceptance, approval or accession;
c   any date of entry into force of this Convention in accordance with Article 13 thereof;
d   any reservation made in pursuance of the provisions of Article 17, paragraph 1;
e   withdrawal of any reservation carried out in pursuance of the provisions of Article 17, paragraph 2;
f   any communication or notification received in pursuance of the provisions of Article 1, paragraph 2, Article 15, paragraphs 2 and 3 and Article 16, paragraphs 1 and 2;
g   any notification received in pursuance of the provisions of Article 18 and the date on which denunciation takes effect.

In witness whereof, the undersigned, being duly authorised thereto, have signed this Convention.

Done at Strasbourg this 27th day of January 1977, in English and in French, both texts being equally authoritative, in a single copy which shall remain deposited in the archives of the Council of Europe. The Secretary General of the Council of Europe shall transmit certified copies of each to the signatory and acceding States.

EEC Draft Directive

(Presented by the Commission to the Council on 9 September 1976)

The Council of the European Communities,

Having regard to the Treaty establishing the European Economic Community, and in particular Article 100 thereof,

Having regard to the proposal from the Commission,
Having regard to the Opinion of the European Parliament,
Having regard to the Opinion of the Economic and Social Committee,

Whereas the approximation of the laws of the Member States concerning the liability of the producer for damage caused by the defectiveness of his products is necessary, because the divergencies may distort competition in the common market; whereas the rules on liability which vary in severity lead to differing costs for industry in the various Member States and in particular for producers in different Member States who are in competition with one another;

Whereas approximation is also necessary because the free movement of goods within the common market may be influenced by divergencies in laws; whereas decisions as to where goods are sold should be based on economic and not legal considerations;

Whereas, lastly, approximation is necessary because the consumer is protected against damage caused to his health and property by a defective product either in differing degrees or in most cases not at all, according to the conditions which govern the liability of the producer under the individual laws of Member States; whereas to this extent therefore a common market for consumers does not as yet exist;

Whereas an equal and adequate protection of the consumer can be achieved only through the introduction of liability irrespective of fault on the part of the producer of the article which was defective and caused the damage; whereas any other type of liability imposes on the injured party almost insurmountable difficulties of proof or does not cover the important causes of damage;

Whereas liability on the part of the producer irrespective of fault ensures an appropriate solution to this problem in an age of increasing technicality, because he can include the expenditure which he incurs to cover this liability in his production costs when calculating the price and therefore divide it among all consumers of products which are of the same type but free from defects;

Whereas liability cannot be excluded for those products which at the time when the producer put them into circulation could not have been regarded as defective according to the state of science and technology ('development risks'), since otherwise the consumer would be subjected without protection to the risk that the defectiveness of a product is discovered only during use;

Whereas liability should extend only to moveables; whereas in the interest of the consumer it nevertheless should cover all types of moveables, including therefore agricultural produce and craft products; whereas it should also apply to moveables which are used in the construction of buildings or are installed in buildings;

Whereas the protection of the consumer requires that all producers involved in the production process should be made liable, in so far as their finished product or component part or any raw material supplied by them was defective; whereas for the same reason liability should extend to persons who market a product bearing their name, trademark or other distinguishing feature, to dealers who do not reveal the identity of producers known only to them, and to importers of products manufactured outside the European Community;

Whereas where several persons are liable, the protection of the consumer requires that the injured person should be able to sue each one for full compensation for the damage, but any right of recourse enjoyed in certain circumstances against other producers by the person paying such compensation shall be governed by the laws of the individual Member States;

Whereas to protect the person and property of the consumer, it is necessary, in determining the defectiveness of a product, to concentrate not on the fact that it is unfit for use but on the fact that it is unsafe; whereas this can only be a question of safety which objectively one is entitled to expect;

Whereas the producer is not liable where the defective product was put into circulation against his will or where it became defective only after he had put it into circulation and accordingly the defect did not originate in the production process; the presumption nevertheless is to the contrary unless he furnishes proof as to the exonerating circumstances;

Whereas in order to protect both the health and the private property of the consumer, damage to property is included as damage for which compensation is payable in addition to compensation for death and personal injury; whereas compensation for damage to property should nevertheless be limited to goods which are not used for commercial purposes;

Whereas compensation for damage caused in the business sector remains to be governed by the laws of the individual States;

Whereas the assessment of whether there exists a causal connection between the defect and the damage in any particular case is left to the law of each Member State;

Where since the liability of the producer is made independent of fault, it is necessary to limit the amount of liability; whereas unlimited liability means that the risk of damage cannot be calculated and can be insured against only at high cost;

Whereas since the possible extent of damage usually differs according to whether it is personal injury or damage to property, different limits should be imposed on the amount of liability; whereas in the case of personal injury the need for the damage to be calculable is met where an overall limit to liability is provided for; whereas the stipulated limit of 25 million European units of account covers most of the mass claims and provides in individual cases, which in practice are the most important, for unlimited liability; whereas in the case of the extremely rare mass claims which together exceed this sum and may therefore be classed as major disasters, there might be under certain circumstances assistance from the public;

Whereas in the much more frequent cases of damage to property, however, it is appropriate to provide for a limitation of liability in any particular case, since only through such a limitation can the liability of the producer be calculated; whereas the maximum amount is based on an estimated average of private assets in a typical case;whereas since this private property includes moveable and immoveable property, although the two are usually by the nature of things of different value, different amounts of liability should be provided for;

Whereas the limitation of compensation for damage to property, to damage to or destruction of private assets, avoids the danger that this liability becomes limitless; whereas it is therefore not necessary to provide for an overall limit in addition to the limits to liability in individual cases;

Whereas by Decision 3289/75/ECSC of 18 December 1975 the Commission, with the assent of the Council, defined a European unit of account which reflects the average variation in value of the currencies of the Member States of the Community;

Whereas the movement recorded in the economic and monetary situation in the Committee justifies a periodical review of the ceilings fixed by the directive;

Whereas a uniform period of limitation for the bringing of action for compensation in respect of the damage caused is in the interest both of consumers and of industry; it appeared appropriate to provide for a three year period;

Whereas since products age in the course of time, higher safety standards are developed and the state of science and technology progresses, it would be unreasonable to make the producer liable for an unlimited period for the defectiveness of his products; whereas therefore the liability should be limited to a reasonable length of time; whereas this period of time cannot be restricted or interrupted under laws of the Member States, whereas this is without prejudice to claims pending at law;

Whereas to achieve balanced and adequate protection of consumers no derogation as regards the liability of the producer should be permitted;

Whereas under the laws of the Member States an injured party may have a claim for damages based on grounds other than those provided for in this directive; whereas since these provisions also serve to attain the objective of an adequate protection of consumers, they remain unaffected;

Whereas since liability for nuclear damage is already subject in all Member States to adequate special rules, it has been possible to exclude damage of this type from the scope of the directive.

Has adopted this Directive;

Article 1

The producer of an article shall be liable for damage caused by a defect in the article, whether or not he knew or could have known of the defect.

The producer shall be liable even if the article could not have been regarded as defective in the light of the scientific and technological development at the time when he put the article into circulation.

Article 2

'Producer' means the producer of the finished articles, the producer of any material or component, and any person who, by putting his name, trademark, or other distinguishing feature on the article, represents himself as its producer. Where the producer of the article cannot be identified, each supplier of the article shall be treated as its producer unless he informs the injured person, within a reasonable time, of the identity of the producer or of the person who supplied him with the article.

Any person who imports into the European Community an article for resale or similar purpose shall be treated as its producer.

Article 3

Where two or more persons are liable in respect of the same damage, they shall be liable jointly and severally.

Article 4

A product is defective when it does not provide for persons or property the safety which a person is entitled to expect.

Article 5

The producer shall not be liable if he proves that he did not put the article into circulation or that it was not defective when he put it into circulation.

Article 6

For the purpose of Article 1 'damage' means:
a   death or personal injuries;
b   damage to or destruction of any item of property other than the
     defective article itself where the item of property
     (i)   is of a type ordinarily acquired for private use or con-
             sumption; and
     (ii) was not acquired or used by the claimant for the purpose
             of his trade, business or profession.

Article 7

The total liability of the producer provided for in this directive for all
personal injuries caused by identical articles having the same defect
shall be limited to 25 million European units of account (EUA).

The liability of the producer provided for by this directive in
respect of damage to property shall be limited *per capita*
— in the case of moveable property to 15,000 EUA, and
— in the case of immoveable property to 50,000 EUA.

The European unit of account (EUA) is as defined by Commission
Decision 3289/75/ECSC of 18 December 1975.

The equivalent in national currency shall be determined by
applying the conversion rate prevailing on the day preceding the date
on which the amount of compensation is finally fixed.

The Council shall, on a proposal from the Commission, examine
every three years and, if necessary, revise the amounts specified in
EUA in this Article, having regard to economic and monetary
movement in the Community.

Article 8

A limitation period of three years shall apply to proceedings for the
recovery of damages as provided for in this directive. The limitation
period shall begin to run on the day the injured person became
aware, or should reasonably have become aware of the damage, the
defect and the identity of the producer.

The laws of Member States regulating suspension or interruption
of the period shall not be affected by this directive.

Article 9

The liability of a producer shall be extinguished upon the expiry of ten years from the end of the calendar year in which the defective article was put into circulation by the producer, unless the injured person has in the meantime instituted proceedings against the producer.

Article 10

Liability as provided for in this directive may not be excluded or limited.

Article 11

Claims in respect of injury or damage caused by defective articles based on grounds other than that provided for in this directive shall not be affected.

Article 12

This directive does not apply to injury or damage arising from nuclear accidents.

Article 13

Member States shall bring into force the provisions necessary to comply with this directive within eighteen months and shall forthwith inform the Commission thereof.

Article 14

Member States shall communicate to the Commission the text of the main provisions of internal law which they subsequently adopt in the field covered by this directive.

Article 15

This directive is addressed to the Member States.

Index

Legislation is grouped under the headings Acts of Parliament, EEC and Statutory Instruments; page references in italics relate to verbatim reproduction from the Statutes. The letter-by-letter system has been adopted. Attention is drawn to a Table of Cases on pp 241-5.